SEVEN CENTURIES OF
POPULAR SONG

Photo: B.B.C.

'Kentucky' Minstrels. From a television production of 1949.

SEVEN CENTURIES OF
POPULAR SONG

A Social History of Urban Ditties

by

Reginald Nettel

WITH 12 PLATES

PHOENIX HOUSE LTD
LONDON

Printed in Great Britain by
The Aldine Press at Letchworth for
Phoenix House Ltd, 38 William IV Street,
Charing Cross, W.C.2.
First published 1956

CONTENTS

ILLUSTRATIONS

PREFACE AND ACKNOWLEDGMENTS

THIS IS A serious book on a topic which cannot by its nature be equally satisfactory throughout. My theme comes in like a lion and goes out like a black sheep, which is exactly what a good writer would avoid.

Yet I have tried to judge popular songs for what they are rather than what they ought to have been, acknowledging that those who want to be entertained have as much right to choose their poison as those who want to be improved. I admit it is more elevating for a writer to lambast the public (and more profitable too) in this age when popular art runs into other channels than print, but I have tried to avoid prejudice by keeping close to comments made at the time the various songs were new. The lowest depths were plumbed a century ago, and in justice to that age I have given Henry Mayhew's comments as he wrote them, restricting myself to a few explanatory footnotes, and, since he was concerned only with the poor, I have given in adjacent chapters the opinions of rich dilettanti and the middle-class reformers. When I move into the present century, however, I begin to feel lonely, for my conclusions—tentative though they be—sit ill with some modern theories. The key I have used—God in the last line of a lyric—will be found in *The Borderland of Music and Psychology* by Frank Howes, but I have forced it into a more complex lock than he, without permission. The urban ditties with which I treat have not the beauty of the songs in the rural tradition dealt with in my previous book,[1] but that is in the nature of the case. I am a townsman and I think I understand the urban point of view.

For illustrations I am obliged to the directors of the British Museum, the Bodleian Library, the British Broadcasting Corporation, Messrs Butlins Ltd, the Blackpool Tower Company, and Messrs H. E. Howarth Ltd, also of Blackpool; Leonard Hibbs & Francis Antony Ltd, the Republic Pictures International Inc. (Gt Britain), and Miss Peggy Coggins of Luton. Permission to quote copyright lyrics has been given by Messrs Campbell Connelly & Co. Ltd, 10 Denmark Street, W.C.2 (*Give Yourself a Pat on the Back* and *The More we are Together*); Messrs Chappell & Co.,

---

[1] *Sing a Song of England* (Phoenix House, 1954).

9

Ltd, for Noel Coward's *Dance, Little Lady* (from *This Year of Grace*) and *Twentieth Century Blues* (from *Cavalcade*), *Brother, can you spare a Dime?* by E. Y. Harburg and Jay Gorney, and *Trees* by Joyce Kilmer. I am obliged to the Herman Darewski Publishing Co. for permission to quote *Champagne Charlie*; Messrs B. Feldman & Co. Ltd for *Don't Dilly Dally* and *We used to gather at the Old Dun Cow*; and Messrs Francis, Day & Hunter Ltd for *Lily of Laguna* and *I Belong to Glasgow*. Quotations from the works of Sir William Schwenck Gilbert are reproduced by permission of the owner of the copyright. A list of books consulted will be found in the bibliography, but the authors of these must not be debited with any of my failings.

I. THE ENGLISH

THERE IS A custom still to be found among the English in their unguarded moments—as, for example, when lightly in their cups —of improvising 'harmony' in a popular song. It is done by some of the singers following the tune at a different pitch, so that there are two lines of tune to be heard, a third or a sixth apart. The Welsh also are fond of this practice, though in their case it is likely to be varied with truer part-singing, for the Welsh have their Eisteddfoddeu and are not ashamed of having voices and musical knowledge superior to that of the common Englishman. This English sense of shame grows more marked as professionals are brought in to criticize and improve amateur singers, but in general it may be said that in the north of England they are still somewhat less inhibited than in the south.

It may be, however, that the southerners are ashamed of the wrong thing. What have they anyway to set against that famous passage of Gerald de Barri (c. 1147–1220), one of the most entertaining writers of his time, who said in his *Descriptio Cambriae*: [1]

In their musical concerts they do not sing in unison like the inhabitants of other countries, but in many different parts; so that in a company of singers, which one very frequently meets with in Wales, you will hear as many different parts and voices as there are performers, who all at length unite, with organic melody, in one consonance and the soft sweetness of B flat. In the northern district of Britain, beyond the Humber, and on the borders of Yorkshire, the inhabitants make use of the same kind of symphonious harmony, but with less variety, singing only in two parts, one murmuring in the bass, the other warbling in the acute or treble. Neither of the two nations has acquired this peculiarity by art, but by long habit, which has rendered it natural and familiar; and the practice is now so firmly rooted in them, that it is unusual to hear a simple and single melody well sung; and what is still more wonderful, the children, even from their infancy, sing in the same manner. As the English in general do not adopt this mode of singing, but only those of the northern counties, I believe that it was from the Danes and Norwegians, by whom these parts of the island were more frequently invaded, and held longer under their dominion, that the natives contracted their mode of singing as well as speaking.

[1] In *Rerum Britannicarum Medii Aevi Scriptores*, I. xxxvi.

We can argue for ever about what Gerald meant by the 'soft sweetness of B flat', but there can be no doubt that he heard Yorkshiremen singing from ear in two lines of melody, and that the Welsh sang in more than two parts. We can learn also that in the southern parts, where Saxon influence was greatest, a different tradition obtained. Modern scholarship supports the observation of Gerald, though it was not until the fifteenth century that a name was given to this type of singing—*gymel*, or twin song.

So we have evidence of an important contribution from Britain towards the development of music as an art, and from a reliable source. Giraldus Cambrensis—to give him his Latinized name— (Gerald the Welshman)—was born of a Norman father and a Welsh mother, both of high birth. He studied and lectured in Paris, and became Court Chaplain to Henry II in 1184; he was a friend of Stephen Langton, Archbishop of Canterbury, leader of the opponents to King John, and one of the reputed writers of the hymn for Whit Sunday *Veni Sancte Spiritus*; and was a contemporary with such men of culture as Geoffrey of Monmouth, William of Malmesbury, and John of Salisbury, greatest scholar of them all—a Saxon Englishman by birth, secretary to Thomas Becket, and finally Bishop of Chartres. The twelfth century was a vital age in learning and the arts.

There was greater variety of taste in music in the twelfth century than may at first be supposed. When William the Conqueror overcame Harold in 1066 he could not thereby alter all the customs of the land, or suppress the language. Anglo-Saxon society had had its scops and gleemen, who were singers or reciters of their history and lore. The oldest poem remaining to us in English is *Widsith*, or *The Far-traveller*, the legend of a minstrel of the Dark Ages. The Norman conquerors, however, had little use for Saxon legends, which could hardly be relied on to proclaim the honour of their invaders, and they believed, as ardently as the Saxons, in the power of song to inspire men. It is on record that William of Normandy's minstrel Taillefer (the Cleaver of Iron) begged permission at the battle of Senlac to lead the charge, and—remarkable indeed, since this was William's right—permission was granted, as Wace records:

> Taillefer qui mult bien chantout
> Sor un cheval qui tost alout
> Devant le duc alout chantant
> De Karlemaigne e de Rollant
> E d'Oliver e des vassals
> Qui morurent en Rencevals.

Quant il orent chevalchie tant
Qu'as Engleis vindrent apreismant:
'Sire,' dist Taillefer, 'merci!
Io vos ai longuement servi.
Tot mon servise me devez.
Hui se vos plaist le me rendez.
Por tot guerredon vos requier
E si vos voil forment preier
Otreiez mei que io ni faille
Le premier colp de la bataille.'
Li dus respondi: 'Io l'otrei.'

Taillefer rode forward, throwing his sword in the air and catching it by the hilt, even as a drum-major will do today with his staff, and he sang of Charlemagne, Roland, and Oliver until he fell in the fight.

The language is archaic but of importance because it carried the art of the troubadours and trouvères [1]—the development of the ideal of romantic love. The Court of Eleanor of Aquitaine saw a great advance in the march of civilization, especially as it affected men's behaviour towards women. Eleanor was a woman of strong character, and as wife of Henry II ruled in England as well as in France; her son Richard Cœur-de-Lion was famous as a singer, and trouvère art must have had a hold in England; however, in tracing the development of popular song in English, we are drawn temporarily at any rate away from the Court to the country—not to the peasantry but to the thought of men of understanding. Our first example dates from somewhere about 1225 and is monodic—i.e. the tune is a line of melody, unaccompanied, to words bearing unmistakable Anglo-Saxon influences:

Mirie it is while sumer ylast,
    With fughles song,
Oc nu necheth windes blast
    And weder strong;
    Ei, ei, what this nicht is long,
    And ich with wel michel wrong,
Soregh and murne and fast.

Standards of domestic comfort were improving, but men were very close to nature in whatever walk of life they knew. The clothes

[1] Troubadours lived in southern France and trouvères in northern France.

both of men and women were thick, with gowns descending to the feet, and sleeves long—the whole fur-trimmed and worn with a hood. Summer must have come each year with a welcome warmth and ever fresh delights for the eye. Men were not sentimental about it, but sang truly from the heart. The most famous song of all time dates from the thirteenth century, with English and Latin words, and it is a tune which we can still sing today with relish. It tells of the cuckoo, of the springing seed, and the young beasts in the field calling after their dams.

> Sumer is icumen in,
>   Lhude sing cuccu!
> Groweth sed, and bloweth med,
>   And sprin'th the wude nu—
>   Sing cuccu!
>
> Awe bleteth after lomb,
>   Lhouth after calve cu;
> Bulluc sterteth, buck verteth,
>   Murie sing cuccu!
>
> Cuccu, cuccu, well singes thu, cuccu.
>   Ne swike thu naver nu.
> Sing cuccu, nu, sing cuccu,
>   Sing cuccu, sing cuccu, nu.

The manuscript containing this song belonged to Reading Abbey, and is supposed to be in the handwriting of John of Fornsete;[1] but even if he wrote the manuscript there is no guarantee that he was the composer. In the same collection are three polyphonic instrumental works, in dance rhythms (as also is the song). The song is remarkable in many ways. On the manuscript are directions for performance, written in Latin, of which this is a translation.

Four companions may sing this rota. But it ought not to be rendered by fewer than three, or two at the least, in addition to those who sing the bass. Now it is sung thus: the others keeping silent, one begins, with those who sing the bass, and when he shall have arrived at the first note after the cross, another begins; and so on with the rest. And each one shall pause at the written rests, and not elsewhere, for the space of one long.

[1] Forncett is in Norfolk.

The composition is therefore a four-part canon on a ground bass, and as such a fine piece of scholarship, but besides this it catches up in a remarkable way the simple joy of the common man. Some have contended that it must be a folk-song arranged as a continuous round (or rota) by skilled musicians, but it is not necessary to assume such an origin. Monks were children and secular men before they became monks, and must have known the Ionian mode upon which the Church frowned but which the minstrels used freely. That Ionian mode (nicknamed *modus lascivus*) is our common major mode, and the mode in which *Sumer is icumen in* was written. This must be our justification for quoting the Reading rota as an example of popular music. One may even compare it with styles of composition practised in Limoges and at Notre Dame. Comparison can easily be made, for *Sumer is icumen in* and the contemporary songs *Alleluia psallat* and *Marionette dance* are all available on a gramophone record,[1] but the fact remains that, judged by modern standards, the Reading song of summer is superior to them all.

'Judged by modern standards.' How often we hear that phrase! Yet is it historically honest to use it? Do we, for example, think of the major scale as being frolicsome or licentious by nature? Think of all the glum music we have heard in the major mode! We must go to thirteenth-century art for understanding of thirteenth-century songs.

The mediaeval mind may be compared with mediaeval architecture—always reaching heavenwards and working to finer and finer points, but in the buildings are innumerable little reminders of daily life: contemporary figures, serious, comical, even ribald, and formal designs worked out in the mind of the craftsman by meditation on the quality of his materials and the nature of his tools. (One can see how design changes as the chisel comes into use, and how the use of compasses tends to seduce the craftsman from the truly functional character of his traditional style.) One may even see demons tucked away in corners of a church, and know that these must have been familiar to the priests as well as to the people. To us they are possibly obscene, but the mediaeval sense of humour was more direct than ours, even as mediaeval minds were at once more pious and more cruel. They lived with demons, but would have fled in horror from our modern unbelief; their evils were heretical, but still based on supernatural beliefs. Material belongings of all were shared with the church and with the overlords, who took their dues in kind and had to house and use them. The link between nature and human society was thus in the work that fell

[1] H.M.V. series, *History of Music in Sound.*

to hand. Buildings, goods, and music were produced by practical experiment. It is useless to look for theoretical bases of *Sumer is icumen in*; they were not in contemporary textbooks but in musical practice.

Sumer is icumen in has two sets of words—English and Latin. So we have an example of educated men using the vernacular for an art product at a time when that language was socially inferior. The Church used Latin and the Court spoke Norman French; all proceedings in the law-courts being conducted in French until 1362. Thirteenth-century songs in English must therefore be accepted as popular in the sense that they employed the vulgar tongue, remembering, however, that this was known to men of trained intelligence.[1] The monasteries were closed communities, often, as in the case of Reading Abbey, drawing tithes from the people of prosperous towns without discharging their full responsibilities towards their supporters. This cleavage between the people and the monks was a source of dissatisfaction in which the parish clergy were often on the side of the people. Into this situation came the preaching friars—belonging to their several orders and vowed to poverty and service even as the monks were, but going among the people, serving them in their own environment, and therefore very welcome among a folk with spiritual needs not fully catered for by all monastic communities. The time was not yet ripe for Chaucer's verse, but the link between educated poets and people was already being forged in these lyrical English songs.

The happy theme of summer we have noted already, but it must not be assumed that popular songs played only with pleasant themes; the spiritual longing of mankind was ever revealed in his pointing upwards to God, and every man knew that he could not escape the day when he must meet his Maker face to face. This was a great theme in mediaeval song—the thought that while on earth one owed duty to one's overlord, and he in his turn to the king, but on the Day of Reckoning all men were equal before God.

There is a fine monodic song which all should hear who wish to know how men felt in their most serious mood at this period, *Worldes blis ne last no throwe* [2] It is a reminder that though men feared God they were ever conscious of their guilt, and that worldly prosperity too often implied selfishness or worse.

---

[1] There is an account of literary work in Middle English to be found in any history of English literature, and *Sumer is icumen in* is generally mentioned, but the popular songs are not treated with the attention they deserve.

[2] H.M.V. series, *History of Music in Sound*.

The thirteenth century must indeed be regarded as an important period in the development of the English as a thinking nation, even though the more marked results were not to come until the century following. The friars certainly proved invaluable. The first Dominicans in Oxford came from Bologna in 1221 to convert the Jews, of whom there were many in Oxford. The reputation of this city for learning was already known abroad, though the position of the Oxford students was precarious. Paris was the starting-place of the first English students who came to Oxford in 1167, but whether the University of Paris expelled them or Henry II recalled them we cannot tell. They were desperately poor, of little or no benefit to the trade of the prosperous city of Oxford, and the Jews charged them exorbitant rates of interest for loans. It was probably to protect themselves from hostile citizens and the landlords of the inns that the poor scholars were obliged to band themselves together and establish their own 'halls' or living places.[1] Instruction could be obtained in plenty from scholars living in the city. The friars probably saved the infant university from extinction by the prestige which they gave to learning and good works. A city tired of the proximity of the great Abbey of Osney and infested with starveling scholars responded to the lead given by Dominican friars. Franciscans (who aided the poor and the sick—even those suffering from leprosy) came in 1224, Carmelites and Augustinians followed.

The earliest colleges arose in the second half of the thirteenth century. One must not think of a university, however, as a building or group of buildings, but as a gild or corporation—a community of people met together for the exchange of learning. The scholars were of many types, including the light-hearted *scholares vagantes*, liable to turn up in any town in Western Europe, to start a discussion in hall, market-place, or ale-house, and to compose songs on any subject, sacred or secular, or mix the two with little reverence. Their part in the production of popular songs must have been considerable. They wrote in Latin, and from one of them comes the greatest drinking song in history:

> Meum est propositum
> In taberna mori,
> Vinum sit oppositum
> Morientis ori,

[1] Later, colleges. Only one of the original 'halls'—St Edmunds—now remains in Oxford.

> Ut dicant, cum venerint
> Angelorum chori:
> 'Deus sit propitius
> Huic potatori'.

Translations usually given are inadequate because they cannot trans-pose the pun implied in the last line (*potatori* in a well-known phrase which would normally read *peccatori*) but the following (by whom I cannot say) at least attempts the task:

> I would die where I would dine,
> In a tavern to recline;
> Then would angels pray the glibber:
> 'God have mercy on this bibber'.

The *vagantes* were often thorns in the flesh of the established churchmen, and were not denounced without good reason, but they had their place in the spread of learning as well as song. They were a foil to the austerity of the stricter clergy, even as the adoration of the Virgin Mary was a foil to the sense of sexual guilt which beset men. Christianity disapproved of sexual relations outside the tie of Holy Matrimony, but sexual relations went on outside that tie. The clergy could not marry, the soldiery took what they could seize, and women were regarded either as daughters of Eve, tempters of men from their higher aspirations, or necessary evils. Into such a paradoxical situation came a great wave of popular worship of the Mother of Christ—a woman perfect even as her Son was perfect. It is now impossible to estimate the influence of the Virgin Mary in the thirteenth century, but on the lowest estimate of all—the money spent on her shrines—there has been no cult to equal it. Not until the vast expenditure on modern warfare has it been equalled. Adoration of the Virgin grew during the grim years of the Crusades until all Christian armies, even when fighting against each other, called on Notre-Dame for aid. Such information is significant but transitory; the true influence of the Virgin was on men's thoughts and on their art. There is a well-known sequence [1] entitled *Angelus ad Virginem* which appears in a thirteenth-century manuscript as a monodic song, the words in Latin with an English translation added:

> Angelus ad Virginem
> Subintrans in conclave,
> Virginis formidinem
> Demulcens, inquit, 'Ave!

[1] See note p. 19.

Ave regina virginum;
Coeli terraeque Dominum
   Concipies
   Et pares
   Intacta
Salutem hominum;
Tupor ta coeli facta,
Medela criminum.'

The English version runs:

Gabriel from evene King
Sent to the maide swete
Broute hire blisful tiding
And faire he gan hire greten:
'Heil be thu ful of grace arith,
For godes sone this evene lith
   For mannes loven
   While man becomen
   And taken
Fles of the maiden birth,
Maken fre for to maken
Of sene and deules mith.'

With the mention of *Angelus ad Virginem* we are on familiar ground, for Chaucer, in *The Milleres Tale*, associated it with his poor scholar, Nicholas, of Oxenford.

And all above ther lay a gay sautrye
On which he made a-nightes melodye,
So swetely that al the chamber rong,
And *Angelus ad Virginem* he song.

The tune is fairly well known as a carol and can be found in modern books.[1] There is, besides the one-part version already mentioned, a two-part setting dating from the late thirteenth century and a three-part setting from the fourteenth century.[2]

The Church, as the repository of learning, had most to do with keeping records of early music and training performers of ecclesiastical music, but there were also the jongleurs—professional entertainers

[1] Cf. *The Oxford Book of Carols* (1947). No. 52. Record, H.M.V. *History of Music in Sound.*

[2] *Angelus ad Virginem* is really a sequence, which is a form of composition evolved from an extension of the last syllable of the Alleluia in the Mass and Office. These extensions were elaborated into strophes, repeated, formed into melodic structures, and eventually given words.

who practised music as well as any other art likely to entertain any company. One cannot generalize about these entertainers; they might offer anything from acrobatics to bear-dancing. Certainly they were a grave menace to the moral principles which the Church taught, and the more so because the people were always liable to be seduced by clever tricks, frivolous music, and carnal allurements. So the sterner moralists denounced the jongleurs or minstrels; they were forbidden the sacrament, could not be buried in holy ground, or even be married. Needless to say they bred like rabbits, and the more they were ill-treated the more sinful they became. The situation was a parallel in ecclesiastical law to that in civil law concerning hunting rights. The people were forbidden to kill the king's deer, and those who were caught at this practice were punished by the loss of property, a hand, or even with the loss of life itself; such people often became outlaws, and by the nature of the circumstances went on shooting the king's deer, and sometimes the king's men, who were assistants in the royal sport of hunting. By all accounts the unlawful hunters were good archers, and certainly popular among ballad-singers and their audiences. There was then in much the same way a cleavage between the intellectual musicians and the folk-musicians at this time, but one cannot condemn all minstrels. Some of them became associated with troubadours, who sang of deeds of chivalry, and, especially in the earlier years of the twelfth century, were socially acceptable. The story of Richard I, and of his minstrel Blondel, who went through Europe singing a song known only to Richard and himself, until at last he heard his king answer from his dungeon with the same tune, is well known. It is a pity history cannot verify the facts, but the tale is excellent as tales go.

The most important development in the art of music during the fourteenth century was the appearance in Paris of Philippe de Vitri's treatise called *Ars Nova*, which facilitated the writing of flexible melody. In England this was championed by Richard de Bury, Lord Chancellor and Bishop of Durham, and a close friend of Edward III. With the work of such men, and the presence of men of genius like Langland and Chaucer, the humanistic spirit of the age found permanent expression. The best of English popular music came in the fifteenth century, just after Chaucer's verse, and may in part be attributed to the influence of Henry V, the hero of Agincourt, and himself a composer of music.[1]

[1] The Old Hall MS. (late fourteenth century) contains a *Sanctus, Benedictus,* and *Gloria in Exelsis* by 'Roy Henry'. Wooldridge assumed these to be by Henry VI, but Bukhofzer more reasonably claims them for Henry V.

The best-known song of his reign is indeed the *Agincourt Carol*, though this is not of Henry's composition. Most likely it is the work of a churchman, but in any case it violated Henry's command that praise should be given for the victory to God alone.[1] The custom was to welcome a hero with all the pageantry that colourful age could invent. In it the returning hero and his men were the principal figures, riding in procession through the streets. At favourable points along the route (places where the street turned sharply were best, for a 'sight' placed there could be seen by the victors in procession as they approached) 'sights' were contrived. Henry was welcomed in the City of London by a 'heavenly host' singing *Benedictus qui venit*, from a scaffold, or 'pageant', erected in the street; by 'Patriarches synging *Cantate Domino*' on another pageant; by 'twelve apostles, a choir of angels (singing *Nowell, nowell*)'; and by a choir of beautiful virgins singing in English 'Welcome, Henry the fifte, Kynge of Englond and of Fraunce'.

The attraction was primarily visual, with music as an important subsidiary to the ceremony. Such things must not be done half-heartedly—nor were they—but should contribute to the 'worship' of the occasion. In fact all art was purposive at such times. The *Agincourt Carol* was not written for this grand entry into London, but it came out soon afterwards.[2] It is not a folk-song, but popular music, written for a time when men were proud of the recent achievements of their king and countrymen, and it was taken up by the populace in that spirit. The song starts with a 'burden' in Latin which is partly repeated at the end of each verse, and then fully repeated in three parts to the same words:

> *Deo gracias Anglia,*
> *Redde pro victoria.*
> Oure kynge went forth to Normandy,
> With grace and myght of chyvalry,
> Ther God for him wrought mervelusly,
> Wherefore Englond may call and cry
> *Deo gracias.*

[1] '. . . Neither would he suffer any ditties to be made and soong by minstrels of his glorious victorie, for that he would have the praise and thanks altogether given to God.' (Holinshed.)

[2] Bodleian Library. MS. Arch. Selden, B.26, f.17. There is a recording also available in the H.M.V. *History of Music in Sound.*

Deo gracias Anglia,
Redde pro victoria.

He sette a sege, the sothe for to say,
To Harflu tovne with a ryal aray;
That tovne he wan and made a fray,
The Fraunce shall rywe tyl domesday.
       Deo gracias.

       Deo gracias Anglia,
       Redde pro victoria.

Then went oure kynge with all his oste,
Thorwe Fraunce, for all the French boste;
He spared no drede of lest ne moste
Tyl he come to Agincourt coste.
       Deo gracias.

              Chorus: *Deo gracias Anglia,* etc.

Than forsoth, that knyght comely,
In Agincourt feld he fought manly;
Thorw grace of God most myghty
He had bothe the felde and the victory.
       Deo gracias.

              Chorus.

Ther dukys and erlys, lord and barone,
Were take and slayne, and that wel sone;
And summe were lad to Lundone,
With joye and merthe and grete renone.
       Deo gracias.

              Chorus.

Now gracious God he saue oure kynge,
His people, and alle his well-wyllynge;
Gef hym good lyfe and gode endynge,
That we with merth nowe sauely sing,
       Deo gracias.

This is the form of the English carol; a song with a burden announced at the very beginning and repeated after each verse. We shall meet more of them. Meanwhile rid your mind of the cant that a carol is a Christmas hymn, and pray for the salvation of the man who arranged the *Agincourt Carol* to fit Kipling's *Recessional*. Think of the original song again, but try to do so in a way more in keeping with its historical importance. It is not merely a boastful song, but a record of the spirit of the English when emerging as a nation.

For a modern Englishman to boast of his country's songs may suggest chauvinism, but nothing can be more certain than that the English songs of the early fifteenth century were regarded with favour throughout France and Italy. Copies of them are to be found in many continental libraries. Dunstable's *O Rosa bella* is, however, that great composer's only song to Italian words; the English love songs of his period to which we refer are set to English words. *Go, Hert, hurt with Adversite*, and *Now wolde I fayne* are gems of English-style polyphony. Lovely, too, is the song illustrated facing page 61:

Alas departynge is ground of woo,
 Odyr songe can y not synge;
But why part I my lady fro,
 Sith love was caus of our metyng?
The bitter terys of hire wepying
 Myne hert hath perishid so mortaly,
That to the dethe hit will me brynge,
 But if y se hire hastily.

II. WITHIN THE TOWNS

IT IS EASY ENOUGH to understand how rural life goes on in the same way throughout the ages; here men are tillers of the soil, making use of the gifts and vagaries of nature much as their fathers have done; it is not so easy to recognize in the townsman a similar continuance of his way of life, because between him and the forces of nature there are mechanical devices and protections which seem to place him in a modern world of his own creation.

Yet the view may be shortsighted. The countryside today is very different from what it was before the great enclosures of land in the eighteenth century, and if the towns have recently accepted chromium plating and electric lighting, these serve the same trades that Piers Plowman described in the fourteenth century:

> I saw in this assembly, as ye shall hear after.
> Bakers and brewsters and butchers many,
> Wool-websters and weavers of linen,
> Tailors and tinkers and toilers in markets,
> Masons and miners and many other crafts,
> Of all kinds of labourers leapt forth some,
> As dykers and delvers that doth their work ill . . .

These are trades still pursued, even to the diggers of roads who disturb the traffic and as often as not take no great pride in their work. In the markets are the stall-holders, and at the fairs the rolling, bowling, or pitching shysters; on a race-train one may even meet the thimble-riggers, playing the same old trick we see represented in a mediaeval painting. Street musicians are not now so numerous as they were, but their decline in numbers has happened only within the last twenty years. At all times these have presented a problem to civic authorities, never really solved.

The problem of the wandering entertainers, as that of the cheapjacks and the tricksters with whom they were associated at fairs, was that they were all there on one day and gone the next. Law and order were difficult to maintain in a gathering which attracted many strangers, all out for money. In many places the ordinary civic government was disbanded for the period of the fair, and a court of pie-powder instituted.[1] Justice was served on the spot, quickly and hilariously; stocks and whipping-post stood in the centre of affairs, and the prison not far off. Times were hard; times were cruel; times were also merry.

The city of Chester is a good example of the continuation of urban tradition. If the city is not as old as the Dee on whose banks it stands, it has anyway some two thousand years of civilization in evidence within its walls. At the Conquest it had a gild of merchants —a constitution in some ways similiar to that of modern municipal corporations—and by ancient usage (confirmed in several charters) the mayor and recorder held crownmote and portmote courts, with jurisdiction in the crownmote over all crimes save that of high treason, the mayor having the power to pass sentence of death, and order execution, independently of the Crown.[2] Because of Chester's strategical position as a barrier against the marauding Welsh, it was strongly held by resolute men; William the Conqueror bestowed it on Hugh Lupus, who substituted Benedictine monks for the secular canons previously installed there, and thus gave us that wonderful architecture still to be seen at Chester Cathedral. Hugh Lupus also granted to the abbey the right of a fair, to be held outside the abbey gateway. The monks could set up booths and rent them to traders, who were forbidden for the duration of the fair to trade elsewhere within five miles of the city. Fourteen days before the commencement of the fair a wooden hand—emblem of open trading and clinching a bargain—would be suspended from the Pentice, adjoining St Peter's Church, where it would remain for the twenty-one days of the fair. While it hung there, non-freemen of the city were permitted to trade. The monopoly of the trade gilds was thus temporarily broken.

During a fair in the year 1212, while the city was full of traders and their hangers-on, an alarm was received from Ruddlan in Flint that Earl Randulf de Blunderville and his men were besieged by the Welsh; the castle of Ruddlan was strong, but the Welsh were numerous enough to contain it. The Constable of Chester at that time was Roger de Lacy—known as 'Roger of Hell' for he was that sort of man—who deserves credit, however, for a most ingenious plan to

[1] Despite their special nature they were true courts of record—*civis pedis pulverisati*, governed by statute 17 Ed. IV, c.2 (1477–8), which is still in force.

[2] There was also the Pentice Court, which could give judgment on personal actions to any amount, from which records were removable to the Portmote Court by command of the mayor without writ. The Municipal Reform Act of 1834 made the Recorder the judge.

raise the siege of Ruddlan. One may perceive that he dared not leave
Chester unpoliced while so many strangers were crowding the city,
especially as there were among them a multitude of jongleurs—
buffoons, tumblers, fiddlers, and their women. These were without
the law—vagabonds, unfree and excommunicated—who had
nothing to lose by rape and pillage if they could not be controlled;
he therefore ordered his son-in-law Hugh Dutton to gather some
of the riff-raff of the fair and march them against the Welsh. This
Hugh Dutton did. With a mighty clamour the minstrels—who
were, after all, the aristocracy of the riff-raff—led the motley army
towards Ruddlan. The Welsh saw them afar off, were astonished at
their number, and fled.

From this incident arose apparently the first attempt to organize
the musical profession, for de Lacy and Dutton claimed rights of
patronage and authority over minstrels and others in the Chester
area, who in their turn were granted a much-needed protection and
certain privileges. Minstrels or other itinerants having a licence
from these or their descendants were not accounted 'rogues, vagabonds, and sturdy beggars', and such protection was valuable.
The right of the Duttons was accepted in other parts of the country
when attempts were made to form gilds or companies of musicians;
it is implied in the charter granted by Charles I in 1636 to 'The
Marshall, Wardens, and Cominalty of the Arte and Science of
Musick in Westminster in the County of Middlesex', who
were granted leave to practise their art all over England except
in Cheshire. There were town gilds of musicians established in
many places, as at Norwich, York, Beverley, and Canterbury.
The Worshipful Company of Musicians still meets in London
to dine.

No modern union could teach anything to a mediaeval trade gild
about the assertion of rights and privileges. These gilds won their
charters from the king for the control and enjoyment of their professions. A Minstrels' Charter of Incorporation, granted in 1469 by
Edward IV, gave its members power 'to examine the pretentions of
all who exercised the minstrels' profession, to regulate, govern, and
punish'; its government was to be in the hands of a marshal and two
wardens to be appointed annually. The similarity of this corporation
to the universities will be obvious; the universities were in fact
mediaeval corporations in the best sense. By their rules, gilds of
minstrels sought to regulate entry into the profession by control
of apprentices and examination of candidates for admission, to
maintain its reputation by ensuring that nobody did a job without

getting the proper rate of pay, and also that no member of the profession imposed himself on company which did not want him. He must not carry his instrument through the streets uncased, or play in the streets at night.

In no way were such rules at variance with the general notion of good professional behaviour in the days when a mayor might be warned solemnly by his corporation that to be seen carrying home the weekly joint was unbefitting to the dignity of his office, and when no merchant was permitted to sell his goods by candle-light. Any master who broke the rules of his gild, by paying the wrong wages, charging the wrong price, selling inferior goods, or permitting his journeymen to do shoddy work, was 'presented' to the mayor, who had the power to withdraw his licence to trade. Strictly, the mayor was accountable to the king through the high sheriff, but in practice a town could, through its corporation, offer in most matters the justice of its own burgesses, and could defend their interests by craft or, if necessary, by force of arms, against other corporations, against avaricious prelates, or against oppressive nobles. The Mayor and Corporation of London could stand up for their rights against the king himself. In this way the rights of fairs granted originally to the Church were bought by the corporations, or new charters were obtained from the king. The functions of local government were taken over by the townsmen. Among them were the town bands or waits, originally watchmen at the gates, who played on instruments of the oboe family; [1] their responsibilities increased as their towns grew in importance, until some of their bands became famous, especially that at Norwich. They had their liveries, and particular tunes by which they were known (a device now used in radio entertainment and called 'signature tune'). They had silver chains about their necks, some of great value, and were expressly allowed to perform at night.

The waits were therefore a special class of minstrel, and, opinions being what they were in a gild-directed community, they kept themselves select; the Chester waits were a separate body from the Fraternity of Minstrels. Segregation had its perils, however, for in 1502 five of the London waits petitioned the corporation that the 'mynstrels' would not allow them to 'trade' within the city unless they became members of the Craft. Gild fought gild, not always (or indeed often) with physical weapons, but with legal arguments based on the liberties granted under their charters. Similarly a town

---

[1] Also the waits used fiddles, cornetts, trumpets, and sackbuts (trombones). The early oboe-type instrument was called the 'wayte-pipe'.

found means to protect its freemen from molestation in other towns, generally by an appreciation of nuisance value. Mayors and corporations spent much of their time writing threatening letters to other local government officials, as, for example, when in 1350 a London vintner was owed £20 by a Colchester man who died; the mayor thereupon wrote to the bailiffs of Colchester, desiring them to order the man's executors to pay up, 'in such a manner as they would wish their folk to be treated when repairing to London in like case or weightier; otherwise their folk would certainly be annoyed when repairing to London, owing to their default; and may the Lord have them in their keeping and increase their honours'.

Above all, civic dignity must be preserved.

None of it was done for love; business was business; things could go hard with a man who offended the dignity of a gild or corporation. So when, in 1594, Robert Gryce, one of the Doncaster waits, was assaulted by a citizen and his servant (one wonders if he had been practising his office to the detriment of the citizen's sleep?) Gryce went to London and took out a writ in the Court of the Queen's Bench. This was a clever move by a man who doubted if he would get judgment in his own city; but what of civic dignity? It was 'agreed at a Common Council, held in the Guildhall, that Robert Gryce, one of the Waits of the town, be displaced from the said office because he had sued the Queen's writ out of the Queen's Bench to bind to the peace William Clark of this town and William Battye his servant, instead of demanding the writ at the hands of the Mayor or other justice of the peace within this town, to their great discredit and disgrace'.[1]

Some of the 'signature tunes' of the waits have been preserved for us.[2] *London Waits* is to be found in John Playford's *The Dancing Master*; the Tower Hamlets used two Hornpipes, Oxford a Gavotte, Warrington a Minuet, York another Hornpipe.

At Christmas it was the privilege of the waits to go round to the houses of the citizens and receive their benefice for duties supposedly carried out satisfactorily during the year.[3] At Lincoln, where there were three waits,[4] it was their duty to 'Cry Christmas' by singing

---

[1] J. C. Bridge, *Town Waits and their Tunes*. Proceedings of the Musical Association (1927–8), p. 72.

[2] Most of these are seventeenth- and eighteenth-century tunes, and so later than the time of which we are now writing.

[3] From this custom survives the present-day habit of calling carol-singers 'waits'.

[4] Coventry in 1423 had four, Leicester had three in 1524, Norwich five or six, Chester three or four, Bristol four, London City nine (to equal the number of the Muses).

a traditional song in the characters of three wise men, or 'senators' as they were called:

1st Senator:

> The Aungells with myrthe the schepperdes did obey,
> When they sang Gloria in Excelsis in tunes mystical
> The byrdes with solemnyte sang on every spray,
> And the beastes for joye made reverence in every stall.

2nd Senator:

> Therefore with a contrite hart let us be merye all,
> Having a steadfast faith and a love most amyable,
> Disdayning no man of power great or small
> For a crewell oppressor is nothying commendable.

3rd Senator:

> That is the chief cause hither we were sent,
> To gyve the people warning to have all things perfitly,
> For they that do not, breaketh Mr Mayor's commandment,
> And according to the order, punysshed must they be.

Apart from the waits, many individual minstrels under the control of their gilds had an assured place in mediaeval town life. At Beverley in Yorkshire may be seen the gallery they had built. These obviously were not vagabonds but men of some corporate wealth with an accepted status in the town.

What did the minstrels play and sing? Here the evidence is by no means so clear as the pictorial evidence of what they wore. It was characteristic of trade gilds that they kept close their trade secrets, and to write down a tune would be a means of passing it into unqualified hands. This behaviour would apply to such as were organized, but not all were so lucky; many popular musicians were outside the protection of the gilds and the nobility who patronized the higher class of entertainers; as likely as not few of these could read music; they would be folk musicians in the broader sense of depending on oral transmission of their songs, but not completely dependent on the common stock of folk-song since they were capable of inventing their own tunes. The line between communal music and popular individual compositions was difficult to draw at this period, but not even the tightest regulated gild could stop a good tune from being remembered. Between the folk-songs and the

B

professional minstrels' songs stood the carols, with their communal
burdens and educational narrative lines:

> *Nowell, Nowell, Nowell, Nowell!*
> *This is the salutation of the angel Gabriel.*
> Tidings true there be come new,
> Sent from the Trinity
> By Gabriel to Nazareth,
> City of Galilee;
> 'A clean maiden and pure virgin,
> Through her humility,
> Hath conceived the person second in Deity.'

This comes from a manuscript of the early fifteenth century [1]
containing carols, drinking songs, and satires against shrewish
women. The word 'nowell' in English was always used as a combined greeting and shout of joy within the carol, and should not
be confused with the French word 'noël', which is the name for a
Christmas song. An English carol may not be a song for Christmas,
but the popularity of the Virgin Mary was such that carols on the
Annunciation and Nativity outnumbered all others.

> When that he presented was
>   Before her fair viságe,
> In most demure and goodly wise
>   He did to her homáge;
> And said, 'Lady, from heaven so high,
>   That Lordés heritage,
> For he of thee now born will be,
>   I'm sent on his messáge.'

> 'Hail, virgin celestial,
>   The meek'st that ever was!
> Hail, temple of the Deity!
>   Hail, mirror of all grace!
> Hail, virgin pure, I thee ensure,
>   Within a little space,
> Thou shalt conceive, and Him receive
> That shall bring great soláce.'

[1] Sloan MS. 2593.

> Then bespake the virgin again
>   And answered womanly:
> 'Whate'er my Lord commandeth me
>   I will obey truly.'
> With '*Ecce sum humillima*
>   *Ancilla Domini;*
> *Secundum verbum tuum*'
>   She said, '*Fiat mihi*'.

By a strange mistake, due to a freak of bookbinding, the tune of this carol was associated with verses completely out of character with it.[1] The actual cause of this mistake need not be retailed here, but we may remark the difficulty of deciding what makes a minstrel's song and what a folk-song; the song which follows has been claimed by eminent scholars for both classifications respectively. It is in carol form, with the burden given in full at the beginning and repeated after each verse. Wright, editing the collection of *Songs and Carols, No. 73*, for the Percy Society in 1841, claimed it for a minstrel's song, but Sir E. K. Chambers claimed it for a folk-song. This difference of classification may, however, be due to the emergence of definite opinion on the nature of folk-song which took place in the latter half of the nineteenth century, but cannot explain the reversal of opinion by R. L. Greene, in *Early English Carols*, 1935. Greene holds that it is not a folk-song, though good for improvisation. He supports his view with Cecil Sharp's statement that he never heard a true drinking-song sung by genuine folk-singers. My reason for classifying it as a popular song, but not a folk-song, lies in a proverbial rhyme quoted by Greene from John Ray in 1678. It is far too clever (in the townsmen's sense) to be a folk proverb:

> He that buys land buys many stones;
> He that buys flesh buys many bones;
> He that buys eggs buys many shells;
> He that buys good ale buys nothing else.

Now for the drinking song:

> *Bryng vs in good ale, and bryng vs in good ale,*
> *Fore our blyssyd Lady sake, bryng vs in good ale.*

[1] See R. L. Greene (ed.), *The Early English Carols* (1935). See also W. Chappell, *Popular Music of the Olden Time* (1855), where both sets of words are made to fit the tune!

Bryng vs in no browne bread, fore that is mad of brane,
Nore bryng vs in no whyt bred, fore therein is no gane,
But bryng vs in good ale.

Bryng vs in no befe, for ther is many bonys,
But bryng vs in good ale, for that goth downe at onys,
And bryng vs in good ale.

Bryng vs in no bacon, for that is passyng fate,
But bryng vs in good ale, and give vs inough of that.
And bryng vs in good ale.

Bryng vs in no mutton, for that is often lean,
Nore bryng vs in no trypys, for they be seldom clene,
But bryng vs in good ale.

Bryng vs in no eggys, for ther are many schelles,
But bryng vs in good ale, and gyve vs nothing ellys.
And bryng vs in good ale.

Bryng vs in no butter, for therin are many herys,
Nore bryng vs in no pygges flesch, for that will make vs borys.
But bryng vs in good ale.

Bryng vs in no podynges, for therein is all Godes good,
Nore bryng vs in no veneson, for that is not for oure blod.
But bryng vs in good ale.

Bryng vs in no copon's flesch, for that is often dere,
Nore bryng vs in no doke's flesch, for they slober in the mere.
But bryng vs in good ale.

About 1850 was discovered a commonplace book, long hidden behind a bookcase, written by Richard Hill, who was a London grocer's apprentice in the earliest years of the sixteenth century, when he started to compile the book. His master, John Wyngar, became alderman of the City in 1493 and Lord Mayor in 1504, so his apprentice Richard Hill must have been well in the midst of affairs. This is borne out by the nature of the subjects in which he was interested, cultural and practical. Both are mixed up in the book, and indicate quite clearly the mind of a young man destined for a townsman's responsibilities. Hill's education was a good deal broader than that of a country gentleman of that time, and certainly was not bounded by what the clergy would have taught him; his book contains pious thoughts, but instead of dominating his life they form merely one aspect of it. Hill knew English, French, and Latin; he could enjoy literature in these three tongues and noted down forms of business letters in the modern ones; he had a knowledge of legal codes sufficient to guide him in the purchase of land or letters of attorney; he took part in arranging civic feasts like those of the Lord Mayor at the Guildhall, and so he knew the qualities of wines, of cooking recipes, and how to brew good ale. Besides these he noted the simple facts needed for a business career, such as weights and measures, and home remedies for a poisoned dog or a cut finger (the latter based on good, strong, sticky ale). He was a man with a rich sense of humour, and a collector of satires as well as carols; a man of many parts, civilized in the true sense of being able to bear his full part in a responsible urban society. He married, wisely, the daughter of Harry Wyngar, haberdasher, in 1518, choosing for his helpmate one who was equally versatile in her interests, able to manage a wealthy middle-class household, help to entertain his business acquaintances, and hold her own in good company. Many such men in the city of London could truly 'walk with kings, nor lose the common touch'. Richard Hill was a man of substance and integrity, but a merchant, given to thinking first in terms of profit and loss. Up and down the country were men such as he in all the growing mercantile towns; their character has been perpetuated in legendary phrases like 'Proud Preston', 'Canny Newcastle', 'A York Bite' (for clever snatching of the lion's share of a profit), and 'A Bristol Man's Gift' (for something no longer wanted by the owner, presented in the hope of securing future favour). These were the men who controlled life in the towns— who could stand up for themselves against their competitors, or stand together against a common enemy. The Court had to respect them on occasion and the Church in its decline had to give way to them.[1]

We see their influence in development of the English drama, as the gilds took over the control of the pageantry at holiday times. Every craft had its patron saint: that of grocers was St Anthony; of tanners, St Clement; of shoemakers, St Crispin; of carpenters, St Joseph; of weavers, St Stephen. Even the beggars had an interest in St Giles, the patron saint of cripples. Saints' days were public

[1] At the Dissolution of the Monasteries many bought from Henry VIII lands previously owned by monastic orders.

holidays, and there were plenty of them. If there is a case to be made out for a merry England in the fourteenth and fifteenth centuries, this is it, not in the seclusion of the sheep runs on the hills. The Houses of York and Lancaster met on the battlefield, the Church was grown notoriously corrupt, but Chester, Coventry, Beverley, York, Wakefield, Norwich, and Newcastle-on-Tyne, to name only the most famous, had their great cycles of miracle plays performed by the members of their gilds, with high stages, or 'pageants', drawn through the streets to recognized stations. At Chester:

They began first at the abbey gates, and when the first pageant was played, it was wheeled to the high cross before the mayor, and so to every street. So every street had a pageant playing before it at one time, till all the pageants for the day appointed were played. When one pageant was near ended, word was brought from street to street, that so they might come in place thereof, exceedingly orderly, and all the streets have their pageants before them, all at one time playing together; to see which plays was great resort and also scaffolds and stages made in the streets in those places where they determined to play their pageants.[1]

This was popular art in the true sense, done by the people and for the people. If the times were largely anti-clerical the people were not anti-Christian. The eternal threat of the Day of Judgment still held men's thoughts, as in the interlude of the *Three Queens and the Three Dead Men.*

1st Queen. I am afeared.
2nd Queen.   Lo, what I see?
3rd Queen. Me thinketh it be devils three!
1st Corpse. I was well fair.
2nd Corpse.   Such shalt thou be.
3rd Corpse. For Godes love, be-ware by me.

The use of music in these miracle plays was much as we have it in the later Elizabethan drama, though simpler in form. Songs could be used to create atmosphere, to hold an emotional situation for a longer period, or bring a scene to an effective close. Nowhere in a miracle-play is music more effectively used than in the Coventry play of *The Nativity*:

---

[1] Ernest Rhys, Introduction to *Everyman and Other Miracle Plays* (1930).

Angels sing 'Gloria in Excelsis Deo'.

3rd Shepherd:

> Hark, they sing above the clouds so clear!
> Heard I never of so merry a choir.
> Now gentle brother draw we near
> To hear their harmony?

1st Shepherd:

> Brother, mirth and solace is come us among
> For, by the sweetness of their song,
> God's Son is come, whom we have looked for long,
> As signifieth this star we do see.

2nd Shepherd:

> Glory, *Gloria in Excelsis*; that was their song;
> How say ye fellows! said they not thus?

1st Shepherd:

> That is well said, now go we hence
> To worship that child of high magnificence;
> And that we may sing in his presence,
> *Et in terra pax omnibus.* (*sic*)

The Shepherds sing:

> As I rode out this enderes' night,
> Of three jolly shepherds I saw a sight,
> And all about their fold a star shone bright;
> They sang 'Terli, terlow';
> So merrily the shepherds their pipes can blow.

The scene changes to the stable at Bethlehem, with Joseph, Mary, and the Holy Child. Then the shepherds' song is again used to end this scene, before the entry of the two prophets.

> Down from heaven, from heaven so high,
> Of angels there came a great company,
> With mirth, and joy, and great solemnity,
> They sang 'Terli, Terlow';
> So merrily the shepherds their pipes can blow.

The origin of the word 'carol', as also of the word 'ballad', was to describe a dance, but in course of time the dance movements were restricted and finally went out of use, but the dancing rhythms still persist in traditional carol tunes. There is always an austere side of religion which will denounce dancing as wanton, and it is at such times that the cultural influence of secular institutions is most valuable to the art. The Church had been weakening in moral fibre for two centuries before the Reformation in England, but increasing its worldly wealth; austerity and luxury were at war within its body. But the years immediately before the Reformation did not see the start of this internal struggle; it had been implicit in Christian behaviour from the early days of the monasteries. If a community vows itself to poverty and to self-abasing toil, it cannot help but create wealth for which it has no use. The wealth can be given away —as some of it was—but the remainder will accumulate and have to be managed according to the laws which govern the preservation of wealth. So these men, vowed to take little or nothing from the common fund, yet devoting their lives to humble work, reclaimed waste land and so made it valuable, raised great houses and wrought within them fine works of art. It is not to be charged against them without excuse that they sometimes became greedy, for the possession of wealth and the skill required to manage it throw great temptation in the way of men. Such temptation was by no means confined to the Church, as we know from the great wealth obtained by wool merchants; there are the great Cotswold churches—Northleach, Chipping Camden, Burford, and Fairford—to prove it, and a description of the factory system employed in Newbury by the famous John Winchcombe—'Jack of Newbury'.

> Within one room, being large and long,
> There stood two hundred looms full strong;
> Two hundred men, the truth is so,
> Wrought in these looms all in a row.
> By every one a pretty boy
> Sat making quills with mickle joy;
> And in another place, hard by,
> An hundred women merrily
> Were carding hard with joyful cheer,
> Who singing sat with voices clear,
> And in a chamber close beside,
> Two hundred maidens did abide . . .
> These pretty maids did never lin,
> But in that place all day did spin.[1]

[1] Thomas Deloney, *Jack of Newbury*, ed. F. O. Mann (1912).

The 'poet', Thomas Deloney, lived later,[1] but he was a weaver and knew his subject—and his public! Let us therefore keep in mind the two conflicting forces in men's minds during the great age of the carols—acquisition of wealth and Christian humility, for the time was to come when this conflict would debase all popular art.[2] In the fifteenth century the perfection of such verses as these was possible:

> I sing of a maiden
>   That is makeless;
> King of all kings
>   To her son she ches.
>
> He came all so still
>   Where his mother was,
> As dew in April
>   That falleth on grass.
>
> He came all so still
>   To his mother's bower,
> As dew in April
>   That falleth on flower.
>
> He came all so still
>   Where his mother lay,
> As dew in April
>   That falleth on the spray.
>
> Mother and maiden
>   Was never none but she;
> Well may such a lady
>   Godes mother be.

Great poetry was still to come, but it lost the universality of such lines as these. The art of the carol came to perfection in the fifteenth century, and owes much to the best-selling quality of an ideal of womanhood.

These things must be mentioned not because they are part of the orthodox history of music in England, but because they are particularly relevant to our theme of the special history of popular music. The great music of the middle sixteenth century in England was

---

[1] John Winchcombe, *d.* 1520; Thomas Deloney, ? *b.* 1543.
[2] See Chapter XIV.

seriously diverted as a result of the Reformation; the Church had to start a new line, and high-grade secular music was subjected to influences stemming from the Italian Renaissance, but popular music went its way. We have mentioned the waits of Norwich; part of their duty was to welcome distinguished strangers at the gates of the city. In 1578 Queen Elizabeth entered Norwich where 'at the gate of the city were placed the loud musick, who cheerfully and melodiously welcomed Her Majesty into the city, this song being sung by the best voices in the choir':

> The dew of heaven drops this day
> > On dry and barren ground,
> Wherefore at fruitful hearts I sing
> > Of drum and trumpet sound.
> Yield what is due, show what is meet,
> > To make our joy the more,
> In our good hope and her good praise,
> > We never saw before.

> Full many a winter have we seen
> > And many storms withall,
> Since here we saw a king or queen
> > In pomp and stately pall.
> Wherefore make feast and bow quite still,
> > And now to triumph fall;
> With duty let us show goodwill
> > To glad both great and small.

> The dew of heaven drops this day, etc.[1]

There is integrity in this song. One feels that the writer of the verse really meant what he said, which is more than can be claimed for the writers of many welcome odes for royalty. Small wonder that the Norwich waits were famous. When Sir Francis Drake wished for music to accompany him on his ill-fated voyage to Corunna in 1589, he asked the permission of the Mayor and Corporation of Norwich for their waits to go with him as his private band. Of the six waits, only two returned. Eleven years later we have further evidence—this time from a comedian in Shakespeare's players—of the fame of the Norwich choir and waits. Will Kemp

---

[1] J. C. Bridge, *Town Waits and their Tunes*, Proceedings of the Musical Association (1927–8), p. 83.

danced the Morris from London to Norwich for a wager, and left an account of his journey. In this way did he arrive:

Passing the gate . . . I got throw that narrow preaze into the open market-place; where on the cross, ready prepared, stood the City Waytes, who not a little refreshed my weariness with toiling thorow so narrow a lane as the people left me: such Waytes (under *Benedicite* be it spoken) fewe Citties in our Realme have the like, none better; who besides their excellency in wind instruments, their rare cunning on the vyoll and violin, theyr voices be admirable, everie one of them able to serve in any Cathedral Church in Christendoome for Quiristers.

We must not leave the story of the common minstrels, however, on this high note, without any consideration of its bass. The waits were musicians employed by the burgesses of their town; they had the mayor's licence to perform; without that, where would they have been? As likely as not whipped through parish after parish under a statute of that very queen whom we have seen so loyally welcomed by the waits of Norwich:

All fencers, bearwards, common players in interludes and minstrels, not belonging to any baron of the realm or towards any other honorable personage of greater degree . . . which . . . shall wander abroad and have not licence of two justices of the peace . . . shall be deemed rogues, vagabonds and sturdy beggars.[1]

As the 'Third Senator' among the Lincoln waits would have expressed it:

That is the chief cause hither we are sent,
To gyve the people warning to have all things perfitly;
For they that do not, breaketh Mr Mayor's commandment,
And according to the order, punysshed must they be.

[1] 14 Eliz. c.5, 1572.

III. TUDOR FANCY

NOBODY IN THE SIXTEENTH CENTURY would have doubted that even a wait had an immortal soul, but they would certainly have denied that his music should be made a reason for the display of it. A wait was required to make music for a definite purpose, as when a visiting dignitary had to be honoured, or when the town made holiday. He was even required to make music at certain times of the day and night on the same principle that the town clock now strikes the hours. Nor was a wait different from other professional musicians in accepting his lot. 'He who pays the piper calls the tune.' It has been left for modern musicians to enforce the claim that they will make better music if they make the music they like best to make, whether their audiences like it or not.

This does not mean that the waits produced bad music.[1] The public wanted money's worth, then as always, and a minstrel of any class who could give a display of skill on suitable occasions was sure of reward. Rewards to minstrels were often greater than those given to the Church for special occasions, much to the disgust of the clergy. Yet the two could agree in principle, for both minstrel and monk made music respectively for ceremonies of greater importance than the music which served them. Of church music, 'Let the precentor or singer who sings surpassingly comport himself in his office', says a clerical directive,[2] 'which is a source of delight and pleasure to God, the angels and mankind, with reverence and modesty. Let him sing with such sweetness and devotion that all the brethren may find in his behaviour a pattern for the religious life.' The art of the precentor was purposive, and pride in one's skill was inconsistent with true holiness; when William of Evere, tenth Abbot of Croxden, enlarged the monastic library in 1303, he had transcriptions made of the books, but if a monk 'showed pride about his work, he was to be punished by a course of bread and water'. It was on the right of the artist to take pride in his work, and to profit by it, that Church and secular musicians could not agree. Display was ungodly, except it be wholly for the glory of the Lord.

[1] Thomas Morley dedicated his *Consort Lessons* of 1599 to the (London) Lord Mayor's Wayts. He must, therefore, have held their playing in respect.
[2] *Observations of the Priory of Barnwell*, Cambridge; cf. F. H. Crossley, F.S.A., *The English Abbey* (1939).

Among the gentry of the sixteenth century music was practised, but again with a distinct understanding of its function in society; it was good to make music for one's solace or recreation among friends, but the public display of one's skill sullied the 'worship' of a person of rank: 'A gentilman, plainge or singing in a commune audience, appaireth his estimation: the people forgettinge reuerence, when they behold him in the similitude of a common seruant or minstrell', said Sir Thomas Elyot. One of the purposes of music was to increase the public estimation of a gentleman, to command for him the reverence of the common people, whose stations in life required them to respect great men even as all men were required to worship God. Undoubtedly it did this. We can accept the ceremonial use of music for the glorification of a ruler without question (and there are innumerable songs like the *Agincourt Carol* and the Norwich waits' song of welcome to Queen Elizabeth I to prove it), but we may also see how music not intended for such ceremonies could yet enhance the popularity of a monarch. There is in existence a sixteenth-century composition attributed to Henry VIII, who certainly loved music and was both practitioner and composer; the song referred to may not be by him, but it is typical of the life he lived among his personal friends, with music, dancing, and hunting activities proper to one of his station:

> Pastime with good company
> I love, and shall until I die;
> Grudge who will, but none deny,
> So God be pleased, this life will I,
>   For my pastance
>   Hunt, sing and dance,
>   My heart is set;
>   All goodly sport
>   To my comfort,
> Who shall me let?

> Youth will needs have dalliance,
> Of good or ill some pastance;
> Company me thinketh of the best
> All thoughts and fantasies to digest;
>   For idleness
>   Is chief mistress

Of vices all;
Then who can say
But pass the day
Is best of all?

Company with honesty
Is virtue—and vice to flee.
Company is good or ill,
But every man hath his free will;
The best I sue;
The worst eschew;
My mind shall be,
Virtue to use,
Vice to refuse,
I shall use me.

This was called *The King's Ballad*. It proclaimed a joy in society which civilized men and women found especially welcome in the sixteenth century, when after the disbanding of the private armies of the nobility under Henry VII civilization advanced more rapidly. Domestic architecture improved; houses were warmer, lighter, more tastefully decorated; women were safer from molestation, though they still had to marry whom their parents chose; the age of the English madrigal was soon to arrive, and domestic life in the upper and middle classes offered all the facilities for its culture. People set a new ideal of domestic happiness for themselves, and they liked to know that their ideals were those of the leaders of fashion.

This cut both ways; if the gentry projected their own beliefs into their conception of the character of the king, the king gained in popularity and influence as a result of it. Henry VIII was a tyrant, self-willed and ruthless, but in his relations with the country at large he secured an impressive measure of willing support. The monasteries were looted and nobody's hands were clean about that business, but Henry needed a divorce, a new source of wealth, and the Church needed reform. If Henry coveted the lands held by monastic orders, so did his people, and since Henry sold these estates to the upper and middle classes, they were favourably disposed to him. Wealth and influence accumulated in the hands of astute men, and social life responded. The sixteenth century saw the flowering of a great new civilization based on domestic life, in which music had a most honourable part; it was cultivated, as Nicholas Young stated, 'among gentlemen and merchants of good accompt', and found its best expression in the madrigal and instrumental fantasia, or 'fancy'. With these we are not primarily concerned in this book, but they should be considered nevertheless by all its readers.[1] Meanwhile, the story of the popular songs may be continued, starting again from the current view of Henry VIII.

A song to be sung in the evening is called a serenade; a song intended to be sung in the morning is an aubade. So much for modern terminology; but in the sixteenth century they had common English phrases which were probably taken from the name of well-known songs and so described exactly what was meant in good English. A song of departing was a 'Loath to depart', and an aubade was a 'Hunt's up':

> The hunt us up, the hunt is up,
>   And it is well-nigh day,
> And Harry our King has gone hunting
>   To bring his deere to baye.
>
> The east is bright with morning light,
>   And darkness it is fled;
> And the merie horn wakes up the morn
>   To leave his idle bed.
>
> Beholde the skyes with golden dyes
>   Are glowing all around;
> The grass is green, and so are the treen,
>   All laughing at the sound.
>
> The horses snort to be at the sport,
>   The dogges are running free;
> The woddes rejoice at the mery noise,
>   Of hey tantara tee ree!
>
> The sunne is glad to see us clad
>   All in our lusty greene,
> And smiles in the sky as he riseth hye
>   To see and to be seene.
>
> Awake, all men, I say agen,
>   Be mery as thou maye,
> For Harry our king has gone hunting,
>   To bring his deere to baye.

[1] There is no dearth of books on the Elizabethan madrigal. E. H. Fellowes's *English Madrigal Composers* (1921) is essential, and Wilfrid Mellers's *Music and Society* (1946).

The popularity of this song can be estimated by the number of parodies or variations on its theme. In 1533 an Act was passed for the suppression of 'fond books, ballads, rhimes, and other lewd treatises in the English tongue'; and in 1537 one John Hogan was prosecuted under this act for a political parody sung to the tune of *The Hunt is up*. The printing press had already begun to prove itself a mixed blessing, but in comparison with later history the craftsmen who followed William Caxton were men of integrity, well worthy of the honour which later was to be popularly attributed to men of their trade—'the Fourth Estate'. For a polite but nevertheless sincere example of a hunt's up the following is typical:

> The hunt is up, the hunt is up,
>   Awake, my lady free;
> The sun hath risen from out his prison,
>   Beneath the glistering sea.

> The hunt is up, the hunt is up,
>   Awake, my lady bright;
> The morning lark is high, to mark
>   The coming of day-light.

> The hunt is up, the hunt is up,
>   Awake, my lady fair;
> The kine and sheep, but now asleep,
>   Browse in the morning air.

> The hunt is up, the hunt is up,
>   Awake, my lady gay;
> The stars are fled to the ocean bed,
>   And now it is broad day.

> The hunt is up, the hunt is up,
>   Awake, my lady sheen;
> The hills look out, and the woods about
>   Are drest in lovely green.

> The hunt is up, the hunt is up,
>   Awake, my lady dear;
> A morn in spring is the sweetest thing
>   Cometh in all the year.

The hunt is up, the hunt is up,
Awake, my lady sweet;
I come to thy bower at this loved hour,
My own true love to greet.[1]

The song is purposive, but delightful art.

It is possible to follow the course of popular song right through the sixteenth century showing how the good taste of the time gained for England the complimentary title 'A nest of singing-birds'. Of recent times Parry [2] has expressed the opinion that vulgarity in music is created when a song is taken out of its true environment into another. Thus, a music-hall song may be good of its type and proper enough in its place, but take it out of the music-hall or the streets and put it in a church service and the result would be most objectionable. Similarly, good church music transferred to the theatre would become insincere in its new environment. The use of the word 'vulgar' in such a context perhaps gives a clue to Parry's reasons, for the word in his day implied a debased type of mind, whereas originally it meant 'the common people' without necessarily implying reproach. 'The vulgar tongue' was not a term for profane speech, but for the language common to a whole nation. In the sixteenth century, song would not be so generally subject to Parry's theory; there is too much evidence to the contrary. Already we have seen how a plain-song melody could be sung by the shepherds in a miracle play, and be absolutely right for its purpose.[3] It was proper for the common people to know simple plain-song, and natural for them to believe that it was the sort of song to which the angels would sing *Gloria in excelsis*. In more sophisticated settings, however, the theory of Parry could apply, and it was true that the Church had constant trouble with musicians who introduced wanton styles of singing into the Church ritual, or, even into the Mass itself, tunes which bore secular associations. This was the great age of many-voiced ecclesiastical music, of intricate part-singing, of the interweaving of many melodies together in counterpoint. The various melodies were woven round a known melody, which by right should have been one of the traditional melodies of the Church —and often was—but secular melodies were used, bearing such names as *L'homme armé* (*The Armed Man*) or *Les nez rouges* (*The Red Noses*). These were of course of French origin; in England

[1] Quoted from Chappell's *Popular Music of the Olden Time* (1855), Vol. I, p. 61.
[2] Sir C. Hubert H. Parry, *Style in Musical Art* (1911), Introduction.
[3] See Chapter II, extract from the Coventry *Nativity Play*, p. 35.

there was a song beloved not only of the people but of eminent musicians, used as the fixed melody or structural basis for the music of the Mass; in it a shepherd yearns for the coming of spring:

> Westron wynde, when will thou blow
> The smalle rain down can rain?
> Christ, if my love were in my arms
> And I in my bed again!

John Taverner's Mass on the tune of this song is undoubtedly great music.[1]

In this process of composition the tune of *Westron Wynde* lost some of the character of popular music. The elaborate music of the polyphonic Mass was for skilled singers and men of good musical education. Moreover, while the Latin rite was enhanced by such music, the style was difficult to apply to English words, and, as we know, the middle of the sixteenth century saw a change indeed when Henry VIII dissolved the monasteries and re-established the Church with the use of the English language. John Taverner himself was an early convert to protestantism, for which he was punished as a heretic by Cardinal Wolsey. Being at that time Master of the Children at Wolsey's own college at Oxford (then called Cardinal College —now Christ Church), Taverner was imprisoned in 'a deep cave under the ground of the same Colledge, where their salt fyshe was layde, so that through the fylthe stincke thereof, they were all infected'. Taverner was released, for musicians were traditionally supposed not to understand religious doctrine, in consequence of which they could be forgiven a little irresponsibility which would amount to heresy in normal men.

The case of John Merbecke, organist of St George's Chapel, Windsor, also is interesting. With three companions, Merbecke was found guilty of heresy and condemned to be burnt at the stake. This sentence was carried out on Merbecke's companions but not on Merbecke.[2] His judges even tried in their way to be kind.

'Take this man and have him to the Marshalsea, and tell the keeper that it is the council's pleasure that he treat him gently; and if he have any money in his purse (as I think he hath not much) take it from him, lest the prisoners do take it; and minister it unto him as he shall have need.'

Next day a messenger from Gardiner, Bishop of Winchester, visited Merbecke and tried to get him to betray his friends. This

---

[1] *Tudor Church Music*, ed. E. H. Fellowes (1923), Vol I.
[2] Foxe's *Book of Martyrs* errs when it says Merbecke was burnt at the stake.

Merbecke refused to do; he was put in irons and ultimately brought before the bishop:

'Merbecke, wilt thou cast thyself away?'

'No, my lord.'

'Yes; thou goest about it, for thou wilt answer nothing. What a devil made thee meddle with the Scriptures? Thy vocation was another way, wherein thou hast a goodly gift, if thou did'st esteem it.'

'Yes, I do esteem it, and have done my part therein according to the little knowledge that God hath given me.'

'And why the devil did'st thou not hold thee there?'

As for Taverner, he became one of Thomas Cromwell's agents in the Reformation in East Anglia, giving up music for other entertainments:

'Accordyng to yor lordshippes comaundment the Roode was burned the vii daye of this monethe beynge also the market daye and A sermone of the blake ffreyre at the burnynge of hym who did expresse the cause of his burnying and the ydolatry comytted by hym whiche sermone hathe done moche good and hathe turned many mennes hartes ffrome yt.' [1]

So much for musicians being harmless! John Merbecke, on the other hand, stuck to his music long enough to demonstrate in his *Booke of Common Praier Noted* how the ritual of the Anglican services could be set to a style of plain-song suitably adapted to English words. The promise was not carried far enough, however, for Merbecke never got on to the Psalms; becoming a Calvinist, he forswore polyphony; he rejected the art of which he had proved himself a master, and only in the twentieth century has his music for the Anglican Church come to be properly understood.

This diversion into the biography of two able musicians is not wholly irrelevant to our theme, for at the root of the matter was the fact that in the Latin Church the music had become divorced from the understanding of the people; elaborate polyphony was admirable for the great choirs, but not an art into which the congregation could enter, as in plain-song. This opened the inevitable split in musical opinion—the rift between 'highbrow' and 'lowbrow', in our modern objectionable terms—with the reformers insisting on the canticles and the psalms as the only authoritative hymns acceptable in the church services,[2] the psalms were paraphrased into ballad-style verses. These metrical psalms were certainly popular.

[1] Letter from John Taverner to Lord Cromwell, 11 September 1538.

[2] Only one of the hymns of the ancient Church appears in the English Prayer Book —*Veni, creator Spiritus* (in the Ordinal of 1552).

Thousands sang them together at St Paul's Cross in London. Some of the original tunes are still in use, with the word 'old' in their title to signify that they belong to Day's first complete publication of Sternhold and Hopkins's metrical psalms [1]—we all know the *Old Hundredth* (actually from Geneva), the *Old 113th*, and the *Old 124th*. As for the words, Psalm 100 in the English Prayer Book version reads: 'O be joyful in the Lord, all ye lands: serve the Lord with gladness, and come before his presence with a song.'

Rendered into metre this became:

> All people that on earth do dwell,
> Sing to the Lord with cheerful voice;
> Him serve with mirth, his praise forthtell,
> Come ye before him and rejoice.

The verse enabled the simple words to be easily remembered, and the sense was that of holy writ, 'Very mete to be used of all sorts of people privately for their godly solace and comfort, laying aparte all ungodly songes and ballades, which tende only to the nourishing of Vice, and corrupting of youth.' The thought was holy, though the style of composition was close to that of the ballads which the author condemned. The style was not to be condemned for its familiarity, however; that is a form of musical snobbery from which the Puritans seem to have been remarkably free; there were, however, lapses from the dignity of such poetry as that of the *Old 100th*. Psalm 22 contains this passage: 'Many oxen are come about me: fat bulls of Basan close me in on every side. They gape upon me with their mouths: as it were a ramping and a roaring lion.'

Put into verse this became:

> So many buls do compass me,
> That be full strong of head;
> Yea, buls so fat, as though they had
> In Basan field been fed.

> They shall heap sorrow on their heads,
> Which run as they were mad;
> To offer to the idle gods.
> Alas, it is too bad.

Certainly it keeps to the text, and is simple. It was the work of

---

[1] *The Whole Booke of Psalms collected into English Meter* (1562).

an educated man exerting himself 'for that the rude and ignorant in song, may with more delight, desire, and good will, be moved and drawn to the goodly exercise of singing the psalms, as well in common places of prayer where all together with one voice render thanks and praises to God, as privately by themselves or at home in their houses.'

But 'alas, it is too bad'! Many a vagrant minstrel could be 'tied to the end of a cart, naked, and be beaten with whips throughout the same market town or other place till his body be bloody by reason of such whipping',[1] and still be able to invent a better verse.

Do not, therefore, place too much faith in the poetic gifts of the educated. Fancy is in the heart, not in the head, as they well knew in the Elizabethan playhouses.

There came out of the grammar schools and the universities, in the second half of the sixteenth century, young men with a passion for life and the New Knowledge of the Renaissance; they were not professional men of literature, for there was no reputable literary profession in those days; there were, however, the professions of music and the theatre, into which these men entered; their lyrics differed widely from those of the old miracle plays, and the theatres themselves lay without the jurisdiction of the London magistrates, on the other side of the Thames; here the passions of men had their amplest vent, and in the enjoyment of life they revelled:

> I cannot eat but little meat,
>   My stomach is not good;
> But sure I think that I can drink
>   With him that wears a hood.
> Though I go bare, take ye no care,
>   I nothing am a-cold;
> I stuff my skin so full within
>   Of jolly good ale and old.
>
>   Back and side go bare, go bare;
>   Both foot and hand go cold;
>   But, belly, God send thee good ale enough,
>   Whether it be new or old.
>
> I love no roast but a nut-brown toast,
>   And a crab laid in the fire;
> A little bread shall do me stead;
>   Much bread I not desire.

[1] 22 Henry VIII, c. 12 (1530–1).

No frost nor snow, no wind, I trow,
   Can hurt me if I wold;
I am so wrapped and thoroughly lapp'd
   Of jolly good ale and old.

       Back and side go bare, go bare, etc.

And Tib, my wife, that as her life
   Loveth well good ale to seek,
Full oft drinks she till ye may see
   The tears run down her cheek:
Then doth she trowl to me the bowl,
   E'en as a maltworm should,
And saith, 'Sweetheart, I took my part
   Of this jolly good ale and old.'

       Back and side go bare, go bare, etc.

Now let them drink till they nod and wink,
   E'en as good fellows should do;
They shall not miss to have that bliss
   Good ale doth bring men to;
And all poor souls that have scour'd bowls
   Or have them lustily troll'd,
God save the lives of them and their wives,
   Whether they be young or old.

       Back and side go bare, go bare;
       Both foot and hand go cold;
       But, belly, God send thee good ale enough,
       Whether it be new or old.

This jovial drinking song was used in the play *Gammer Gurton's Needle*.[1] Its rhythm and its sentiments are intended to appeal to a wide range of opinion, such as is necessary for the success of a popular song.

The official attitude towards the drama was equivocal; it was admitted that the drama could have an uplifting effect on men's minds, and even a moral elevation, but it also drew to the playhouses much bawdy company, who liked a wanton love-scene or a spate of bloody vengeance. Without doubt that which they saw in an Elizabethan playhouse raised passions which in a civilized state

[1] The song is older than the play, and probably by a cleric.

should be kept under control, while a new variant of t̶
moralist, calling himself 'Puritan', appeared; his sect hel̶
that the reformation of the Church under Elizabeth was
plete; that unscriptural and corrupt ceremonies were retai̶
pre-Reformation times. Knowing only too well how m̶̶ were
conceived and born in sin, the Calvinist section of the Puritans (by
far the most influential) saw salvation only in the grace of God;
man was too weak an instrument to effect his own, but he could
listen to the voice of conscience, read the Bible, and submit himself
to strict discipline. The Puritans were not opposed to all music,
nor to all drama, but, like the metrical psalms, these must be purposive, and reason should be the guide. Shakespeare knew the type:
'Thinkest thou because thou art virtuous there shall be no more
cakes and ale?'

The Puritan policy was a valuable contribution to an age when
humanistic thought was the fashion at Court, in the universities,
and in the arts generally. Once it had been the highest function of
great art to praise God; now it was fashionable to find merit in pagan
authors, to play with the virtues of heathen deities, heroism in
divine emperors, and wisdom in nature; much of it was artificial,
but artificial in the Elizabethan sense of being well wrought:

> Under the greenwood tree
> Who loves to lie with me,
> And turn his merry note
> Unto the sweet bird's throat;
> Come hither, come hither, come hither;
> Here shall he see
> No enemy
> But winter and rough weather.

Jaques:

More, more! I prithee, more.

Amiens:

It will make you melancholy, Monsieur Jaques.

Jaq:

I thank it. More! I prithee, more. I can suck melancholy out
of a song as a weasel sucks eggs. More! I prithee, more.

Ami:

My voice is ragged; I know I cannot please you.

Jaq:

>I do not desire you to please me; I do desire you to sing.
>Come, more; another stanza; call you 'em stanzas? [1]

The song itself creates the atmosphere for a scene in which a company of exiled courtiers can philosophize on the reality of nature as opposed to the shams of the Court; but they are not of the countryside, like William and Audrey in the same play; the exiles are products of the New Learning; they are interested in music as an art, and in the relation of music to the emotions, and of the cultivation of the music and emotions for their pleasurable effect—even the pleasure of relishing the unpleasant, which is an acquired taste: 'I do not desire you to please me; I do desire you to sing.'

Classical philosophy is beautifully expressed in *The Merchant of Venice*:

Jessica:

>I am never merry when I hear sweet music.

Lorenzo:

>The reason is, your spirits are attentive;
>For do but note a wild and wanton herd,
>Or race of youthful and unhandled colts,
>Fetching mad bounds, bellowing and neighing loud,
>Which is the hot condition of their blood;
>If they but hear perchance a trumpet sound,
>Or any air of music touch their ears,
>You shall perceive them make a mutual stand,
>Their savage eyes turn'd to a modest gaze
>By the sweet power of music; therefore the poet
>Did feign that Orpheus drew trees, stones, and floods;
>Since nought so stockish, hard, and full of rage,
>But music for the time doth change his nature.
>The man that hath no music in himself,
>Nor is not moved with concord of sweet sounds,
>Is fit for treasons, stratagems, and spoils;
>The motions of his spirit are dull as night
>And his affections dark as Erebus:
>Let no such man be trusted. Mark the music. [2]

The presentation of classical lore in so attractive a guise was characteristic of the age. One can find flaws in the theory. Was John Taverner a man without music in his soul when he turned to

---

[1] *As You Like It*, II. v.   [2] *The Merchant of Venice*, v. i.

persecution of the clerics? Or was John Merbecke, when he gave up his fluid plain-song style for metrical psalms? We all know highly moral people who cannot tell one tune from another, and we have all heard of musicians like Liszt and Wagner whose sexual adventures acquainted them with strange bedfellows. One cannot generalize on such evidence, but in Shakespeare's day it was good to associate music with man's soul, and to believe that through music the mind also could be enriched.

In a playhouse containing little scenery, where lighting effects were impossible on the main stage, music was a valuable medium for creating atmosphere and holding a mood in the imagination of the audience. Shakespeare asks for music to increase our awe of the supernatural, be it heavenly or heretical. He brings in lyrics to hold a pleasant social scene, to tell of love in its lighter moods, or to end a scene effectively. Sometimes the lyric is simplicity itself, to be heard today with a tune traditional in the theatre:

> When that I was and a little tiny boy,
>   With hey, ho, the wind and the rain;
> A foolish thing was but a toy,
>   For the rain it raineth every day.
>
> But when I came to man's estate,
>   With hey, ho, the wind and the rain;
> 'Gainst knaves and thieves men shut their gates,
>   For the rain it raineth every day.
>
> But when I came, alas! to wive,
>   With hey, ho, the wind and the rain;
> By swaggering could I never thrive,
>   For the rain it raineth every day.
>
> But when I came unto my beds,
>   With hey, ho, the wind and the rain;
> With toss-pots still had drunken heads,
>   For the rain it raineth every day.
>
> A great while ago the world begun,
>   With hey, ho, the rain and the rain;
> But that's all one, our play is done,
>   And we'll strive to please you every day.[1]

Shakespeare ends his play on a simple human theme sung by a clown, and he uses the last verse of the song to say farewell to his

---

[1] *Twelfth Night*, end. Record, *Shakespeare Songs*, H.M.V. ALP 1265.

audience. He is in fact doing what any wandering ballad-singer would do—adding verses to the tune to suit his purpose. The tune decides the form—the verses carry the thought. Again the tune is used in *King Lear*, in a very different situation. In a scene portraying mighty anger, in which the elements join with Lear to shake the soul, the Fool sings:

> He that has and a little tiny wit,—
> With a hey, ho, the wind and the rain,—
> Must make content with his fortunes fit,
> For the rain it raineth every day.[1]

The temptation to treat madness as a horrific stage display is great indeed, and some there were who never got beyond that treatment, but Shakespeare could call up the mysterious belief that madness was a visitation of some supernatural agency, and had therefore in it some aspect of the divine. The Fool in Lear ends the scene not with his snatch of song, but with a double-edged prophecy.

The insane escape from this oppressive world into one where true-life discords are resolved. With Lear the discords were a result of ingratitude, with Ophelia, of thwarted sex. So Ophelia escapes into a dream world conveyed to the audience very forcibly by snatches of popular songs: *How should I your true love know? Tomorrow is St Valentine's Day, And will he not come again?* It says much for the common songs of the day that they could be used so well to pierce the tough exterior of conventional thought and prick the man beneath. Free love was a constant problem in a society which believed in the giving of sons and daughters in marriage as a form of family contract. Hormones know no law; sons could be disinherited and daughters starved, shut up, and beaten, but some of them—like Kate in *The Taming of the Shrew*, Beatrice, or thirteen-year-old Juliet, could nevertheless be very determined. Love songs, therefore, were a power in human actions—innocent in simple folk, who were less subjected to the wiles of scheming parents than their betters; so love songs about the peasantry had an attractive ring:

> It was a lover and his lass,
> With a hey, and a ho, and a hey nonino,
> That o'er the green corn-field did pass,
> In the spring-time, the only pretty ring time,
> When birds do sing, hey ding a ding, ding;
> Sweet lovers love the spring.

[1] *King Lear*, III. ii.

Think of the song as the musician would think of it. He has got his first verse and a tune to fit. Now the tune becomes the pattern to which the words for the remaining verses must comply. So the following verses keep close to the rhythm of the original pattern, and the important words come in the same places in the tune.

Verse one, line one: 'lover', 'lass'.
Verse two, line one: 'acres', 'rye'.
Verse three, line one: 'carol', 'hour'.

But in the last verse the rhythm of thought is thrown forward to the previous strong accents of the tune—on the words 'therefore' and 'present', but without any alteration of the tune; the musical instinct is paramount. This is characteristic of the age—an age when music and language were equally organic:

> Between the acres of the rye,
>   With a hey, and a ho, and a hey nonino,
> These pretty country folks would lie,
>   In the spring-time, the only pretty ring time,
> When birds do sing, hey ding a ding, ding;
> Sweet lovers love the spring.
>
> This carol they began that hour,[1]
>   With a hey, and a ho, and a hey nonino,
> How that life was but a flower
>   In the spring-time, the only pretty ring time,
> When birds do sing, hey ding a ding, ding;
> Sweet lovers love the spring.
>
> And therefore take the present time,
>   With a hey, and a ho, and a hey nonino,
> For love is crowned with the prime
>   In the spring-time, the only pretty ring time,
> When birds do sing, hey ding a ding, ding;
> Sweet lovers love the spring.[2]

One can sense this one-ness of verse and melody not only in the songs to be found in Shakespeare's plays but in all the works of Elizabethan composers. Shakespeare thought according to the fashion of his time, as also did his audiences; if the artistic standard was high, it was because popular taste would accept that standard.

---

[1] It is not a carol, but that word had now lost its definite meaning.
[2] *As You Like It*, v. iii.

One should not think of good songs as being morally superior in a
puritanical sense; there is plenty of evidence that some of the most
beautiful love songs were accepted as stimulants of wantonness:

Sir Toby Belch:

> Come on; there is sixpence for you; let's have a song.

Clown:

> Would you have a love-song, or a song of good life?

Sir Toby:

> A love-song, a love-song.

Sir Andrew Aguecheek:

> Ay, ay; I care not for good life.

Clown (sings):

> O mistress mine! where are you roaming?
> O stay and hear; your true-love's coming,
>   That can sing both high and low.
> Trip no farther, pretty sweeting,
> Journeys end in lovers' meeting
>   Every wise man's son doth know.
>
> What is love? 'tis not hereafter;
> Present mirth hath present laughter;
>   What's to come is still unsure;
> In delay there lies no plenty,
> Then come kiss me, sweet and twenty,
>   Youth's a stuff will not endure.

Sir Andrew:

> A mellifluous voice, as I am true knight.

Sir Toby:

> A contagious breath.

Sir Andrew:

> Very sweet and contagious, i' faith.

Sir Toby:

> To hear by the nose, it is dulcet in contagion. But shall we

make the welkin dance indeed? shall we rouse the night-owl in a catch that will draw three souls out of one weaver? shall we do that?

Sir Andrew:

An you love me, let's do 't; I am dog at a catch.[1]

So the three of them weave their separate souls into an endless canon, in the style we have already seen in the round (or rota) *Sumer is icumen in*; but the way of the catch and the song *O Mistress Mine* were to be very different; catches were to enliven boozy stag-parties, while *O Mistress Mine* graced the pages of *Queen Elizabeth's Virginal Book* in a setting by William Byrd, and graced Thomas Morley's *First Booke of Consort Lessons*, for a variety of instruments playing together. This book contains arrangements of madrigals, some by Morley himself, and arrangements of tunes well known in the theatres, like *Goe from my Window*, *O Mistress Mine*, and the two tunes which the citizen and his wife ask the theatre musicians to play in Beaumont and Fletcher's *The Knight of the Burning Pestle* —called *Lacrimae* and *Balowe*. The Elizabethan age saw a marvellous flowering of the arts, and in this display the popular songs of the theatres had their place along with the choicest blooms from musical Italy and the no less attractive music of the English school. But now the greatest art was not directed towards the glory of God alone, but for the glory of mankind; for we, too, moved like music in an ordered universe. One should not confound in singleness the part he should bear in the whole, but take heed of the lesson of music:

Mark how one string, sweet husband to another,
Strikes each in each by mutual ordering,
Resembling sire and child and happy mother,
Who, all in one, one pleasing note do sing:
    Whose speechless song, being many, seeming one,
    Sings this to thee: 'Thou single wilt prove none.'

[1] *Twelfth Night,* II. iii.

IV. DELONEY'S ENGLAND

'IN THE DAYES of King *Henry* the first, who was the first King that
instituted the high Court of Parliament, there liued nine men, which
for the trade of Clothing, were famous throughout all England.
Which Art in those daies was held in high reputation, both in respect
of the great riches that thereby was gotten, as also of the benefite
it brought to the whole Common-wealth: the yonger sons of
Knights and Gentlemen, to whom their Fathers would leaue no
lands, were most commonly preferred to learn this trade, to the
end that thereby they might liue in good estate, & driue forth their
daies in prosperity.

'Among all Crafts this was the onely chiefe, for that it was the
greatest merchandize, by which our Countrey became famous
through all Nations. And it was verily thought, that the one halfe
of the people in the land liued in those daies therby, and in such
good sort, that in the Common-wealth there were few or no beggars
at all: poor people, whom God lightly blesseth with most children,
did by meanes of this occupation so order them, that by the time
they were come to be sixe or seuen yeares of age, they were able
to get their owne bread: Idlenesse was then banished our coast, so
that it was a rare thing to heare of a thiefe in those daies. Therefore
it was not without cause that Clothiers were then both honoured
and loued, among whom these nine persons in this Kings daies were
of great credit, viz. *Tho. Cole* of *Reading, Gray* of *Glocester, Sutton*
of *Salisburie, Fitzallen* of *Worcester,* (commonly called *William* of
Worcester) *Tom Doue* of *Excester,* and *Simon* of *South-hampton,*
alias *Supbroath:* who were by the King called, The sixe worthy
Husbands of the West. Then were there three liuing in the North,
that is to say, *Cutbert* of *Kendall, Hogekins* of *Hallifax,* and *Martin
Byram* of *Manchester.* Euery one of these kept a great number of
seruants at worke, spinners, carders, weauers, fullers, dyers, sheer-
men, and rowers, to the great admiration of all those that came into
their houses to behold them. . . .'

So begins the tale of *Thomas of Reading, or the Sixe Worthie
Yeomen of the West,* by Thomas Deloney, who died in 1600.[1] He

---

[1] F. O. Mann. *D.N.B.* says 1607.

is thought to have been originally a silk-weaver from Norwich—a city made famous in commerce by the Flemish and Walloon Protestant refugees who brought that trade to Norwich. Certainly Deloney was a silk-weaver, and a Protestant; his hatred of Roman Catholics is everywhere apparent in his writings, and it is as a writer and not as a silk-weaver that he is notorious. He never was famous. Deloney represents a type of scribbler all too common in our semi-literate world—the writer for the public. He wrote stories like *Thomas of Reading* and *Jack of Newbury*—screeds extolling the virtues of large-scale capitalism and the acquisition of power through wealth—and ballads made to coax reluctant pence from cunning men's pockets. He played this market for all he could, and he died poor.

Yet Deloney knew his England. He knew her towns and their inhabitants, their industries and their pride. He knew what the ignorant wanted to believe, and how to dress it up for a cheap press. A course in modern journalism would cost more than *The Works of Thomas Deloney*,[1] but it cannot better demonstrate the subtle art of blurb. Deloney lived at a critical time in the history of publishing. It is well known that when William Caxton first set up his press near Westminster Abbey in 1477 he had made a reasonable fortune as a merchant in the Low Countries, had learnt the new art of printing in Cologne, and came to England to practise this art as a retired man's hobby. He printed good books, translated in many cases by himself from the originals, and looked for his business to the gentlemen drawn to Westminster by their obligation to serve in Parliament.[2] After Caxton's death, his business was continued by one of his apprentices, Wynkyn de Worde, and the craft then diverged along two lines of policy: (*a*) the learned publications, best represented by those of the printers Richard Pynson and Thomas Berthelet, and (*b*) the popular publications consisting of small books running into larger editions for a growing middle-class public, for which Wynkyn de Worde catered. Wynkyn de Worde's publications were better printed than Caxton's—his type-faces very neat —but he was a man of business more than of literature, who printed good books because he had to beat his competitors in the City of London, where he himself had set up his presses.

It follows that this policy could meet with another sort of competition—the cheap and nasty. The printed ballads of the sixteenth century were descended from the minstrels' songs; we can see the

---

[1] Modern edition ed. Francis Oscar Mann, Clarendon Press (1912).
[2] An irksome duty in those days.

relationship clearly enough through Autolycus in *The Winter's Tale*.[1]

Clown:

> What hast here? Ballads?

Mopsa:

> Pray now, buy some: I love a ballad in print o' life, for then we are sure they are true.

Autolycus:

> Here's one to a very doleful tune, how a usurer's wife was brought to bed of twenty money-bags at a burden; and how she longed to eat adders' heads and toads carbonadoed.

Mopsa:

> Is it true, think you?

Autolycus:

> Very true, and but a month old.

Dorcas:

> Bless me from marrying a usurer!

Autolycus:

> Here's the midwife's name to 't, one Mistress Taleporter, and five or six honest wives that were present. Why should I carry lies abroad?

Mopsa:

> Pray you now, buy it.

Clown:

> Come on, lay it by; and let's first see more ballads; we'll buy the other things anon.

Autolycus:

> Here's another ballad of a fish that appeared upon the coast on Wednesday the fourscore of April, forty thousand fathom above water, and sung this ballad against the hard hearts

[1] IV. 3.

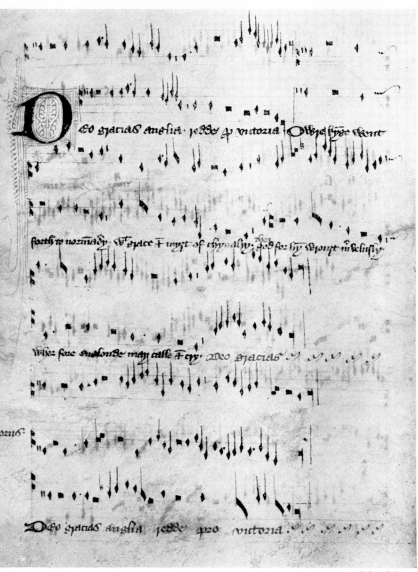

Deo gracias anglia redde pro victoria. Owre kynge went

forth to normandy. with grace & myzt of chyualry. ther god for hym wrouzt mervelusly.

wher fore englonde may calle & cry. deo gracias.

Deo gracias anglia redde pro victoria.

The Agincourt Carol. Early fifteenth century.

Bodleian Library

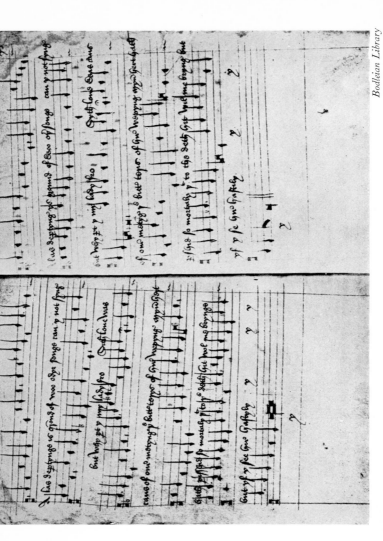

Alas, Departynge. Early fifteenth-century English love-song. The upper of the two voices is given on the left, the lower on the right.

of maids: it was thought she was a woman and was turned into a cold fish for she would not exchange flesh with one that loved her. The ballad is very pitiful and as true.

Dorcas:

Is it true, too, think you?

Autolycus:

Five justices' hands at it, and witnesses more than my pack will hold.

Clown:

Lay it by too: another.

Autolycus:

This is a merry ballad, but a very pretty one.

Mopsa:

Let's have some merry ones.

Autolycus:

Why, this is a passing merry one, and goes to the tune of *Two Maids Wooing a Man*: there's scarce a maid west-ward but she sings it: 'tis in request, I can tell you.

Mopsa:

We can both sing it: if thou'lt bear a part thou shalt hear; 'tis in three parts.

Dorcas:

We had the tune on 't a month ago.

Autolycus:

I can bear my part; you must know 'tis my occupation; have at it with you.

A merry song, a song about a freak of nature, and a song about a moneylender's wife's sad fate (though no doubt it served her right), all still wet from the press and guaranteed true; worthy indeed to compare with the Loch Ness Monster and the Flying Saucers of the twentieth century! Enterprise! What boots it if Autolycus is the plainest of frauds, so that only rustics as dense as Clown and Mopsa fail to catch him out? Shakespeare's audience was not composed of clowns, but of smart fellows from a great commercial city, not to be taken in so easily; and Autolycus is

c

a good stage character anyway, with a head full of townsmen's notions, including the commonest of all, that a townsman can outwit a rustic every time.

Therein lies a strain of Bankside guile. To hold an audience it is advisable to tell them what they want to be told, and every man loves his little prejudices. This is the art of popular entertainment, and though we may value Shakespeare sufficiently to believe that he was raised by his genius above the pettier prejudices of his fellow players, the taint was there. Only by their licence were the Earl of Leicester's men protected from a harsh law which would have branded them rogues and vagabonds; the City Corporation would not have a theatre within its jurisdiction; in such circumstances it was a good business policy to emphasize one's superiority over the common rabble, at any rate in one's advertisements.

So thought Will Kemp, who advertised himself with his famous dance from London to Norwich, and published his own account of the exploit in his *Nine Daies Wonder* of 1600. No doubt this was authentic, but that would not stop other ballad-mongers from 'improving' on it. Kemp had to defend his publication and make a

request to the impudent generation of Ballad-makers and their coherents, that it would please their Rascalities, to pity his pains in the great journey he pretends; and not fill the country with lies of his never-done-acts, as they did in his late Morrice to Norwich. To the tune of *Thomas Deloney's Epitaph*.

I have made privy search, what private Jigmonger of your jolly number hath been the Author of these abominable Ballets written of me.

I was told it was the great Ballad-maker, T. D., alias Thomas Deloney, Chronicler of the memorable lives of the Six Yeoman of the West, Jack of Newbury, the Gentle Craft, &c., and such like honest men, omitted by Stow, Holinshed, Grafton, Halle, Froissart, and all the rest of those well deserving writers.[1]

Thomas Deloney had but recently died, but during his lifetime his reputation as prince of balladeers seems to have been accepted. Kemp calls him their 'General'. One may expect then to find a filthy flow of obscenity published by 'D.T.', but it is not so. There was a market for such things in the jigs, but in a wide appeal to the people—women as well as men—there was need of moral censure of the common vices. Just as Shakespeare's audiences thought themselves masters of the tricks of Autolycus but would not be associated with him, so all men liked to hear a salacious rhyme with a little moral sauce to give it greater relish. The trick was not easy;

[1] See F. O. Mann, *Deloney's Works*, Introduction, p. xiii.

it had to be learned; but Thomas Deloney had no peer in this technique. In Chapter II of *The Gentle Craft*[1] appears this *Curtizans Song of Venice*,[2] rather in the style of an Elizabethan jig:

Ladies:

      Welcome to *Venice*, gentle courteous Knight,
        Cast off care, and entertain content.
      If any here be gracious in thy sight,
        Do but request, and she shall soon consent:
      Loues wings are swift, then be not thou so slow;

Hugh:

      Oh that faire *Winifred* would once say so.

Ladies:

      Within my lap lay down thy comely head,
        And let me stroke those golden locks of thine,—
      Looke on the teares that for thy sake I shed,
        And be thou Lord of any thing is mine,—
      One gentle looke upon thy Loue bestow,—

Hugh:

      Oh that faire *Winifred* would once say so.

Ladies:

      Embrace with ioy thy Lady in thine armes,
        And with all pleasures passe to thy delight:
      If thou dost think the light will work our harmes,
        Come, come to bed, and welcome all the night;
      There shalt thou find what Louers ought to know,

Hugh:

      Oh that faire *Winifred* would once say so.

Ladies:

      Giue me those pearles as pledges of thy Loue,
        And with those pearles the fauour of thy heart,—
      Do not from me thy sugred breath remoue,
        That double comfort giues to euery part:
      Nay stay Sir Knight, from hence thou shalt not go.

Hugh:

      Oh that faire *Winifred* would once say so.

[1] Shoemaking.
[2] Venice was in the sixteenth century the city of luxurious pleasure *par excellence*.

This surely is a model of the art of having one's cake and eating it, and it goes on in the succeeding prose:

When *Sir Hugh* had heard this song, and therewithall noted their wanton gestures, he began to grow suspitious of their proffers, and, thinking in himselfe, that either they sought his destruction, as the Syrens did to *Vlysses*; or they intended to make a prey of his purse, as *Lais* did of her louers: and therefore supposing some Adder to lie lurking under the fair flowers of their proffered pleasures, he determined the next morning after (with speed) to depart from the City. So when he had with good discretion auoided their company, while he lay tormented with restless thoughts on his still tossed bed, began thus to meditate.

Now I wel see mine own vanity . . .

The trick is to play on the conflict of naughty desires and a puritanical conscience.

Understand this trick of how to whip up two conflicting emotions about the same situation and there is money in story-telling. It may not be great literature, but it will sell. One of the neatest bits of titillation in Deloney's *Jack of Newbury* is in the first chapter, where his master's widow, having saucily sent about their business a parson, a tailor, and a tanner who came with gifts to woo her, invited her journeyman Jack to supper, had her maid put him in her late husband's bed, and came to him in the night because her feet were cold. In the morning she ordered Jack to go with her to do business in the town. In the town she turned into a church to pray for luck in her business, but had previously warned the priest that she was to be married that morning; her prayers ended, and no bridegroom arrived, she thereupon told the priest that she would marry her man Jack. There was no love in the match; the widow had need of a steady worker to manage her business, and Jack accepted the custom of the time that marriage was convenient in these circumstances. She gave him hell, but died in due course and left him the business, to the reader's great delight, for had he not been faithful to her and her interests in this adversity?

What the affairs of state were to kings, the success of business was to the middle classes; careful management of business was combined with careful management of home life—for both went on under the same roof. The steady virtues of the trading classes were related to the sober virtues of puritanism, and thus a climate of opinion developed in a society growing politically more important. Deloney would have been horrified, however, to learn that within fifty years of his death the Puritans would have become a political party, have waged a civil war, and executed the king. Deloney's patriotism and loyalty to the Crown were patent, whether he dealt with popular history or with current affairs. When Henry VIII's visit to Newbury is related in Deloney's book [1] the opportunity arrives for a welcome ode demanding not only expression of loyalty but of the moral qualities which were making England great:

Loe here presented to your Roiall sight,
The figure of a flourising Common-wealth:
Where vertuous subjects labour with delight,
And beat the drones to death which liue by stealth:
  Ambition, Enuie, Treason, loathsome serpents be,
  Which seek the downfall of this fruitfull tree.

But Lady Prudence with deep searching eye,
Their ill intended purpose doth preuent,
And noble Fortitude standing alwaies nye,
Dispersed their power prepar'd with bad intent.
  Thus are they foild that mount with meanes vnmeet,
  And so like slaues are trodden under feet.

If the great writers Stow, Holinshed, Froissart, Hall (whom Shakespeare read) failed to mention the great merchants whose history so intrigued Deloney's readers, they were writing only part of history, and the part they missed is the part necessary for a true understanding of the events of the seventeenth century. Kings were not the only men to be admired. Why should a prince disdain to be a craftsman? Writers had missed their opportunities, for tradesmen were numerous, literate, and liked to think themselves important:

Of craft and craftsmen, more and lesse,
  The *Gentle Craft* I must commend,
Whose deeds declare their faithfulnesse,
  And hearty loue unto their friend:
The *Gentle Craft*, in midst of strife,
  Yeelds comfort to a carefull life.

A Prince by birth I am indeed,
  The which for Loue forsook this Land;

[1] *Jack of Newbury*, Chapter 3.

And when I was in extreme need,
   I took the *Gentle Craft* in hand,
And by the *Gentle Craft* alone,
   Long time I liu'd being still vnknown.

Our shoos we sowed with merry notes,
   And by our mirth expelled all mone:
Like Nightingales, from whose sweet throats,
   Most pleasant tunes are nightly blown;
The Gentle Craft is fittest, then,
   For poore, distressed Gentlemen.

Their minds do mount in courtesie,
   And they disdain a niggards feast:
Their bodies are for Chiualry,
   All cowardnesse they do detest.
For Sword and Shield, for bowe and Shaft,
   No man can stain the *Gentle Craft*.

Yea sundry Princes sore distressed,
   Shall seek for succour by this Trade:
Whereby their griefs shall be redrest,
   Of foes they shall not be afraid.
And many men of fame likewise
   Shall from the *Gentle Craft* arise.

If we want money ouer night,
   Ere next day noon God will it send,
Thus may we keep our selues upright,
   And be no churl vnto our friends:
Thus do we liue where pleasure springs,
   In our conceit like petty Kings.

Our hearts with care we may not kill,
   Mans life surpasseth worldly wealth,
Content surpasseth riches still,
   And fie on knaues that liue by stealth:
This trade therefore both great and small
   The *Gentle Craft* shall euer call.

So Deloney played on the wishes of the people whom he hoped would buy his ballads. His was not the lowest of markets, for he issued his ballads in sets, called 'garlands', thereby offering a larger assortment at once and receiving a higher price. His prospective customers were the tradsmen, their journeymen and apprentices; the men who had raised their status in society through the power of their gilds and corporations. Their dignity must be fed, and their prejudices too. It was no part of the gilds' responsibility to consider the financial wishes of the workers; these took wages decided by the gild without reference to their opinion.[1] To defy the ruling of the masters would have been plain rebellion, quickly put down. Deloney always describes the workers as happy, singing at their work, and holding their master in proper respect. His commonwealth was in fact ideal; anyone who interfered with business was a rebel indeed. So into Deloney's *'Strange Histories . . . Verie pleasant either to be read or sunge, and a most excellent warning for all estates'*, comes the story of how *'Wat Tiler* and *Jack Straw*, rebelled against king *Richard* the Second'. It is interesting for the moral tone which pervades the whole. Here is the ending:

> Into the Cittie came they then,
>   like rude disordered franticke men:
> They robbed the Churches euerie where,
>   and put the Priests in deadly feare.
> Into the Counters then they get,
>   where men imprisoned lay for debt:
> They broke the doors and let them out,
>   and threw the Counter bookes about,
> Tearing and spoiling them each one,
>   and Records all they light vpon.
> The doores of *Newgate* broke they downe,
>   that prisoners ran about the towne:
> Forcing all the Smithes they meete,
>   to knocke the yrons from their feete:
> And then like villaines void of awe,
>   followed *Wat Tylor* and *Jack Straw*.
> And though this outrage was not small,
>   the King gaue pardon to them all,
> So they would part home quietly,
>   but they his pardon did defie:
> And being all in *Smithfield* then,
>   euen three score thousand fighting men,

---

[1] The gilds supported charities and built almshouses for the poor, but would not have admitted a right of fair wages other than by their own decision.

Which there *Wat Tylor* then did bring
 of purpose for to meete our king.
And there withall his royall grace,
 sent *Sir John Newton* to that place:
Vnto Wat Tylor willing him,
 to come and speak with our young king,
But the proud Rebell in despite,
 did picke a quarrell with the knight.
The Mayor of *London* being by
 when he beheld this villanie:
Vnto *Wat Tylor* rode he then,
 being in midst of all his men:
Saying Traytor yeelde tis best;
 in the Kings name I thee arrest:
And therewith to his Dagger start,
 and thrust the Rebbell to the heart.
Who falling dead vnto the ground,
 the same did all the host confound:
And downe they threwe their weapons all
 And humbly they for pardon call.
Thus did that proud Rebellion cease,
 and after followed joyfull peace.

This goes to the tune of *The Miller would a-wooing ride*. It does not, however, agree with the popular opinion of Wat Tyler, who certainly led a revolt of desperate men, but was no match for the clever advisers of the king. It may well be that Deloney had learnt his lesson, for the Elizabethan authorities could act quickly enough if they thought a ballad might lead to a breach of the peace:

In the next Year [1] Sir Stephen Slany, Maior, in the Month of July was brought to his hands a certain Ballad, containing a Complaint of great want and Scarcity of Corn within the Realm. And forasmuch as it contained in it certain vain and presumptuous matters, bringing in the Queen, speaking with her People Dialogue wise in very fond and undecent sort (as the said Maior in his letter, wrote also to the Lord Treasurer shewed) and Prescribing Order for the Remedying of this Dearth of Corn; which was extracted, as it seemed, out of a Book, published by the Lords last Year, but done in that Vain and indiscreet manner, as that thereby the Poor might aggravate their Grief, and take occasion of some Discontentment: therefore he thought fit to acquaint the said Lord, that he called

---

[1] 1596. Stow, ed. Strype, 1720, *Survey of London*, Bk v, p. 333; see F. O. Mann *Deloney's Works*, Introduction p. ix.

before him both Printer and the Party by whom it was put to print; who pretended a licence for it. But that finding it to be untrue, he committed him to one of the Counters, and took Sureties of the printer himself for his appearance.

.   .   .   .   .

The maker of this scurrilous Ballad was one Delonie, an idle Fellow. . . . Him the Maior also was in search for, but could not find him; as he signified also the said Lord, and sent him a copy of the foresaid Ballad.

Deloney was obviously safer in writing ballads about the death of traitors to the realm (and these could, after all, be more blood-thirsty and unrestrained), or 'Of the strange and most cruel Whippes which the Spanyards had prepared to whippe and torment English men and women: *which were found and taken at the ouerthrow of certaine of the Spanish Shippes*, in July last past, 1588.' It goes to the tune of *The Valiant Soldier*:

> Al you that list to looke and see
>   what profite comes from *Spayne*
> And what the Pope and Spanyards both
>   prepared for our gayne.
> Then turne your eyes and bend your eares,
>   and you shall heare and see,
> What courteous minds, what gentle harts,
>   they beare to thee and mee.
>
> They say they seek for *England's* good,
>   and wish the people well:
> They say they are such holie men,
>   all others they excell.
> They bragge that they are Catholikes,
>   and Christes only Spouse:
> And what so ere they take in hand,
>   the holie Pope allowes.
>
> These holie men, these sacred Saints,
>   and these that thinke no ill:
> See how they sought, against all right,
>   to murder, spoyle, and kill.
> Our noble Queene and Countrie first,
>   they did prepare to spoyle:
> To ruinate our liues and lands,
>   with trouble and turmoyle.

* C

And not content by fire and sword
  to take our right away:
But to torment most cruelly
  our bodies night and day.
Although they ment with murdring hands
  our guiltlesse bloud to spill:
Before our deaths they did deuise
  to whip us first their fill.

And for that purpose had preparde
  of whips such wondrous store,
So straungely made, that sure the like
  was neuer seen before,
For neuer was there Horse, nor Mule,
  nor dogge of currish kinde,
That euer had such whips deuised
  by any sauadge minde.

One sorte of whips they had for men,
  So smarting fierce and fell:
As like could neuer be deuisde
  by any deuill in hell.
The strings whereof with wyrie knots,
  like rowels they did frame,
That euery stroke might teare the flesh
  they layd on with the same,

And pluck the spreading sinewes from
  the hardned bloudie bone,
To prick and pearce each tender veine,
  within the bodie known.
And not to leaue one crooked ribbe,
  on any side vnseene:
Nor yet to leaue a lump of flesh
  the head and foote betweene.

And for our seelie women eke,
  their hearts with griefe to clogge,
They made such whips wherewith no man
  would seeme to strike a dogge:
So strengthened eke with brasen tagges,
  and filde so rough and thin,
That they would force at euery lash
  the bloud abroad to spinne.

Although their bodies sweet and fayre
    their spoyle they ment to make:
And on them first their filthy lust
    and pleasure for to take.
Yet afterward such sower sauce
    they should be sure to finde
That they shoulde curse each springing branch
    that cometh of their kinde.

Perhaps this is enough of Deloney's righteous sadism and flat-footed verse to take at one dose, but he was an artist nevertheless. Who but a genius could end such a ballad on this note?

What printed Bookes were sent about,
    as filled their desire:
How *England* was, by Spanyards wonne,
    and *London* set on fire.
Be these the men that are so milde,
    whom some so holie call:
The Lord defend our noble Queene
    and Countrie from them all.

Anger is the object, and hatred, for the Armada had been beaten before this was written. If we would see England in danger we should turn to an earlier ballad:

O noble England,
    fall downe vpon thy knee:
And praise thy God with thankfull hart
    which still maintaineth thee.
The forraine forces,
    that seekes thy vtter spoile:
Shall then through his especiall grace
    be brought to shameful foile.
With mightie power
    they come vnto our coast:
To ouer runne our countrie quite,
    they make their brags and boast.
In strength of men
    they set their onely stay:
But we, vpon the Lord our God,
    will put our trust alway.

Such lines must have made men catch their breath. With an Armada in the Channel, God is not a name to be tossed about as an oath in an alehouse. Deloney's style is hardly, however, epical:

> The Lord no doubt is on our side,
> which soone will worke their fall.

Deloney, true, is up to his old tricks, and now he is playing on the emotion of fear; fear employed, however, in its two related senses of alarm and awe; fear of the Spaniards and fear of God, with no doubt as to which force was the stronger. In time of war, and especially under threat of invasion, such an appeal is just what the people want; it may not be great poetry, it may not be wholly altruistic, but it gives heart to the nation; it tells them what they hope is true:

> Lord God almightie,
> which hath the harts in hand
> Of euery person to dispose,
> defend this English land.
> Bless thou our Soueraigne
> with long and happie life:
> Indue her Councel with thy grace,
> and end this mortell strife.
> Give to the rest,
> of Commons more and lesse:
> Louing harts, obedient minds,
> and perfect faithfulnesse.
> That they and we,
> and all with one accord:
> On *Sion* hill may sing the praise,
> of our most mightie Lord.

FINIS

LONDON

Printed by John Wolfe,
for Edward White,
1588.

V. PURITAN STIMULUS

IF WE SEEK a scapegoat for any decline in taste during the seventeenth century there is one to hand—the Puritans. They broke down the organs in the churches and closed the theatres, denounced maypole dancing, and made the Christmas feast into a fast. They must be bad! They cut off King Charles's head, therefore they must be criminal, for was it not a royal prerogative to cut off heads?

Among the results of this seeking for a scapegoat is the theory that the Puritans were in principle opposed to all music except the trumpet, the drum, and the Jew's harp. Percy A. Scholes, however, in his book *The Puritans and Music*, has mustered an imposing array of facts to prove that excepting in matters pertaining to religion and morals the Puritans were tolerant of the taste of others in music, and that many of the most influential Puritans were themselves fond of the art. Cromwell, Milton, and Bunyan certainly were, and many others of less fame. Already we have read of a Puritan—Thomas Deloney—who was not only fond of music but had a gift for balladry. He died, however, in 1600, while Elizabeth was still on the throne, and never knew the full force of dissension which came in the reigns of the Stuarts. Deloney's loyalty was never in question with regard to his country—in fact he almost tripped over himself in his zeal to be patriotic; the Catholics were his enemies and his queen's; Deloney, uncrowned king of cheap literature in Shakespeare's day, might be thought a national asset!

But if we seek a true description of English life in the reign of Elizabeth we shall find Deloney partial. The rising cost of living and spread of vagabondage and beggary were serious problems; Edward VI had passed a law in 1547 [1] condemning 'foolish pity and mercy' shown to persistent vagrants, and prescribing branding and slavery as remedies. It could not be carried out effectively because the public conscience would not tolerate the brutality it implied. Elizabeth in 1572 [2] gave magistrates permission to assess the punishment of beggars and ordered culprits to be branded on the shoulder. Overseers were created by this Act to superintend the relief of the poor (for since the Dissolution the Church had not the resources to maintain the poor even when it had the will). The Act of 1597 [3] lays down the rights and duties of the overseers, and

---

[1] 1 Ed. VI, c. 3.   [2] 14 Eliz. c. 5.   [3] 39 Eliz. c. 3.

orders their appointment by the justices; it is part of the social legislation drafted by a committee of the Commons in Elizabeth's reign, preliminary to the most important Poor Law of 1601.[1]

This is the great poor law of Elizabeth, *the* poor law *par excellence*, and its twenty sections deserve careful study. The most important of all is s. 1, ordering the churchwardens and four, three, or two substantial householders to be nominated each year as overseers of the poor, and imposing on them the duty of maintaining and setting to work the poor, the funds being provided by taxation of 'every inhabitant, parson, vicar, and other and every occupier of lands, houses, tithes impropriate and propriations of tithes, coalmines, or saleable underwood'.

Two acts of 1609–10 [2] are designed to prevent the misuse of apprenticing charities and to ensure that all the laws not put in execution shall be so put in operation forthwith. They order that houses of correction shall be built, and the constables shall search out rogues in each parish, and apprehend vagrants and shall take them before the justices who shall commit them to the house of correction. 'Lewd women who have bastards' and parents leaving their children chargeable to the parish are to be committed to the same establishment.[3]

Such provisions were harsh, but harsher still were to come in the 'enlightenment' of later history. Tyrannical as Elizabeth I may have been (and the Tudors were far more tyrannical than the Stuarts), she and her Parliament were hammering out a means of government based on an appreciation of the facts. Long ago dues had been paid largely in kind, and, stored in the owners' barns, had been available for relief of the poor or distribution at Christmas. So long as this situation obtained, customary charity was practicable, but when dues came to be paid in money, this was carried to the towns and spent there, often in lavish entertainment, dress, or political jobbery, while the localities which provided the means for these extravagances remained as tributaries, liable to dry up first in times of distress. Here was a theme to catch the public ear, and if Thomas Deloney found it expedient to ignore it (or to praise the middle-class townsmen) there were plenty of others ready to give it expression:

> Christmas is my name, far have I gone,
>   Have I gone without regard;
> Whereas great men by flocks there be flown,
>   There be flown to London-ward.

---

[1] 43 Eliz. c. 2.   [2] 7 Jac. I, cc. 3 and 4.
[3] W. E. Tate, *The Parish Chest* (1946), pp. 190–1.

There they in pomp and pleasure do waste
That which old Christmas was wonted to feast,
Houses where music was wont to be found,
Nothing but bats and owlets do sing,
    Welladay, welladay,
    Welladay, where should I stay?

Christmas beef and bread is turned to stones,
    Into stones and silken rags,
And Lady Money sleeps and makes moans,
    And makes moans in misers' bags.
Houses where pleasure once did abound,
Naught but a dog and a shepherd is found,
Houses where Christmas revels did keep
Now are become habitations for sheep;
    Welladay, welladay,
    Welladay, where should I stay?

This song of *Christmas's Lamentation* belongs to the reign of James I. We shall do well to keep it in mind when we try to unravel the twisted knots of seventeenth-century polemics. They had inherited these abuses from Tudor days.

The seventeenth century abounds with songs having a bias for or against the new ideas which were affecting the thought of all at that time. No longer was the simple man who wished to know the word of God deprived of the opportunity of finding out for himself. The Authorized Version of the Bible dates from 1611, but it was only the completion of a design initiated in the early sixteenth century, well expressed by William Tindale: 'If God spare my life, ere many years I will cause the boy that driveth the plough to know more of the Scriptures than you do.' Not less important is the passage in the preface to Day's edition of the metrical psalms of Sternhold and Hopkins:

For that the rude and ignorant in song, may with more delight, desire, and good will, be moved and drawn to the goodly exercise of singing the psalms, as well in common places of prayer where all together with one voice render thanks and praises to God, as privately by themselves or at home in their houses. I have set here in the beginning of this book of psalms, an easy and most plain way and rule, of the order of the notes and keys of singing, which commonly is called the scale of music, or the gammut. . . .

This is the beginning of popular musical education, or at any rate the first attempt to teach the rudiments of written music to all, for the metrical psalms of Sternhold and Hopkins soon came to be bound in one volume with the *Book of Common Prayer*.

. . . Thou shalt understand, gentle reader, that I have (for the help of those that are desirous to learn to sing) caused a new print of note to be made with letters to be joined to every note. Whereby thou mayest know how to call every note by its right name, so that with very little diligence (as thou art taught in the introduction printed heretofore . . .).

A most worthy ambition, but note the easy persuasion by which the rude and ignorant in song are to learn to read music with very little diligence. There are always responsibilities to be accepted where the ignorant are to be made literate. Once they learn to read who knows what ideas they will pick up? The spread of madrigal singing in the Elizabethan homes owed much to the method of teaching to read music which was then in vogue, but such music was taken up by people of means, with some social refinement; we ought not to overlook the humbler form of the catch, which spread far wider than the madrigal, into the taverns, even, where madrigals were certainly not the rule.

Every child knows the round *Three Blind Mice*. It first appears in print in Ravenscroft's *Deuteromelia* of 1609, which was a sequel to the same publisher's *Pammelia; Musickes Miscellanie, Or Mixed Variety of Pleasant Roundelayes and Delightful Catches of 3, 4, 5, 6, 7, 8, 9, 10, Parts in One*. The three voices in singing *Three Blind Mice* enter one after the other, catching up the tune at the right time to make a harmonious effect; that 'catching up' is the origin of the word 'catch' applied to a musical composition. A catch is an endless canon. *Three Blind Mice* is fun to sing, and its humour innocent. John Ravenscroft, indeed, has all sorts of themes for his catches, each immediately attractive.

It would be surprising in the age of Shakespeare if the humour of the pun were absent from these compositions, and indeed it is not; a catch by Baldwin runs:

> Adam catch'd Eve by the furbelow,
> And that's the oldest catch we know.
> Oh, ho, did he so? [1]

There are two puns in the first two lines—one on the double meaning of the word 'catch' and the other on the word 'furbelow',

[1] Record, *Allegro*, ALX 3008.

which cannot possibly apply to Eve's dress. We are offered a euphemism for a sexual characteristic, and a euphemism must always be suspected of hiding a snigger. When the Authorized Version of the Bible was written the word 'concubine' was plain English, and so was the decent word 'mistress', but in time the word 'mistress' became a euphemism for 'concubine' and by this association a couple of good words have become tainted with the sneers of the illiterate. These pitfalls are inseparable from popular education; are in fact part of the responsibility which reformers must accept in the hope that such distortions of meaning will pass away in time. The age which gave us the harsh polemics of the seventeenth century gave us also the beauty of *The Pilgrim's Progress*. The interesting factor about the period is that mankind was encouraged to think for itself and stand up for the right to hold an individual opinion, at least among the Independent section of the Puritans, who grew in influence. The dangers were as obvious to the Presbyterians as to Archbishop Laud, but nobody could turn back the clock to mediaeval times.

The honest opinion of humble folk is often a thing of beauty. Folk-songs offer us many examples of this, but with these we are not here concerned. There is a song of the early seventeenth century, however, which comes from the north of England (Westmorland is mentioned in one of the verses), not a folk-song, but very close to the sentiments these songs display: [1]

> A north-country lass up to London did pass,
>   Although with her nature it did not agree,
> Which made her repent and so often lament,
>   Still wishing again in the north for to be;
>   O the oak and the ash, and the bonny ivy tree,
>   Do flourish at home in my own country.

> Since that I came forth of the pleasant north
>   There's nothing delightful I see doth abound,
> That never can be half so merry as we
>   When we are a-dancing of *Sellenger's Round*;
>   O the oak and the ash, and the bonny ivy tree,
>   Do flourish at home in my own country.

> I like not the Court, nor to City resort,
>   Since there is no fancy for maids such as me;

[1] The tune, called *Quodling's Delight*, first appears as an instrumental piece by Giles Farnaby in the *Fitzwilliam Virginal Book*.

Their pomp and their pride I can never abide,
  Because with my humour it doth not agree.
    O the oak and the ash, and the bonny ivy tree,
    Do flourish at home in my own country.

At wakes and at faires, being rid of all cares,
  We there with our lovers did use for to dance;
Then hard hap had I my ill-fortune to try,
  And so up to London my steps did advance;
    O the oak and the ash, and the bonny ivy tree,
    Do flourish at home in my own country.

But still, I perceive, I a husband might have,
  If I to the city my mind could but frame,
But I'll have a lad that is north-country bred
  Or else I'll not marry, in the mind that I am.
    O the oak and the ash, and the bonny ivy tree,
    Do flourish at home in my own country.

A maiden I am, and a maid I'll remain,
  Until my own country again I do see,
For here in this place I shall ne'er see the face
  Of him that's allotted my love for to be;
    O the oak and the ash, and the bonny ivy tree,
    Do flourish at home in my own country.

As the singer perceived, the established way of life still persisting in the country was out of tune with the new manners in the towns, and this despite the fact that even London at that time was a small place by modern standards, with easy access to the countryside. Opinions ran high, and, as we shall see, were resented by many sober people, but one could not get away from them. Pamphleteering kept the presses going, and popular songs appeared with political and religious bias (the two were inseparable) and prophecies were taken seriously—became indeed, a political issue. Where once the Church had been the guide in matters of moral right or wrong, now the Puritans wanted to arbitrate also on what was considered sin, and to punish. Nor were they all; Archbishop Laud tried to exact penance for sexual offences, making the guilty parties—adulterers and fornicators—stand publicly in a white sheet. As might be expected, the sinners threw in their lot with the Puritans against the authority of the Bishops' Courts. It was too easy to shift one's allegiance according to one's interests, and though there is plenty of evidence that men made sacrifices in obedience to their consciences, (otherwise the Civil War would have been a very different type of conflict), in the popular songs of the time the clever men are most in evidence. Frequently they cheated, but they were clever in their way.

> What Booker doth prognosticate
>   Concerning kings and kingdoms' fate,
> I take myself to be as wise
> As he that gazes on the skies;
>   My skill goes beyond
>   The depths of a Pond,
> Or Rivers in the sorest rain;
>   Whereby I can tell
>   All things will be well
> When the King enjoys his own again.

Booker, Pond, and Rivers were popular astrologers, as were Swallow, Dove, and Dade mentioned in the next verse. Booker, before turning to prophecy, had been famous as a maker of fishing tackle, and as an authority on angling, so the song-writer played on a double meaning of Ponds and Rivers in conjunction with Booker's trade. This is the greatest of all Cavalier songs:

> There's neither Swallow, Dove nor Dade
> Can soar more high, or deeper wade,
> Or show more reasons from the stars
> What causes peace, what causes wars.
>   The man in the moon
>   May wear out his shoon
> By running after Charles his Wain;
>   But all to no end,
>   For the times will never mend
> Till the King enjoys his own again.

The next verse refers to the divine right of kings and in its first line dates the song by implication to the year 1643, when Charles was out of London and with his troops facing pockets of Parliamentarians in many parts of the country—Oxford, Bristol, Gloucester, Somerset, Newark, etc. The Parliamentarians fought with local levies who were unwilling to fight except in their own parts of the country, but they were seriously impairing transport on the principal roads. The King's cause was by no means yet lost, and hope was strong among his loyal followers:

> For forty years our royal throne
> Has been his father's and his own,
> Nor is there any one but he
> With right can there a sharer be;
>   For who better may
>   Our high sceptre sway,
> Than he whose right it is to reign?
>   Then look for no peace,
>   For the wars will never cease
> Till the King enjoys his own again.
>
> Though for a time we see Whitehall
> With cobwebs hanging on the wall,
> Instead of gold and silver bright
> That glanc'd with splendour day and night;
>   With rich perfume
>   In every room
> All to delight that princely train;
>   These again shall be
>   When the time we see
> That the King enjoys his own again.

The Puritans never wrote a song of this quality. Their prophecy went another way.

There was, for example, *A Prognostication on W. Laud, late Archbishop of Canterbury* (Laud was beheaded in 1645, so publication of this song was after that event) *written in 1641, which accordingly is come to pass.* 'Prophecy' was called in to sell a popular song, along with a variety of puns:

> My little lord, methinks 'tis strange
> That you should suffer such a change,
>   In such a little space.
> You, that so proudly t'other day
> Did rule the King, and country sway,
>   Must trudge to t'other place.
>
> Remember now from whence you came,
> And that your grandsires of your name
>   Were dressers of old cloth? [1]

---

[1] Laud came of a family of tailors in Reading.

Go, bid the dead men bring their shears,
And dress your coat to save your ears,
   Or pawn your head for both.

The King, by hearkening to your charms,
Hugg'd our destruction in his arms,
   And gates to foes did ope;
Your staff would strike his sceptre down,
Your mitre would o'ertop the crown,
   If you should be a Pope.

The silenced clergy, void of fear,
In your damnation will have share,
   And speak their mind at large;
Your cheese cake cap and magpie gown,
That made such style in every town,
   Must now defray your charge.

Within this six years, six ears have
Been cropt off worthy men and grave,
   For speaking what was true; [1]
But if your subtle head and ears
Can satisfy these six of theirs,
   Expect but what's your due.

Poor people that have felt your rod
Yield *Laud* to devil, praise to God,
   For freeing them from thrall;
Your little 'Grace' for want of grace
Must lose your patriarchal place
   And have no grace at all.

The Commonalty have made a vow,
No oath, no canons to allow,
   No bishop's *Common Prayer*;
No lazy prelates that can spend
Such great revenues to no end,
   But virtue to impair.

Dumb dogs that wallow in such store,
That would suffice above a score
   Pastors of upright will;

[1] As a result of Laud's policy of a strict control of the press, William Prynne, Henry Burton, and John Bastwick were pilloried, had their ears cut off, and were imprisoned.

Now they'll make all the bishops teach,
And you must in the pulpit preach
    That stands on Tower Hill.

When the young lads to you did come,[1]
You knew their meaning by the drum,
    You had better yielded then;
Your head and body then might have
One death, one burial, and one grave,
    By boys—but two by men.

But this I say, that your lewd life
Did fill both Church and State with strife,
    And trample on the crown;
Like a bless'd martyr, you will die
For Church's good; she rises high
    When such as you fall down.

Christian charity has little place in these lines, and the fact that
they were brought out after Laud's death as a boast makes the
situation worse. Laud was not a lewd man, as the last verse would
have us believe, but he was a determined man trusted by the king
because it was felt that the English needed controlling with a stern
resolution. People were thinking for themselves, and some thinking
wrongly; disaster was to be expected if it continued; moreover,
neither Crown nor Church were used to having to argue their case,
and resented the necessity. Firm in their consciences the thinkers,
too, resented dictation by lords temporal and spiritual, and resisted.
Resistance breeds counter-resistance, as the songs show:

Me have of late been in England,
    Vere me have seen much sport;
De raising of de Parliament
    Have quite pulled down de Court;
De King and Queen dey separate
    And rule in ignorance.
Pray, judge, ye gentlemen, if this
    Be à la mode de France.

[1] Warned of the approach of five thousand London apprentices (in 1640) to his
palace at Lambeth, Archbishop Laud was saved. One of the lads—a tailor—was taken
and hanged for the attempt on Laud's life.

A vise man dere is like a ship
    Dat strike upon de shelves;
Dey prison all, behead, and vip
    All viser dan demselves;
Dey send out men to fetch deyr King,
    Who may come home, perchance.
O fy, fy, fy it is, be gar,
    Not *à la mode de France.*

Dey raise deyr valliant 'prentices,
    To guard deyr cause vith clubs;
Dey turn deyr Bishops out of doors,
    And preach demselves in tubs;
De cobbler and de tinker, too,
    Dey vill in time advance;
Gar take dem all, it is (*mort Dieu*)
    Not *à la mode de France.*

Instead of bowing to deyr King,
    Dey vex him vith epistles;
Dey furnish all deyr soldiers out
    Vith bodkins, spoons and vistles;
Dey bring deyr gold and silver in,
    De Brownists to advance,[1]
And if dey be cheat of it all
    'Tis *à la mode de France.*

But if ven all deyr vealth be gone,
    Dey turn unto deyr King,
Dey vill all make amends again,
    Den merrily ve vill sing,
    'Vive le Roy, vive le Roy,' [2]
Ve'll sing, carouse and dance,
De Englishmen have done *fort bon*
    And *à la mode de France.*

The facts touched on in this song date it 1640, when Charles I
had failed to quell the spirit of rebellion in Scotland, and returned

[1] Followers of Robert Brown, who in the reign of Elizabeth I opposed the doctrine of the Established Church. The Independents accepted the main Brownist tenets.
[2] A famous Cavalier song.

to call his fourth parliament in April—known as the Short Parliament, for it was dissolved in the same year—in the hope of getting money to carry on the fight against the Scots; he succeeded only in widening the breach between himself and the Commons. John Pym stated the case of the Puritan Party; Parliament, he said, 'was to the body politic as the rational faculties of the soul are to man'. He urged the two Houses to petition the king for redress of their grievances—any grant of powers to raise money must be deferred until after these had been satisfied. When Charles proposed to raise subsidies Parliament petitioned that he should come to terms with the Scots. Charles saw the unmistakable hand of a usurping authority, so dissolved Parliament before the petition could be voted.

These events are inherent in the verses of the song above quoted, but others even more important appear, in the alarm shown at the thought of popular preachers replacing the clergy (which we may note from the opposite side in the *Prognostication on W. Laud* previously quoted). Both songs also refer to the rioting apprentices in London, and there is in the second song the fear of democracy—the fear that tinkers and cobblers may be voices in the land. It is in such details that the songs are most revealing; and in their partiality—for neither has any depth of judgment.

In a country where men claimed the right of following their individual consciences, uniformity was impossible, and the milestones in seventeenth-century history are marked with arbitrary decisions made by strong men, and the immediate reactions of others. Samuel Butler came out with this:

> What's he that doth the Bishops hate,
> And counts their calling reprobate,
>   'Cause by the Pope propounded?
> And thinks a zealous cobbler better
> Than learned Usher in ev'ry letter,
>   Oh! such a rogue's a Roundhead.

> What's he that doth high treason say,
> As often as his yea or nay,
>   And wish the King confounded?
> And dares maintain that Mr Pym,
> Is fitter for a crown than him?
>   Oh! such a rogue's a Roundhead.

What's he, that if he chance to hear
A little piece of Common Prayer,
   Doth think his conscience wounded?
Will go five miles to preach and pray,
And meet a sister on the way?
   Oh! such a rogue's a Roundhead.

This is a good deal better than the propaganda songs earlier quoted, for only in the last stab does Butler play foul, and in it he makes a charge which is still to be heard against the puritanical.[1] The other sentiments attributed by Butler to the Puritans were founded on fact. But from either side a counter-attack might be expected, or an answer to extremists may even come from their own side. Prynne, as we have seen, was punished for publishing his *Histriomastix, or the Player's Scourge,* wherein he strove to prove that the playhouses were pernicious. Many agreed with him. In 1612 the Middlesex justices forbade the playing of jigs [2] on the stage, because of their coarse sentiments, and, one ventures to hope, because of their lack of artistic merit. (Musical historians who have claimed that Puritan objections to the seventeenth-century theatres centred on the social conditions obtaining in the playhouses and not to the plays themselves, should look again to their briefs.) Prynne attacked dancing in 1634 in remarks which were held to implicate the queen (who certainly loved dancing) and so drew on himself a vicious punishment. His punishment was not a cause for public resentment at first, but only became so when Burton and Bastwick were punished also; the immediate reply to Prynne, which revealed the state of reasonable opinion, was the decision of the gentlemen of the Inns of Court to present a masque of great splendour at Whitehall, as an act of loyalty. These young lawyers were not all of either party, and they had a traditional pride in their official Revels, going back certainly to the reign of Henry VI; the masque they performed in 1634 was Shirley's *Triumph of Peace,* with music by Henry Lawes and Simon Ives. This was a fair reaction to an extremist opinion. We must not look for the suppression of such spectacles after the rise of Puritan rule, for they took place in the private theatres, which were roofed and provided with scenery and 'machines' for bringing on, up, or down the

---

[1] Modern psychologists claim that a puritanical mind always has its obscene side, but some would deny this of the seventeenth-century Calvinists.
[2] The Elizabethan jig was a sung play, the words fitted to one or more common ballad tunes.

actors. The playhouses at Bankside were of a different character, and were closed when the Puritans got control in 1642.

Whereas the distressed Estate of Ireland, steeped in her own blood, and the distracted Estate of England, threatened with a Cloud of Blood, by a Civill Warre, call for all possible means to appease and avert the Wrath of God appearing in these Judgments; amongst which, Fasting and Prayer having bin often tryed to be very effectuall, have bin lately, and are still ejoyned; and whereas publike Sports doe not well agree with publike Calamities, noe publike Stage-playes with the Seasons of Humiliation, this being an Exercise of sad and pious solemnity, and the other being Spectacles of pleasure, too commonly expressing lascivious Mirth and Levitie: It is therefore thought fit, and Ordeined by the Lords and Commons in this Parliament Assembled, that while these sad Causes and set times of Humiliation doe continue, publike Stage-Playes shall cease, and bee forborne. Instead of which, are recommended to the people of this Land, the profitable and seasonable Considerations of Repentance, Reconciliation, and peace with God, which probably may produce outward peace and prosperity, and bring againe Times of Joy and Gladnesse to these Nations.

Reason was behind the Act, applied to a belief in the efficacy of a high seriousness. In 1643 the *Book of Sports* was finally withdrawn and burnt. This declaration of the right of all to suitable recreation on Sundays (the labourers' only free day) after the duty of church-going was completed, had been first issued in 1618 and had aroused a great deal of opposition from all parties. People had a right to be quiet if they so wished on their day of rest, and there was plenty of evidence in the Quarter Sessions that bull- and bear-baiting (as well as morris-dancing) could be rowdy. In 1644, however, Christmas Day fell on a Wednesday, which was a fast-day, and had to be observed as such, and in 1647 Christmas was legally abolished; on 30 January 1649 Charles I was beheaded; in 1650 the Commonwealth Government, like the new broom it was, started on a clean sweep, and among other things set its hand firmly against sin; the death penalty was prescribed for sexual offenders. This law (like the law to make slaves of vagrants, introduced and repealed by Edward VI) proved too unpopular in practice; a few sentences of death were passed, but juries found it against their consciences to help operate this law. The force of public opinion could not be stemmed.

These things are mentioned in the history books as facts relating to Puritan government policy (into which musical taste did not enter except in so far as it affected religious observance), but the history books omit therefore one of the most patent evidences of public feeling. Between January and March 1651 appeared a musical best seller, entitled *The Dancing Master*, issued by John Playford, who had a shop at the entrance to the Middle Temple and addressed his preface to the 'Ingenious Reader', but with a special eye for the gentlemen of the Inns of Court 'whose sweet and ayry Activity has crowned their Grand Solemnities with Admiration to all Spectators'. Already we have noted the popularity and splendour of the traditional revels held annually by the gentlemen of the Inns of Court, and their reaction to Prynne's *Histriomastix*. One cannot brand all lawyers either Puritan or Cavalier, any more than one could brand all families one or the other, for the seventeenth century, we repeat, was an age when men thought for themselves as never before in England; John Playford went straight to his point —a defence of the art of ballroom dancing:

The Art of Dancing called by the Ancient Greeks *Orchestice*, and *Orchestis*, is a commendable and rare quality fit for young Gentlemen, if opportunely and civilly used. . . . Excellent for Recreation, after more serious Studies, making the body active and strong, gracefull in deportment, and a quality very much beseeming a Gentleman.

He depends on reason, for his age was an age when one had to have a serious message. Similiarly, John Milton, in his *Tractate of Education*, justified music with social and physical reasons:

The interim of unsweting themselves regularly, and convenient rest before meat may both with profit and delight be taken up in recreating and composing their travailed spirits with the solemn and divine harmonies of Music heard or learnt . . . which, if wise men and prophets be not extremely out, hath a great power over dispositions and manners, to smoothe and make them gentle from rustic harshness and distempered passions. The like also would not be unexpedient after meat to assist and cherish Nature in her first concoction, and send their minds back to study in good tune and satisfaction.

In addition, Milton's metrical paraphrases of the Psalms show his practical interest in religious music.

John Bunyan's delight in metrical psalms was a typical result of his education by good books—by which we mean the Bible and the various editions of Sternhold and Hopkins's *Whole Book of Psalms, etc.* He found contentment in these though he also knew much other music. So with Izaak Walton—a man of different temperament again, but music gave him the peace of mind he loved, as we can well see in his writing:

Gentlemen, these were a part of the thoughts that then possessed me. And I there made a conversation of a piece of an old catch, and added more to it, fitting them to be sung by us anglers. Come, Master, you can sing well; you must sing a part of it, as it is in this paper.

Here follows the two-part song of Henry Lawes:[1]

> Man's life is but vain
> For 'tis subject to pain,
> And sorrow, and short as a bubble;
> 'Tis a hodge-podge of business
> And money, and care,
> And care, and money, and trouble;
> But we'll take no care
> When the weather proves fair
> Nor will we vex tho' it rain,
> We'll banish all sorrow,
> And sing till tomorrow,
> And angle and angle again.

Peter:

Aye marry, Sir, this is music indeed; this has cheered my heart, and made me remember six verses in praise of musick, which I will speak to you presently:

> Music! miraculous rhetorick, that speak'st sense
> Without a tongue, excelling eloquence;
> With what ease might thy errors be excused,
> Wert thou as truly lov'd as th'art abused!
> But though dull souls neglect, and some reprove thee,
> I cannot hate thee, 'cause the angels love thee.[2]

Piscator and Venator, begging a song from a milk-woman and her daughter, were asked would they like '*Come Shepherds, deck your herds?* or *As at noon Dulcina rested?* or *Phillida Flouts me?* or *Chevy Chase?* or *Johnny Armstrong?* or *Troy Town?*' The song Piscator chooses is *Come, live with me and be my love*, and Venator

---

[1] Record, *Allegro*, ALX 3008.
[2] *The Compleat Angler*, Chapter XVI.

rewards the singers with a compliment: 'I now see it was not without cause that our good Queen Elizabeth did so often wish herself a milkmaid all the month of May'.

This insistence on music and dancing being suitable for the cultivation of good manners is probably the most interesting feature of Commonwealth social life. Before 1640 country house-parties had become romps, with a great fondness for kissing games and amorous pursuing under and over the furniture, so that Richard Burton could make learned fun of it:

Cupid and Death meet both in an inn; and being merrily disposed, they did exchange arrows from either quiver; ever since young men die, and oftentimes old men dote—*Sic moritur Juvenis, sic moribundus amat,* And who can then withstand it? If once we be in love, young or old, though our teeth shake in our heads like virginal jacks, or stand parallel asunder like the arches of a bridge, there is no remedy, we must dance trenchmore for a need, over tables, chairs, and stools, etc. And Princum Prancum is a fine dance. . . .

The Restoration was to see more romps, but in 1650 John Playford was certain of the beneficial effect of dancing as a social accomplishment. 'Trenchmore' is given by Playford as a longways dance for as many as will, no longer a romp over tables and chairs. We have seen previously how an aubade in the sixteenth century was generally called a 'hunt's-up', though this was the name of a particular song also. Variants of *The King's Hunt's Up* come into Playford's *The Dancing Master* as *All in a Garden Green* and *Gathering Peascods*; *The Merry Milkmaids* is a major-mode version of the tune traditionally associated with Ophelia—*Walsingham* —a pre-Reformation shrine of pilgrimage. The song *The Oak and the Ash* gave Playford the tune for the dance *Goddesses,* and another fine dance-tune—*Nonesuch*—is that used for the deplorable propaganda song already quoted—*A la mode de France.* Playford's editions are confusing at times, for he and his successors switched tunes and names of tunes; but they were not really concerned with the trials of future bibliophiles; they were issuing a compendium of ballroom dances with suitable tunes and instructions for performance. They had their reward; *The Dancing Master* became a best seller almost overnight and ran through eighteen editions under John Playford and his successors. No wonder Playford turned from the polemic literature he had issued before 1650—he had found in published music a little gold mine.

As public opinion swung in these austere times towards the recreation of ballroom dancing in a graceful and even stately character, so even the misfortunes of the churches, from which pipe organs were looted by the soldiery, had an influence in some degree perhaps salutary. Some innkeepers bought these organs and had them erected in their taverns. Taverns which catered specially for musical customers were known as 'music-houses'; these engaged players to entertain their customers (or 'guests' at an inn) and from these music-houses may be traced the history of the modern music-halls. The provision of music at an inn was an old custom; minstrels had always visited such places. The minstrels' gilds had tried to stop their members touting for business there, making rules which forbade the going round to inns obsequiously begging 'Would you have any music, gentlemen?' but there were always many minstrels outside the gilds. During the Commonwealth one got a job as best one could; the waits were not disbanded, and some at least found extra employment in the music-houses, for Sir John Hawkins states in his *History of Music* of 1776 how music was provided by

Fidlers and others, hired by the master of the house; such as in the night season were wont to parade the city and suburbs under the title of Waits. . . . Half a dozen of fidlers would scrape *Sellenger's Round*, or *John, Come Kiss Me*, or *Old Simon the King* with divisions, till themselves and their audience were tired, after which as many players on the hautboy would in the most harsh and discordant tones grate forth *Greensleeves*, *Yellow Stockings*, *Gillian of Croydon*, or some such common dance-tune, and the people thought it fine music.

This was written in the elegant days of the late eighteenth century, but opinion in the Commonwealth would not rate such tunes distasteful—nor would we of the twentieth century; it is little to the credit of the Puritans that church organs were relegated to public-houses, and players found for them among the former church organists, but their influence on musical taste in these places may not have been unsalutary. The music-houses were superior pubs; there was usually only one such house in a district which might contain many common taverns. In their strange way the Puritans helped the cause of popular musical education; they were repeatedly accused of 'levelling', but the levelling, after all, did involve raising some sections of society. It was open to gentlemen themselves to buy the organs and set them up in their own houses, as Oliver Cromwell did, and employ a music-master to teach their children. All the organs could have been preserved in that way. As usual, those who shouted loudest about the sins of vandals were not themselves inclined to act in time to counter the vandalism.

If we seek for originality of musical invention during the Commonwealth we shall find it in chamber music. William and Henry Lawes are the best examples, but the styles Milton and Walton so admired had been established before the Commonwealth began. Playford's tunes were old ones, church music was now confined to metrical psalms, and the public theatres were closed; chamber music offered the best opportunities for music of character. There were masques still in use in private houses, schools, and a very special one in 1653, Shirley's *Cupid and Death*, played in London before the Portuguese ambassador and later given a public performance in Leicester Fields.[1] The masque had passed its zenith as a musical entertainment, however, by this time, for its literary content had stolen the stage. The events which claim most consideration in the art history of the Commonwealth are probably the attempts of Sir William Davenant to establish an English form of opera at Rutland House, Charterhouse Square, in 1656. Not a note of the music has survived, but we know enough about the staging and the librettos.

Davenant's first effort was called merely *The First Dayes Entertainment at Rutland House by Declamations and Musick: after the manner of the Ancients*. In it he told his audience not to expect

> To watch the plot's swift change, and counterturn:
> When Time moves swifter than by Nature taught;
> And by a *Chorus* miracles are wrought;
> Making an infant instantly a man:
> These were your plays, but get them if you can.

The entertainment Davenant offered was argumentative; it had something in common with the old welcome entertainments, and something also of the character of a University Act, such as Davenant must have seen in Oxford at the Encaenia celebrations; opera it was not, but Davenant was sounding the depths—if there were any:

> Think this your passage, and the narrow way
> To our Elisian Field, the Opera.

Then came the first serious attempt at 'opera' with an entertainment called *The Siege of Rhodes*, music by Henry Lawes, Matthew

[1] 1659 (after Oliver Cromwell's death).

Locke, Henry Cook, and Edward Coleman, stage settings by John Webb, a pupil of Inigo Jones who applied the principles formerly used by his master in the private theatres; these used perspective, obtained by means of flats set in the foreground representing rocks, behind which were two pillars between which painted shutters could be slid to represent various scenes, and again behind these —visible when the shutters were drawn back into the wings— painted scenery. Changes of scene were made by sliding painted shutters into view before the very eyes of the spectators. But why not? The spectators liked them, and the 'opera' offered them many changes of scene, no doubt because of their novelty. Some of the lines were sung in recitative—an Italian innovation which had, however, been heard to English words in a Jacobean masque, written by the composer Nicholas Laniel.

Let us see the lines Davenant wrote for his recitative.

The scene is the town of Rhodes, besieged. Ianthe (played by Mrs Coleman, wife of Edward Coleman who wrote some of the music and sang the part of Alphonso) enters, dressed in a nightgown. She has been wounded. By courtesy of Solyman, the Sultan, she had been allowed to enter the besieged town with permission to leave again with her husband, Alphonso; Alphonso thought her to have obtained this permission by infidelity, and so refused to leave the city. Ianthe, the wife, has taken part in the fighting, hence the wound, which is not serious. Soon after her entry Alphonso enters, sorely wounded, led in by two mutes:

Alphonso:

<blockquote>
Tear up my wounds! I had a passion, coarse
   And rude enough to strengthen jealousy;
But want that more refined and quicker force
   Which does out-wrestle Nature when we dye.
Turn to a tempest all my inward strife:
     Let it not last,
     But in a blast
Speed this infectious vapour, Life!
</blockquote>

Ianthe:

<blockquote>
It is my lord! Enough of strength I feel
To bear me to him, or but let me kneel?
He bled for me when he achieved for you
This day's success; and much from me is due.
Let me but bless him for his victory,
And hasten to forgive him e'er I dye.
</blockquote>

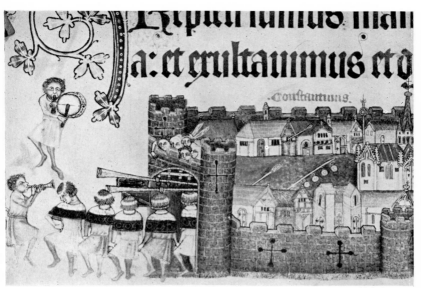

ABOVE. Illumination from the Luttrell Psalter. Minstrels in livery (probably waits) performing a round-dance or carol at a city gate. Early fourteenth century. BELOW. Singing a Catch (eighteenth century). The character on the left is Thomas Augustine Arne.

Baroque Art in the Theatre. The stage of Dorset Garden Theatre during a performance of the masque in Settle's *Empress of Morocco*. Note the music-room above
the proscenium arch. Compare plate facing page 156.

Alphonso:

> Keep back, Ianthe, for my strength will fail
> If on thy cheeks I see the roses pale.
> Draw all the curtains and then lead her in;
> Let me in darkness mourne away my sin.   (*Exeunt*)

Chorus of Souldiers:

> With a fine merry Gale,
>   Fit to fill ev'ry Sail,
> They did cut the smooth Sea
> That our Skins they might flea:
> Still as they landed we forkt them with Sallys;
>   We did bang their silk Shashes,
>   Through Sands and through Plashes,
> Till amain they did run to their Gallies.

There are four verses, but perhaps this one is enough. Is this really heroic opera? We know nothing of the music, for none has been preserved, but what could any musician do with this stuff? The rhymed couplets of Ianthe and Alphonso were presumably set to recitative, but are they what a composer wants from his librettist? They are Davenant's own idea of what was good for an opera, and they are conceived in literary terms—not musical. As for the chorus of 'souldiers', it is popular ballad stuff; if Davenant was not deliberately boiling a common pot he ought to have been. There are further examples, some in the style of patriotic balladry, which Tom Deloney had done better. The following verses are taken from Alphonso's song in the second entry [1] of *The Siege of Rhodes*:

> How bravely fought the fiery French,
>   Their bulwarks being stormed!
> The colder Almans kept their Trench,
>   By more than valour warmed.

> The grave Italians paused and fought,
>   The solemn Spaniards too;
> Study'ng more deaths than could be wrought
>   By what the rash could do.

> .   .   .   .   .

---

[1] The scenes are called 'entries', as in a masque.

D

The cheerful English got renown:
    Fought merrily and fast;
'Tis time, they cry'd, to mow them down,
    War's harvest cannot last.

If Death be rest, here let us dye;
    Where wearieness is all
We daylie get by Victory
    Who must by Famine fall.

The Siege of Rhodes was followed by another 'opera' called *The Cruelty of the Spaniards in Peru*. This goes in for history with an eye on Cromwell's hatred of the Spaniards. Consider, then, the innocent lives of the Peruvians before the Incas brought them to live in cities and build forts.

Whilst yet our world was new,
    When not discover'd by the old;
E'er beggar'd Slaves we grew,
    For having Silver Hills, and Strands of Gold.

Chorus:

We danced and we sung,
    And lookt ever young,
And from restraints were free,
As Waves and Winds at Sea.

Then wildly did we live,
    E'er crafty Cities made us tame:
When each his whole would give
    To all, and none peculiar right did claim.

        Chorus.

When none did Riches wish,
    And none were rich by Bus'ness made;
When all did hunt or fish,
    And Sport was all our Labour and our Trade.

        Chorus.

When Forts were not devis'd,
    Nor Cittadils did Townes devour:
When lowly Sheds suffic'd,
    Because we feared the Weather more than Power.

        Chorus.

When Garments were not worn,
    Nor shame did nakedness resent:
Nor poverty bred Scorn:
    When none could want, and all were innocent.

Chorus:

    We danc'd and we sung,
        And lookt ever young,
    And from restraints were free,
    As Waves and Winds at Sea.

Remember that Davenant was Cavalier in his sympathies, and had obtained, before the closing of the theatres in 1642, a patent from Charles I to build a theatre and present plays and entertainments of music therein. Davenant had now the task of giving stage entertainments in a country where public theatres were illegal. He emphasized the musical nature of his entertainment, calling it 'opera', and played to Cromwell's politics in the plot. But the plot was insincere; Davenant did not understand the nature of Puritan thought, nor of the theory of 'levelling' to which it had led some of its adherents. Cromwell was opposed to the Levellers and sternly put them down, yet here is Davenant in the last years of Cromwell's rule trying to glorify a classless society! The effect is like a modern Conservative trying to write a play for a prize offered by the Communist Party. It does not ring true.

Davenant wrote another 'opera' to use the same scenery as *The Cruelty of the Spaniards in Peru*. It had more of a plot, and though a British sailor 'salutes a Spaniard with his foot', it is poor stuff. Only *The Siege of Rhodes* had any dramatic power. Davenant brought it out again, and John Evelyn wrote in his diary under the date 5 May 1659:

I went to visit my brother in London; and next day, to see a new opera, after the Italian way, in recitative music and scenes, much inferior to the Italian composure and magnificence; but it was prodigious that in a time of such public consternation such a vanity should be kept up or permitted. I, being engaged with company, could not decently resist the going to see it, though my heart smote me for it.

Again the same argument, that it is not proper to support such vanity in times of public consternation. Evelyn was not politically Puritan. His sympathies were with 'the King across the water', and he had seen operas in Venice. Evelyn knew what he was saying.

Oliver Cromwell was now dead and the Commonwealth left without a leader strong enough to guide or enforce a policy. The Restoration was in sight. What, then, were the results of the Puritan experiment in government, as regards the art of music? Had a few more years of Puritan rule obtained it is fair to say that the Church of England tradition in music would have been broken. The loss to music due to the closing of the theatres was less, for the masques and chamber music went on. Mrs Samuel Pepys had a maid named Mary Ashwell who delighted Samuel 'all along telling us some parts of their maske at Chelsea school, and I find she hath a most prodigious memory, remembering so much of things acted six or seven years ago'. Since the date of this entry in Pepys's diary is 26 April 1663, Mary must have learnt her parts in these masques during the Commonwealth. Again on 15 September 1667 Pepys wrote, 'there comes Mr Pelling, with two men, by promise, one Wallington and Piggott, the former whereof, being a very little fellow, did sing a most excellent bass, and yet a poor fellow, a working goldsmith, that goes without gloves to his hands. Here we sung several things. They supped with me, and so broke up'.

It was sufficiently rare for a working man to be able to sing well in a consort for Pepys to marvel at the fact, yet poor Wallington, as a fellow singer in the consort, supped with Mr Pepys of the Navy Office! We know from other sources that Wallington sang well and composed music of inferior merit—some of which, however, was published. Levelling was not officially a Puritan policy, but raising the standard of literacy and musical ability among the poor was approved and encouraged. Before the Commonwealth, madrigals had been sung by 'gentlemen and merchants of good accompt';[1] after the Commonwealth the way was open for the musical clubs which were to flourish right through the eighteenth century.

[1] Nicholas Yonge, *Musica Transalpina* (1588).

VI. PEPYS'S ENGLAND

SAMUEL PEPYS GLANCED from his prayer-book in the direction
of my Lady Castlemaine, but his voice betrayed no hint of any
naughty thought in the next 'Amen'. How changed were the times
now that the king enjoyed his own again!

> Four and twenty fiddlers all in a row,
> And there was fiddle, fiddle,
> And twice fiddle, fiddle,
> 'Cause 'twas my lady's birthday,
> Therefore we kept holiday,
> And all went to be merry.

The austere years were ended, at least in the Court; the organ
pealed, and the singing men could 'rejoice in the Lord alway'; but
the twenty-four violins were something special at Westminster—to
be seen there only on great occasions. Their regular duties were in
the royal household, or half of their number in the theatre at times.

For the English drama had raised its head again. Out from their
seclusion came some of the old players who had trod the boards
in Ben Jonson's time, to whom were now gathered a company of
young aspirants and the new actresses. *O tempora; O mores!*

For the king liked music, the theatre, and women. So did Samuel
Pepys. They had this also in their favour, that sword and Bible
authority had had their chance, and had made themselves unpopular;
Pepys could go to a play without the risk of a raid by troopers who
might (in Cromwell's time) mulct him of three pounds eight
shillings and sixpence on the spot. Now there were two playhouses
within a short distance of each other—one in Vere Street, Clare
Market, and the other in Portugal Street, Lincoln's Inn Fields,
and if Samuel did not like the play at one of these he could walk out
after the first act and try his luck at the other. Patrons did not pay
until after the first act, so Etherege could complain:

> From one Playhouse, to the other Playhouse,
> And if they like neither the Play nor the Women,
> They seldom stay any longer than the combing
> Of their Perriwigs [*sic*] or a whisper or two with a
> Friend; and then they cock their Caps, and out they
> Strut again.[1]

[1] *She Wou'd if she Could* (1668).

Pepys did this on 7 January 1667–8, but it was not his custom. Neither was it his habit to run up a credit account at a playhouse as some of the gallants would do; Pepys was not a gallant. These swashbuckling characters had been put down during the Commonwealth, when duelling was forbidden, but they had come into vogue again with the Restoration. Another type was appearing, however, called the 'beau', who affected a new distinction in dress, a powdered peruke and a lazy drawl; he would beware the entrance to a quarrel, but was no coward. The beau had manners—perhaps he emphasized them overmuch, but he was to have his rightful place in English social history. Then there were the ladies—masked, and free with their current stock of oaths—whom Samuel liked to think were all ladies of the Court, though there was no guarantee of this, and, according to the actors, sober husbands in the city had their doubts also:

> They say their Wives learn ogling in the Pit;
> They'r from the Boxes taught to make advances,
> To answer stolen sighs and naughty glances.[1]

Yet Samuel Pepys was a jewel among playgoers—a man who liked a good play. He made a friend of the actress Mrs Knepp (he always spelt her name Knipp) and hated her interfering husband, but the play was the thing for Samuel. This trait could hardly go unnoticed. Moreover, he was spending at the rate of £1,154 a year in 1666, 'which is a sum not fit to be said that I should spend in one year', he drove in his coach (with his sword across his knees, for in the devastated area left by the Great Fire lurked desperate men), and he had his little vessel on the sea. These things cannot be hid, and it is not therefore surprising that Tom Killigrew the actor sought him out:

This done, T. Killigrew and I to talk: and he tells me how the audience at his house is not above half so much as it used to be before the late fire. That Knipp is like to make the best actor that ever come upon the stage, she understanding so well: that they are going to give her £30 a year more. That the stage is now by his pains a thousand times better and more glorious than ever heretofore. Now, wax-candles, and many of them; then, not above 3lbs. of tallow: now, all things civil, no rudeness anywhere; then, as in a bear-garden: then, two or three fiddlers; now, nine or ten of the best: then, nothing but rushes on the ground, and every

---

[1] Shadwell, *The Lancashire Witches* (1681), Epilogue.

thing else mean; now, all otherwise: then, the Queen seldom and the King never would come; now, not the King only for state, but all civil people do think they may come as well as any. . . . That he hath ever endeavoured in the late King's time, and in this, to introduce good musique, but he never could do it, there never having been any musique here better than ballads. And says, 'Hermitt poore' and 'Chiny Chese' [1] was all the musique we had; and yet no ordinary fiddlers get so much money as ours do here, which speaks our rudeness still. . . . And he tells me plainly that the City audience was as good as the Court, but now they are most gone.[2]

Behind all this was the need for money. Killigrew was finding difficulty in getting payment from hangers-on of the Court, to whom he made his strongest appeal. The Puritan rule was no more, but still the middle classes disapproved of the theatres. They went on special occasions, for Pepys noticed them there, but generally about Christmas time; they were not regular supporters of the drama, and preferred spectacular shows to what the Restoration dramatists called wit. Spectacular shows were costly, and so the actors were always in need of capital. Mr Pepys was fond of Mrs Knipp and her music. A fool and his money are soon parted. So Tom Killigrew talked about his theatre and about Mrs Knipp's prospects, and about the wonderful new Italian *castrati*, 'so tall, that Sir T. Harvy said well that he believes they do grow large by being gelt as our oxen do, and one woman well very dressed and handsome enough, but would not be kissed, as Mr Killigrew, who brought the company in, did acquaint us.' [3] The only thing wrong with Tom's scheme was that Samuel was no fool.

Musical standards were to be raised; ballads were to go and Italian opera singers to have their due. It did not work out like this, for Charles II would not pay regularly what he had promised the Italians, and the English singers knew how to hold their own. Yet this was a great period for English music—the last great period we were to have until the twentieth century dawned. One name alone would justify this claim to greatness in the seventeenth century— the name of Henry Purcell. We know him as a musician of the Court, the theatres, Westminster Abbey, and a Chelsea girls' school, equally at home with grand or light music.

Samuel Pepys was born in 1633 and died in 1703, so the ten years covered by his diary (1659-69) represent but a small part of his life's experience. He lived through the Puritan experiment in government,

---

[1] *Chevy Chase.*   [2] *Diary*, 12 February 1666–7.
        [3] *Diary*.

the Restoration, the Revolution of 1688 which ended James II's occupation of the throne, and when Pepys died Anne was queen. He thus saw a great deal more of English history than the diaries reveal. He missed very little, from the public indignities done on Cromwell's body at Tyburn (by men who regarded themselves as superior to the Puritans) to being himself sworn in as a justice of the peace for Middlesex, Essex, Kent, and Southampton, 'with which honour I did find myself mightily pleased, though I am wholly ignorant in the duties of justice of the peace. I went to Monsieur L'Impertinent (Mr Butler) to a dancing meeting in Broad Street, at the house that was formerly the glass-house, Luke Channell master of the school, where I saw good dancing'. Next day he drank tea for the first time, and so on.

Luke Channell was well known. He it was who had arranged the dances for Shirley's masque of *Cupid and Death* done during the Commonwealth, and he seems to have been sufficiently famous to be parodied in the theatre. Durfey's [1] *Love for Money, or the Boarding School* contains a character named Luke Cheynell, a hop-merchant. 'Hop-merchant' was slang for dancing-master. In this play we are shown how the dancing-master employed his art to teach deportment and good manners to young ladies; he does it to a song:

> Make your honours, Miss, tholl, loll, loll,
> Now to me, Child, tholl, loll, loll,
> Aiery and easy now, tholl, loll, loll,
> Very well done, Miss, tholl, loll, loll,
> Raise up your body, Child, tholl, loll, loll,
> Then you in time will rise, hoh, tholl, la.

> Bear your hips swimmingly, tholl, loll, loll,
> Keep your eyes languishingly, tholl, loll loll,
> Zouns! Where's your ears now? tholl, loll, loll;
> Leave off jerking, tholl, loll, loll,
> Keep your knees open, tholl, loll, loll,
> Else you will never do, hoh, tholl, la.

Since this is a comedy, the ladies must be awkward and rebellious. The boarding-school must be made ludicrous for the theatre wits,

---

[1] Thomas Durfey had a gift for making verses in the ballad styles, and his published collection *Wit and Mirth, or Pills to Purge Melancholy* is important in the history of popular song.

with the girls escaping to get themselves in trouble in the city. The Princess None-so-Fair (called Nonsey) does so with her friend Glozy (played by a man):

Nonsey:

> I'll ne'er go home again, that's flat.
> Maids are not here confined to Rules,
> As at your Whoreson Boarding Schools.

Glozy:

> How silly is the Shock and Pomp
> That's practised there by every Romp.

A 'romp' was a clumsy girl, or a tomboy. The moral tone of *Love for Money* is what we may expect from its title, or its songs; parody had its uses and abuses. There was a popular song in those days from Shadwell's *Psyche* with music by Matthew Locke which ran:

> The Delights of the Bottle and Charms of old Wine,
> To the Power and the Pleasure of Love must resign;
> Though the Night in the Joys of good Drinking be past,
> The Debauches but till the next Morning will last;
> But Love's great Debauch is more lasting and strong,
> For that often lasts a Man all his life long.

> Love and Wine are the Bonds that fasten us all;
> The World, but for these, to confusion would fall;
> Were it not for the Pleasures of Love and good Wine,
> Mankind for each trifle their Loves would resign;
> They'd not value dull Life, nor could live without thinking,
> Nor would Kings rule the World, but for Love and good Drinking.

Durfey turns it into this:

> The delights of the Bottle, and the Charms of the Drab,
> When they pour out their pleasure will make a man mad.
> All the night in deep healths and loud curses is spent,
> Which the dull silly Fop the next day does repent.
> And Love's sweet debauch in a moment is gone,
> But leaves a damned Pox to last all the life long.

* D

Love and Wine rule the Swords that shed so much Blood.
All the World, but for them, would grow virtuous and good
Were it not for the Witchcrafts of Wenching and Wine,
Madam —— would be poor, and my Lord would be fine,
But she now keeps her Coach, and can live without thinking,
And damns her Debauch with his Wenching and Drinking.

This a young woman might expect at the worst, but if she were educated in one of the reputable boarding-schools situated in the pleasant villages grouped round London, she would have as good a chance of a marriage acceptable to her parents as their means and social position warranted, for she would have the background of an eligible debutante:

Here blest with Innocence and peace of Mind,
Not only bred to Virtue, but inclined,
We flourish, and defy all human kind.
Art's curious garden thus we learn to know,
And here secure from nipping Blasts we grow.
Let the vain Fop range o'er yon vile lewd Town,
Learn Playhouse Wit, and vow 'tis all his own;
Let him Cock, Huff, Strut, Ogle, Lye and Swear
How he's admired by such and such a Player;
All's one to us, his Charms have here no power,
Our hearts have just the temper as before;
Besides we show we live by strictest Rules,
Our Nunnery-door is charmed to shut out Fools;
No Love-toy here can pass to private view,
Nor China-orange cram'd with Billets dew,
Rome may allow strange things to please her Sons,
But we are Protestants, and English Nuns,
Like nimble Fawns, and Birds that bless the Spring,
Unscar'd by turning Times we dance and sing;
We hope to please, but if some Critick here,
Fond of his Wit, designs to be severe,
Let not his patience be worn out too soon,
And in a few years we shall be all in Tune.

This epilogue to Purcell's opera *Dido and Aeneas* was written by Durfey and spoken by Lady Dorothy Burke, who afterwards became the first wife of Alexander Pendarves, whose character and method of choosing a wife we may learn from the life of his more famous future partner, Mary Granville; [1] he was then an elderly man, dirty in his habits, ill-tempered, gouty, and a sot; Mary was seventeen. The business of marriage had to be carefully conducted, especially after the Restoration, when family fortunes, already once reversed in the Great Rebellion, were again reshuffled. Lands and titles, sons and daughters, were basic commodities.

As for their musical skill, the young ladies in the boarding-schools had to learn the graces and flourishes commonly employed at that time in all sophisticated music, be it for church, theatre, or home. So, in *Love for Money*, a music master tries to teach Molly —another 'romp'—how to sing a trill: she does it badly:

A plague; what, with your mouth full of bread and butter? for shame: empty your Chops, miss. There's a Trill for the Devil.

There were trills above and trills below a note; trills fast or slow; trills ending with a turn; appoggiaturas from above or below a written note; *messa di voce*—which was the control of the volume of a sung note; an effect called 'anticipation', which we should call *portamento*, for it meant sliding to a note, especially if it implied a dissonant interval; then there was the 'dragg', where a wide leap from a high to a low note would be covered by a series of down-the-scale jerks to a rhythm indicated by such words as 'shudder' or 'never'—and the music and the words were closely related in the style of singing. Descriptions of late seventeenth- and early eighteenth-century *bel canto*—the art of beautiful song—may actually read like descriptions of the effects heard today from American crooners, but the element of taste is not transferable in print, and singing had to be carefully learnt in a great Italian tradition.

We use the word 'baroque' to describe the elaborate art of this period, but the word in use at the time was 'heroic'. The 'heroic' couplet, 'heroic' history-painting, 'heroic' opera. The ornamentation was part of the whole; it failed in its object when it became merely an encrustation on the surface of the work. Art was not to be used to present the facts of history but to aggrandize them. In the course of time this art became outmoded and the term 'baroque' applied as a word of reproach. It has now come back into favour. Dryden outlined the theory of the heroic in the prefaces to his plays, into which scheme Purcell's music fitted. Beside Dryden, however, should be put the name of Elkanah Settle, with whom Purcell also

[1] Later Mrs Delaney, whose letters throw so much light on eighteenth-century social life.

collaborated. Settle regarded himself as a rival of Dryden in the theatres. His 'heroic' style went to the extreme, as is demonstrated in the illustrations to printed editions of his play *The Empress of Morocco*. These give not only Settle's scenery but also the only known pictures of the interior of the Dorset Garden theatre, where the most elaborate plays were staged. Settle ended his days as a showman in the annual fair of St Bartholomew, producing there some of his elaborate settings, and possibly affording in this way an historical link between the great transformation scenes of the masques and the modern pantomime.

The English language presented problems difficult to reconcile with Italian practice, but Henry Purcell had a natural genius for the effective use of consonants and short vowels. Dryden theorized on the place of music in opera, and at first tended to crack the whip to his musical collaborator, but in the end he came round to the view that the poet must give way to the musician in the arrangement of sounds.

But the numbers of Poetry and Vocal Musick, are sometimes so contrary, that in many places I have been oblig'd to cramp my verses, and to make them Rugged to the Reader, that they might be Harmonious to the Hearer: of which I have no reason to repent me, because these sorts of Entertainment are principally designed for the Ear and the Eye; and therefore in Reason my Art on this occasion, ought to be subservient to his.

The passage quoted comes from Dryden's dedication of the 'opera' *King Arthur*. It is not an opera, but a design in verse, music, dancing, and spectacle, to catch the ears of a numerous public. So it had to be on a patriotic theme.

Come if you dare, our Trumpets sound;
Come if you dare, the Foes rebound.
We come, we come, we come, we come,
Says the double, double, double Beat of the Thundering Drum.

This is not good on the printed page, as Dryden well knew, but the effect with Purcell's music is admirable for its purpose on the stage. When this poet and this composer were in agreement even the threadbare tradition of British patriotic songs took on rare beauty.

Well might we agree with Dryden:

There is nothing better, than what I intended, but the Musick; which
has since arrived to a greater perfection in *England* than ever formerly;
especially passing through the Artful Hands of Mr Purcel, who has composed with so great a Genius that he has nothing to fear but an ignorant,
ill-judging Audience. . . .

There he goes—snapping at the hand which should feed him,
just like a modern poet. The reasons were much the same; the
public liked sensory effects and intellectual relaxation. Perhaps also
they disliked being called unintelligent, but poets kept on saying
it. In an entertainment called *The Fairy Queen*, which used some of
Shakespeare's rustic characters from *A Midsummer Night's Dream*
in a most un-Shakespearian manner, the author wrote:

> What have we left untry'd to please this Age,
> To bring it more in liking with the Stage?
> We sunk to Farce, and rose to Comedy
> Gave you high Rants, and well-writ Tragedy.
> Yet Poetry, of the success afraid,
> Call'd in her Sister Musick to her aid,
> And, lest the Gallery should Diversion want,
> We had Cane Chairs to dance 'em a Courant.

Purcell wrote a Dance of the Chairs for *Dioclesian*, and the above
quotation from *The Fairy Queen* is from the prologue to a pot-
boiler, but Purcell nevertheless wrote some of his best music for it.
Only the pot did not boil. 'The Court and Town were wonder-
fully satisfied with it; but the Expenses in setting it were so great,
the Company got very little by it.' [1]

We have, therefore, something like a parallel with the problem
besetting twentieth-century culture in which an entertainment of
good artistic quality can only be expected to draw a small audience,
while a spectacular attraction will fill the house with people of medi-
ocre taste, but only after great capital outlay. We may then be
tempted by the old fallacy that history is repeating itself, when in
fact this is not so; for modern technology has devised means of
spreading the product among a wide public by means of the cinema,
radio, and television, and spreading publicity through illustrated

---

[1] Downes, *Roscius Anglicanus* (1708). The libretto may have been the work of
Elkanah Settle.

magazines; these things were not possible in seventeenth-century England, nor were there transport facilities to draw people from the Provinces to the London theatres. The battle between the fashionable wits—who regarded themselves as artistically superior —and the mass of the available public, was much as it is today, but that was all. The middle classes were still the backbone of Puritanism in the seventeenth century, whereas today they are cautious of their reputation without seeking religious justification.

In the seventeenth century there was no monopoly of reason among the wits—that was their vanity; it was an age when all educated classes had learned to think for themselves; none were more given to clear reasoning than the opponents of the theatre. Jeremy Collier in 1698 restated the Puritan view,[1] and let it not be said that he objected to the social atmosphere of the theatres but approved the art; he knew the artistic theory of his times as well as Dryden, and employed it in his attack. Consider his objections to Dryden and Purcell's *King Arthur*:

Now here is a strange Jumble and Hotch-potch of Matters, if you mind it. Here we have *Genii*, and *Angels, Cupids, Syrens,* and *Devils, Venus* and St *George, Pan* and the *Parson*, the Hell of Heathenism, and the Hell of *Revelation*; a fit of Smut, and then a Jest about Original Sin. And why are Truth and Fiction, Heathenism and Christianity, the most Serious and Trifling Things blended together, and thrown into one Form of Division? Why is all this done unless it be to ridicule the whole, and make one as incredible as the other?

Compare this with the Preface to Dryden's opera *Albion and Albanius*, 1681. The gods must keep their proper stations, or the fiction becomes absurd [2]. Now pass on to Collier's criticism of Purcell's employment of music in *King Arthur*:

Now granting the *Play-House Musick* not vicious in the Composition, yet the design of it is to refresh the *Idea's* of the *Action*, to keep *Time* with the *Poem*, and be true to the *Subject*. For this Reason among others the *Tunes* are generally Airy and Gailliardizing: They are contriv'd on purpose to excite a sportive Humour, and spread a Gaiety upon the Spirits. To banish all Scruple, and lay Thinking and Reflection asleep. This sort of Musick warms the Passions, and unlocks the Fancy, and makes it open to Pleasure like a Flower to the Sun. It helps a Luscious

---

[1] Jeremy Collier, *A Short View of the Immorality and Profaneness of the English Stage: together with the Sense of Antiquity Upon this Argument* (1698).
[2] Cf. also Dr Johnson's criticism of *Paradise Lost* in *The Lives of the Poets—Milton* (1779–81).

Sentence to slide, drowns the Discords of *Atheism*, and keeps off the Aversions of Conscience. It throws a Man off his Guard, makes way for an ill Impression, and is most Commodiously planted to do Mischief. A Lewd *Play* with good Musick is like a Loadstone *Arm'd*, it draws much stronger than before.

Collier was right in his facts, according to the theory and artistic practice of the time. He differed from the theatrical profession in the purpose of music; to the musical profession it was right that music should be employed to rouse the passions and serve the sensory delights of the theatre; to Collier the purpose of everything should be the moral elevation of human character.

In such an age lived Samuel Pepys, a respectable civil servant, in touch with the Court but not of it. He did his duty towards the Navy in most difficult times, was a member of the Royal Society at its inception, and sang and composed music. His own music was of inferior merit, and in a declamatory style (reminiscent of Henry Lawes) which was going out of fashion when Pepys wrote it, but he never lost his interest in the art:

This day I bought the book of country dances against my wife's woman Gosnell comes, who dances finely; and there, meeting Mr Playford, he did give me his Latin songs of Mr Deering's, which he lately printed.[1]

The book Samuel purchased was of course Playford's *The Dancing Master*, and the Latin songs composed for two and three voices by Richard Dering had just been published, though Dering had died in 1630. (Dering lived most of his life abroad, a Roman Catholic, yet his Latin motets were Cromwell's favourite music for voices, sung by two boys trained by the Protector's private organist John Hingston.)

The country dances and Dering's motets were in the old styles of the common people and the Latin Church respectively; Pepys's own composition *Gaze not on Swans*, to words from Davenant's *The Siege of Rhodes*, was in the English style of the middle seventeenth century, and may well be the style of music used in Davenant's 'opera', if we but knew it; there was, however, another style coming into vogue during the Restoration, with the king's full approval—the Italian style which had captured the affections of music-lovers all over Europe. Among Pepys's friends was one

Diary, 22 November 1662.

Thomas Hill, who in 1673 lived in Lisbon; Hill recommended to Samuel an Italian musician named Cesare Morelli, who wanted to come to England. 'I am certain', wrote Hill, 'that you will like his voice; his manner of singing is *alla Italiana di tutta perfettiore*.' Pepys, as we know, had been greatly impressed by the Italian singers introduced to him by Thomas Killigrew, and so (with characteristic caution) he offered Morelli a salary of £30 a year to enter his service. This the Italian accepted. Under Morelli's tuition Samuel learnt to set Hamlet's soliloquy *To be or not to be* in recitative. 'I have entertained myself harmlessly with him', said Pepys, 'singing with his lute, till twelve o'clock, when it was time to rest.' Surely an idyllic association of a nature which would not have been officially condemned during the Puritan rule! But now the king enjoyed his own again, and some writers have acclaimed the Restoration as a time of personal freedom! It was in fact a time of intrigue and oppression, as well as of the advancement of science. The year 1678 saw Titus Oates fanning up resentment against Roman Catholics, and poor Morelli was of that faith. He must therefore be a priest incognito, a Jesuit spy—they all were—all Roman Catholics!

Seeing the danger in which Morelli stood, Pepys tried hard to convert him to Protestantism, employing one James Houblon of a well-known Huguenot family to this end, but Morelli's faith could not be broken, and Pepys accordingly sent him into the country out of harm's way.

A year later Pepys himself was taken to the Tower, accused of being in treasonable correspondence with the French Government, and with being a secret Papist—the latter charge solely on the evidence that Morelli was of his household. Pepys's butler gave evidence that Morelli used to say Mass at the Queen's Chapel, had a rosary, certain pictures, and a private door to his room—all declared to be indicative of Jesuitry. Pepys was said to have been often closeted with Morelli to a late hour, singing psalms; no doubt he was, for as we have seen, the psalm-books contained matter for musical instruction. Such was the risk anyone ran in the days when Titus Oates had only to point to a man in a crowd and shout 'Papist', and the whole crowd would fall on the man indicated. Pepys's enemy was one John Scott, calling himself Colonel Scott —a swindler who in the ordinary course of his business Samuel had exposed. In spite of this, Scott was able to trump up a succession of charges against various people. Earlier in the seventeenth century witch-hunting had enjoyed similar immunity; the growing interest in scientific thinking had discounted witchcraft, but the populace still responded to the cry for scapegoats.

The credulity of the people is evident from the popular ballads of the time, of which Samuel Pepys has left a useful collection. Several deal with the Popish Plot and Titus Oates. One of the year 1678 begins:

> Let Traytors Plot on till at last they're undone,
> By hurting their Brains to destroy us.

And even in the reign of William and Mary, when Oates had been exposed and punished long enough for the truth to be apparent, some of the balladeers were still on his side. In the Pepys collection is the following; to the tune of *Greensleeves*:

> Come listen a while both Young and Old,
> While I in brief to you will unfold,
> A Ditty as true as ever was told,
> *Which Nobody can deny.*

> In Seventy-eight the Popish Plot
> Was Private, yet Hellish, and desperate Hot,
> For which some at last did go fairly to Pot,
> *Which Nobody can deny.*

> Some Protestant Lords did strive to devour
> A *Protestant* Monarch who then was in power,
> For which they were decently sent to the *Tower*,
> *Which Nobody can deny.*

It contains many verses, but the above will serve.

Pepys was suspected of Roman Catholicism also because he was known to the Duke of York, afterwards James II; but James was a dour man, anyway, without his brother's facility in tacking to the wind of public opinion. Charles II had his ups and downs; but he was popular; as Dr Wolcot said:

> I own that king
> Was never any very mighty thing;
> And yet he was a devilish honest fellow—
> Enjoyed his friend and bottle, and got mellow.

But the song which best reveals conservative opinion at that time is John Saville's:

> Here's a health unto His Majesty,
>   With a fa, la, la, la, la;
> Confusion to his enemies,
>   With a fa, la, la, la, la;
> And he that will not pledge his health,
> I wish him neither wit nor wealth,
> Nor yet a rope to hang himself.
>   With a fa, lal, lal, la, la, la, la, la, la, la—
>   With a fa, lal, lal, la, la, la, la.[1]

Charles II hid under a veneer of frivolity an able mind, capable of straight thinking and crooked dealing, but he left the Crown more secure than he found it. James II was a man of 'infinite industry, sedulity, gravity, and great understanding, and of a most sincere and honest nature', according to Evelyn. 'He makes a conscience of what he promises, and performs it.' He reigned four years!

His departure was accompanied by a song which started in Ireland amongst the soldiery, and with verses written by Thomas Wharton, spread across the whole of Britain:

> Ho, brother Teague, hast heard the decree?
>   Lillibulero, bullen-a-la;
> That we shall have a new deputy,
>   Lillibulero, bullen-a-la.
>   Lero, lero, lillibulero,
>   Lillibulero, bullen-a-la;
>   Lero, lero, lillibulero, lillibulero, bullen-a-la.

Cutting out the refrain lines to save space, we can follow the argument of the song, such as it is:

> Ho! by my shoul, it is de Talbot,
> And he will cut all de English throat.

> Tho', by my shoul, de English do praat,
> De law's on dare side, and Creish knows what.

[1] Record, Decca LF 1218.

But if dispence do come from de Pope,
We'll hang Magna Charta and demselves on a rope.

And de good Talbot is made a lord,
And he with brave lads is coming aboard;

Who all in France have tauken a sware
Dat dey will have no Protestant heir.

O, but why does he stay behind?
Ho! by my shoul, 'tis a Protestant wind!

Now Tyrconnel is coming ashore,
And we shall have commissions galore.

And he dat will not go to Mass,
Shall turn out, and look like an ass.

Now, now, de heretics all go down,
By Creish and St Patrick, de nation's our own.

The background to *Lillibulero* is interesting. In 1686 James II
concentrated on Hounslow Heath an army of thirteen thousand
men in the hope of overawing London. He began to put Roman
Catholics in key posts in England, and made Richard Talbot Earl
of Tyrconnel and later Lord Deputy of Ireland,[1] with control of
the army in that country and authority to transfer the civil service
posts to Roman Catholics. In 1687 James relaxed the restrictions
on the nonconformists by the issue of his first Declaration of Indulgence,[2] 'suspending the execution of all penal laws for religious
offences, and forbidding the imposition of religious oaths as quali-
fications for office'. Toleration certainly was needed, but in the
process James gave offence to the English Church and the universities; neither did many of the nonconformists trust him, for they
feared the Catholics. In the end, James offended all the old supporters of his father's cause—nobility, gentry, church, and universities—but worse than this, he had an army ready to enforce his
will. In 1688 he issued a second [3] Declaration of Indulgence and
tried to force the Church to implement it. A petition submitted by

[1] 1687.
[2] Charles II had issued a previous one in 1672.
[3] The third, counting that of Charles II.

seven bishops was described by James as 'a standard of rebellion' and he really lost his temper. The clergy for the most part refused to read James's Declaration in their churches, and where they did so their congregations showed disapproval by walking out. The whole country was angry with the king, and he in turn was stubborn enough to imprison in the Tower the seven bishops who had submitted the petition.

It was now the turn for the army to act. James realized, however, that they were most unwilling to do so, and he accordingly sent them back to their country quarters. Then he began to introduce recruits into the English regiments from Tyrconnel's Irish army, and the Irish, besides being Roman Catholics, were the traditional enemies of the English soldiery. Now we can understand the popularity of *Lillibulero*. 'Teague' was slang for Irishman (nowadays the Irishman is called 'Paddy') and 'Ireland shall be ruled by a dog and an ass'. The Talbot crest was a talbot *arg* langued *gu*, so 'Talbot's de dog, and James is de ass,' [1] and England too would be ruled in the same way if the Irishmen were allowed to enter the English ranks, for, as James expected, the Catholic Irish would have no qualms about attacking the English clergy. Such was the temper of the army that officers refused to enroll the Irish recruits (some of these officers were cashiered), while the common soldiers let their feelings be known through the song *Lillibulero*.

As may well be imagined, there were a great many popular political songs during the later seventeenth century, for these were the recognized means by which opinions might quickly and entertainingly be got about. If it was true that 'a lewd *Play* with good Musick', as Jeremy Collier said, was 'like a Loadstone Arm'd', it was equally true that a catchy tune would, with a few gallons of beer and ordinary good luck, start a riot. Nevertheless, these songs served their turn and died; they are to be found in libraries, while the songs which have retained popular affection are such as hold sentiments we can forever approve: *What shall I do to show how much I love her? Come lassies and lads,* and one which may originally have had political echoes, but which has come down to us as a children's song:

> Lavenders blue, diddle-diddle,
>   Lavenders green;
> When I am king, diddle-diddle,
>   You shall be queen.

[1] This verse was added later to those quoted above.

Call up your men, diddle-diddle,
  Set them to work,
Some to the plough, diddle-diddle,
  Some to the cart.

Some to make hay, diddle-diddle,
  Some to thresh corn,
Whilst you and I, diddle-diddle,
  Keep ourselves warm.

In male company the singing of catches was now established in favour among all classes, and in no other form of art, possibly, may the two extremes of the thought of the age be seen so clearly. At the one extreme were the pornographical clevernesses constantly referred to as characteristic of the age but unquotable, and at the other the rounds of Dean Aldrich known to us all: *Hark the bonny Christ Church Bells* and the catch composed by the same author to be sung by three men whilst smoking their pipes. It is untrue to say that few catches of the late Stuart period can be quoted, for there were so many of these compositions that (like the Victorian limericks) a choice can be made. Playford's *Musical Companion* gives one with a hidden subject, the effect of age on sexual desire:

From twenty to thirty, good night and good morrow;
From thirty to forty, good night or good morrow;
From forty to fifty, as oft as ye shift ye;
From thence to three score, once a month and no more.[1]

Henry Purcell certainly composed many catches which would offend against good taste if they were now printed; he gave us many more, however, in the true convivial tradition of the catch, but with power in the poetry:

Drink on till night be spent and sun do shine,
Did not the gods give anxious mortals wine
To wash all care and trouble from the heart?
Why then so soon should jovial fellows part?
Come, let this bumper for the next make way;
Who's sure to live and drink another day?[1]

Sonority was an emotional thrill; unintelligent though intelligible.

[1] Record, *Allegro* ALX 3008.

One took a catch as a cure from thinking, as one took a wench or a bumper:

> To thee, to thee, and to a maid,
> That kindly will upon her back be laid,
> And laugh and sing and kiss and play,
> And wanton out a summer's day,
> Such a lass, kind friends, and drinking,
> Give me, great Jove, and damn the thinking.[1]

Henry Purcell died in 1695. He was the last British composer to compare in merit with his contemporaries abroad until we come to the present century. From the time of Purcell onwards the British took great music from foreigners; light music, however, they were able to make in their own most charming manner. The cleavage between a literary and musical tradition (which arts had at the time of the first Elizabeth been integrated) had shown itself during the life of Samuel Pepys. Purcell brought Dryden round to an appreciation of the need to think of a song lyric in musical terms, but the partnership was short-lived. The misfortune of Purcell's early death is part of the stock-in-trade of musical historians, but more significant is the fact that so many men insisted on the distinction between sense and sensuality, putting the pleasure of sound in the latter class, as an artistic inferior.

[1] Record, *Allegro* ALX 3008.

VII. OPPOSITION

THE ITALIAN SINGERS whom Samuel Pepys met at the house of Lord Brouncker were the Albrice family—Vincenzo, Bartolomeo, and their sister Leonora 'who would not be kissed, as Mr Killigrew ... did acquaint us'. There was also an Italian whom Pepys called Signor Baptista—Giovanni Baptista Draghi, composer and harpsichord player—and later came the inimitable 'Siface' (G. F. Grossi), who sang in the Queen's Chapel. He was a soprano, castrated in childhood (like the Albrice brothers) to retain his high voice, and trained carefully in Italy until fully grown. There came also a woman singer called 'The Baroness', and an Italian who went by a French name—Margarita de L'Épine—and who was a fine player of the harpsichord,[1] singer, and scholar in music. They competed with the English singers on the stage, but the English had the advantage of language, so the main drama employed English players and singers while the Italians were relegated to the singing of songs in their own language between the acts of the English plays. Italian opera, which the foreign singers wanted to introduce, was financially risky, and all efforts to establish it in the London theatres during the seventeenth century failed. For all that, the Italians could sing better than the English actresses, and the public responded. Actresses being what they were, jealousy was inevitable. On 19 January 1704, while Margarita de L'Épine was making her second appearance at this theatre, a disturbance arose in the audience; some of the demonstrators were caught, including one Ann Barwick; this will help to explain a letter received by Christopher Rich (undoubtedly the biggest sharper who ever got control of London's theatres) from Mrs Tofts, an English soprano well-known in that theatre:

Sir, I was very much surprised when I was informed that Ann Barwick, who was lately my servant, had committed rudeness last night at the playhouse, by throwing of oranges, and hissing when Mrs L'Épine, the Italian gentlewoman, sung. I hope no one can think that it was in the least with my privity, as I assure you it was not. I abhor such practices; and I hope you will cause her to be prosecuted, that she may be punished, as she deserves. I am, Sir, your humble servant, Katharine Tofts.

Poor Ann! She did her best, but suffered for being caught.

[1] The strings of the harpsichord were plucked with quills, hence the name L'Épine.

Let there be no mistake; Mrs Tofts could look after her own interest. The following year saw the first attempt at presenting opera in the Italian style in England, in recitative and aria, but the opera—*Arsinoe, Queen of Cyprus*—was translated into English and performed by an English company in which Mrs Tofts appeared. Her Italian rival—the thorny Margarita—sang between the acts! The music was arranged by an incompetent named Thomas Clayton, but *Arsinoe* nevertheless ran for twenty-four performances and another eleven in the following year. The elaborate baroque scenery by Sir James Thornhill may have had a lot to do with the success, but apart from this it is likely that the public wanted opera if they could get it.

In such circumstances we were ready to welcome Handel in 1710, for he was a master of his craft. He came from Hanover and settled among us under circumstances which are a commonplace of musical history, and in 1720, when the South Sea Bubble had made men crazy to invest in any grandiose scheme, came the first permanent project for producing Italian opera; it was called the Royal Academy of Music, after the French fashion, but was in fact a company promoted to exploit Italian *opera seria*. It carried on until 1728, employing Handel among its regular composers, and an expensive array of castrated Italian singers whose voices were superlative—'soprano' and 'contralto' are Italian masculine nouns —raised above the natural voices of men and so associated with classical heroes and gods. The tune we know as Handel's *Largo* was sung in the opera *Serse* by a male contralto, with vocal embellishments not written on the page from which he learnt the song. The singer was paid a high salary because he had been trained to introduce and execute such embellishments. The effect was not by any means simple, as is the version we hear today.

Then, as a foil, came a new art-form—the ballad opera. *The Beggar's Opera*, written by John Gay, was a pot-boiler, a social scourge, a political satire, and a challenge to Italian opera, all in one. The tunes were well known to everybody; catchy, sentimental, 'natural'. The music was arranged for the original performance by Dr Pepusch, a clever musician whose wife was that same Margarita de L'Épine against whom Mrs Toft's hirelings had thrown oranges in 1704. The date of *The Beggar's Opera* was 1728. Between those two dates Italian *opera seria* had come into fashion in England and met its first repulse. Handel said that his operas had been driven off the stage in 1728 by lumps of pudding. *Lumps of Pudding* is the name of the tune used for the final dance in *The Beggar's Opera*! [1]

'I hope I may be forgiven', says the Beggar in his Introduction, 'that I have not made my Opera throughout unnatural, like those in vogue; for I have no Recitative.' Far from exalting the great in his opera, the Beggar made a hero of a highwayman and villains of those in authority, he made his heroine marry for love instead of duty, and parodied the situations fashionable in Italian opera: 'I have introduced the Similes that are in all your celebrated Operas; the Swallow, the Moth, the Bee, the Ship, the Flower, etc.' Then, with a sly dig at Buononcini, in one of whose operas the *prima donna* and *seconda donna* had come to blows on the stage, the Beggar goes on: 'As to the Parts, I have observ'd such a nice Impartiality to our two Ladies, that it is impossible for either of them to take Offence.' We may see the parody of Buononcini's impartiality in the Prison Scene in Act III of *The Beggar's Opera*. The characters are Captain Macheath the highwayman, Lockit the jailor and his daughter Lucy, Peachum the gangster and criminal 'fence', and Polly his daughter. Polly and Lucy both believe themselves to be Macheath's wife, and Lucy has helped him to escape from Newgate Prison. He has been recaptured, however, and in Scene xi we have a delightful vignette of love and duty:

Lockit:

> Set your Heart at rest, Captain. You have neither the chance of Love or Money for another Escape,—for you are order'd to be call'd down upon your Tryal immediately.

Peachum:

> Away, Hussies! This is not a time for a Man to be hamper'd with his Wives. You see, the Gentleman is in Chains already.

Lucy:

> O Husband, Husband, my Heart long'd to see thee; but to see thee thus distracts me!

Polly:

> Will not my dear Husband look upon his Polly? Why hadst thou not flown to me for Protection? with me thou hadst been safe.

---

[1] Recordings of *The Beggar's Opera*: H.M.V. CLP 1052–3, ARGO RG 76, 77, 78.

SONG

Polly:

Hither, dear Husband, turn your eyes.

Lucy:

Bestow one Glance to cheer me.

Polly:

Think with the Look, thy Polly dyes.

Lucy:

O shun me not—but hear me.

Polly:

'Tis Polly sues . . .

Lucy:

'Tis Lucy speaks.

Polly:

Is thus true Love requited?

Lucy:

My Heart is bursting.

Polly:

Mine too breaks.

Lucy:

Must I . . .

Polly:

Must I be slighted?

Macheath:

What would you have me say, Ladies? You see, this Affair will soon be at an end, without my disobliging any of you.

Peachum:

But the settling of this Point, Captain, might prevent a Law-suit between your two Widows.

Macheath is a 'gentleman' to the last, for, as the Beggar admits, 'it is difficult to determine whether (in the fashionable Vices) the fine Gentlemen imitate the Gentlemen of the Road, or the Gentlemen of the Road the fine Gentlemen'; the Captain's attitude to his two wives is clear enough:

> How happy could I be with either,
> Were t'other dear Charmer away!

Only the ladies are not satisfied. Polly flies to sentiment and Lucy to revenge:

Polly:
     I'm bubbled . . .

Lucy:
                  I'm bubbled.

Polly:
     Oh, how I am troubled!

Lucy:
     Bambouzled and bit . . .

Polly:
                  My distresses are doubled.

Lucy:
     When you come to the Tree, should the Hangman refuse,
These Fingers, with Pleasure, could fasten the Noose.

Polly:
     I'm bubbled . . .

Lucy:
                  I'm bubbled.

Polly:
     Oh how I am troubled!

Lucy:
     Bambouzled and bit!

Polly:
                  . . . My distresses are doubled.

The tunes to which these ditties are sung in the 'opera' are *The last time I went o'er the Moor* and *The Irish Trot*. John Gay in writing *The Beggar's Opera* turned everything topsyturvy and showed that, so regarded, it was more true to reason than the political and artistic theories of the day pretended. He used all the tricks we have found in Thomas Deloney's ballads and stories, and this clever satire had more effect on eighteenth-century thought than all the operas of Handel—which, to give them their due, were not intended to provoke thought, but to provide a select entertainment of a high order. In Italian opera one 'saw the world as the world's not'—in comic opera one saw the world distorted, but so obviously a distortion of reality that one longed to take up arms against the satire —as Sir Robert Walpole did—or use it to ridicule the people who were offended by it. *The Beggar's Opera* was socially and historically significant in a way that Italian opera was not.

In no way was this more revealing than in the career of Lavinia Fenton, the actress who played the role of Polly Peachum at its first performance. Rich paid her only fifteen shillings a week when she first sang in *The Beggar's Opera* so she must have had a greater fame as a toast than as a singer. Her voice was pleasant enough for simple ballads but untrained in the subtleties of *bel canto*. That was, however, a thing actually in her favour at Lincoln's Inn Fields, for she sang *naturally*. The town was sick of superior artificiality, just as a large part of the public is sick of high art today.

The Beggar's Opera ran for sixty-two nights in 1728, the last of these being on 19 June. Then on 16 July John Gay wrote to Swift: 'The Duke of Bolton, I hear, has run away with Polly Peachum, having settled £400 a year on her during pleasure, and upon disagreement £200.' Lavinia's social position was now clear—the status of a mistress was distinguished even among the ladies in *The Beggar's Opera*:

Dolly Trull:
> Pray, Madam, were you ever in keeping?

Suky Tawdry:
> I hope, Madam, I ha'n been so long upon the Town, but I have met with some good Fortune as well as my Neighbours.

Dolly Trull:
> Pardon me, Madam, I meant no harm by the Question; 'twas only in the way of Conversation.

Charles Paulet, Third Duke of Bolton, had married Lady Anne Vaughan in 1713, and she was still alive. It was a rational contract with a woman for whom he had no affection, and who had neither beauty nor wit. On the death of his father in 1722 he left her. The Duchess of Bolton lived on until 1751; when she died the Duke immediately married Lavinia Fenton. For twenty-three years a natural affection had kept 'Polly' and Bolton together, though he was twenty-three years older than she. As mistress and wife her manners were always discreet. Like Polly Peachum, with whom she was associated in the popular mind, she had a natural wit and a capacity for natural love:

Polly:

I know as well as any of the fine Ladies how to make the most of myself and my Man too. A Woman knows how to be mercenary, though she hath never been in a Court or at an Assembly. We have it in our Natures, Papa. If I allow Captain Macheath some trifling Liberties, I have his Watch and other visible Marks of his favour to show for it. A Girl who cannot grant some Things, and refuse what is most material, will make but a poor hand of her Beauty, and soon be thrown upon the Common.

But along with this—as every kitchen-wench knew—went the force of nature:

Polly:

Can Love be controul'd by Advice?
   Will Cupid our Mothers obey?
Though my Heart were as frozen as Ice,
   At his Flame 'twould have melted away.

When he kist me so closely he prest,
   'Twas so sweet that I must have comply'd:
So I thought it both safest and best
   To marry, for fear you should chide.

So reasoned Polly Peachum, and every woman in the audience secretly agreed that in her formula lay bliss. Marry for love. *The Beggar's Opera* set the theme in contrast with a contemporary society, where love had to be curbed as an irrational idea, and mercenary interests had to rule; for in the eighteenth century, State affairs—traditionally heroic on the stage—were plainly mercenary; therefore the conflict of love and duty we find in Purcell's *Dido and Aeneas*, with duty conquering and love creating the tragedy, was reversed in comedy; in *The Beggar's Opera*, though the social machine runs according to its construction, we see no justification for that sacrifice of the purer human wishes which its persistence required.

The modern equivalent of this is the play on human souls caught up in a machine-shop environment. The machine will be preserved at all costs—even at the cost of starving human passions.[1] The literary theme insists that these passions will break out in some other direction, as indeed they do. The comic operas of the eighteenth century set a similar problem, but in social life instead of industrial; love would find out the way.

Polly Peachum's sentimentality, however, must not be taken as typical of the best songs of the time, for it was part of Gay's satire. The middle classes, as we have seen, had little respect for the theatres, and the theatres had no more for the middle classes. Money had to be attracted, however, so the actors played up to middle-class morality, and in the process produced a sentimental fashion in goodness which brought the early eighteenth-century theatre no credit. This was the opportunity for Colley Cibber. The Cibbers—Colley and Theophilus—come into the story like villains in a melodrama, but since we are concerned with music, their place is unimportant. Henry Carey, who wrote *Sally in our Alley*, was worth a dozen of them. While magistrates complained that apprentices ran away to become 'gentlemanly' highwaymen under the influence of the glamour radiated by Captain Macheath, the note of sincerity persisted in the song:

Sally in our Alley is natural:

> My master, and the neighbours all,
>   Make game of me and Sally;
> And but for her I'd rather be
>   A slave and row a galley;
> But when my seven long years are out,
>   Oh, then I'll marry Sally;
> And then we'll wed, and then we'll bed,
>   But not in our alley.

The social scene was small enough for men to see it whole, so history, satire, and good sound sense met together in songs which

---

[1] See Chapter XIV, '*Deus ex machina?*'.

everybody could enjoy. The difficulty was in finding a market for these things at a time when the middle classes were suspicious of the theatres and the rich were lavishing their wealth on the Italian opera singers. Hogarth's pictures show us Senesino and the incomparable Farinelli [1] taking their toll of the fop's patrimony, and these things were true; the Italian singers received great sums from private entertainments which the nobility gave, in addition to what they were paid by Handel or the rival Italian opera (called The Opera of the Nobility) set up by Frederick Prince of Wales and the 'Patriots' as a counterblast to the influence of George II and his Whig ministers. By 1737 Handel was in serious financial straits, and his rivals in even worse, for they had to close down completely.

Compared with the Italians the simplicity of the English singers won them admiration, especially among those unable by education or temperament to tolerate the florid style of *opera seria*. Of Lavinia Fenton they sang in the streets:

> Compared with her how flat appears
>   Cuzzoni or Faustina? [2]
> And when she sings I shut my ears
>   To warbling Senesino.

Or, from another angle, hatred of the successful hangers-on of the Whigs brought popularity to such songs as this:

> Great Dames there are that break their Vows
>   As oft as Madam Peachum,
> And greater Robbers than her Spouse
>   Though Tyburn cannot reach 'em.

Envy and hatred may be spurs to satirical expression, but we have to admit that few of the songs from the innumerable ballad operas which popped up in the wake of *The Beggar's Opera* of 1728 had any real merit. Slinging mud, or worse, at public figures is not difficult, but neither is it artistic. There were tunes in plenty used in these ballad operas, but the words had only temporary interest. Apart from this the tunes themselves tended to be maltreated in the process. There is a well-known folk-tune called *Constant Billy* which became in *The Beggar's Opera* the tune used for the song *Cease your Funning*.

[1] Senesino and Farinelli were the most famous of the *castrati*.
[2] The two women singers who came to blows in Buononcini's opera (see p. 117).

Then among the immediate successors of *The Beggar's Opera* was *The Quaker's Opera* which contained a tune called *The Country Garden*, still in use as a folk-dance. The tune ultimately became associated with the poem of *The Vicar of Bray*, the verses of an early eighteenth-century satire of enduring worth, but what has happened to the tune? [1] The tune has become angular—a bad relation to the earlier version. But this must have been about 1770, for earlier than that a Scottish tune, *Bessy Bell and Mary Gray*, had been used for the song of *The Vicar of Bray*. Imitation Scottish tunes had a vogue throughout the century.

The real Vicar of Bray, who changed his coat with the political situation, was Simon Alwyn, who lived in the latter half of the sixteenth century, and 'therefore lived', as Fuller said, 'under Henry VIII, Edward VI, Queen Mary, and Queen Elizabeth; and was first a Papist, then a Protestant, then a Papist, and then a Protestant again.' But in those days the parish clergy mostly kept their cures while the State changed sides, and went with the tide of Reformation and Counter-reformation. The Puritan political experiment had not yet appeared. After this had happened men were not so ready to accept political direction of their faith, and the Restoration efforts at uniformity made the clergy more determined to follow their own consciences. Dissent grew stronger in the years following the return of Charles II. The song of *The Vicar of Bray* is fictional, and typical not of the seventeenth century but of the Church of England in the eighteenth, as its final verses show:

> In good King Charles's golden days
>   When loyalty no harm meant,
> A zealous High Churchman was I
>   And so I got preferment;
> To teach my flock I never missed
>   Kings were by God appointed,
> And damned are those who do resist
>   Or touch the Lord's anointed.

> And this the law I will maintain
>   Until my dying day, sir,
> That whatsoever king may reign
>   I'll be the Vicar of Bray, sir.

[1] For a discussion of these changes see Cecil J. Sharp, *English Folksong—some Conclusions* (1907).

When royal James obtained his crown
  And Pop'ry came in fashion,
The penal laws I hooted down
  And read the Declaration;
The Church of Rome I found would fit
  Full well my constitution,
And had become a Jesuit
  But for the Revolution.

        And this the law, etc.

When William was our King declared
  To ease a nation's grievance,
With this new wind about I steered
  And swore to him allegiance;
Old principles I did revoke,
  Set conscience at a distance;
Passive obedience was a joke,
  A jest was non-resistance.

        And this the law, etc.

When gracious Anne became our queen,
  The Church of England's glory,
Another face of things was seen
  So I became a Tory;
Occasional conformists base,
  I damned their moderation,
And thought the Church in danger was
  From such prevarication.

        And this the law, etc.

When George at pudding-time came o'er,
  And moderate men looked big, sir,
I turned a cat-in-the-pan once more,
  And so became a Whig, sir.
And thus preferment I secured
  From our new faith's defender,
And almost ev'ry day abjured
  The Pope and the Pretender.

        And this the law, etc.

E

Th' illustrious House of Hanover,
And Protestant Succession,
To these I do allegiance swear
While they can keep possession;
For in my faith and loyalty
I never more will falter,
And George my lawful king shall be
Until the times do alter.

And this the law that I'll maintain
Until my dying day, sir;
That whatsoever king may reign
I'll be the Vicar of Bray, sir.

This was well enough in its way, but the faith of a man should
stand steady whatever opinions his rulers might foster, and to act
otherwise is a confession of weakness. It is also a weakness in the
ruler if he cannot rely on his subjects' loyalty without imposing,
or trying to impose on them, views which they cannot conscien-
tiously adopt. The vicar in the song is a turncoat (the song seems
to have been derived from an early one by Ned Ward called *The
Religious Turncoat*, sung to the tune of *London is a fine Town*), but
the old rascal has his tongue in his cheek while he does it; this gives
zest to the song, but it was not the kind of behaviour likely to please
eighteenth-century Dissenters, or the more honest of the Anglican
clergy. Evangelicalism came in the Church of England as a necessary reaction against those of the clergy who took their duties
lightly.

If the clergy were the better for believing what they preached, the
musicians were traditionally expected not to trouble about belief
but to stick to their music. Already we have noticed the surprise
and anger of Gardiner, Bishop of Winchester in the reign of Henry
VIII, when John Merbecke took to Calvinism. (An opposite
example is that of William Byrd in the reign of Elizabeth I, who was
Roman Catholic in his private belief while holding an appointment
in the Chapel Royal.) So long as his music was good for the
Anglican church's purpose they paid his salary. A musician was a
craftsman. But there was nothing to prevent anyone from question-
ing the musician's art, or even making of it an Aunt Sally for doc-
trinal or political purposes. Certainly the Puritans took their aim
at traditional Church music, and Handel had his bellyful of poison

from the Tories. Every crisis in Handel's career during the time he was producing Italian opera in England coincides with a Tory drive against Walpole's government. The year 1728 brought *The Beggar's Opera*, a year after the Tory anger at being cold-shouldered when George II came to the throne; 1734 saw the establishment of a rival opera against Handel's, a year after the reorganization of the Opposition political party known euphemistically as 'The Patriots'.

It shook George Frideric Handel, who was made a scapegoat for his king and Walpole much as Mr Peachum in *The Beggar's Opera* was a scapegoat for the corruption of 1728—only Handel was real and Mr Peachum fictitious.[1] Handel was accused of extortion over the prices of admission to his oratorio *Deborah* at the same time that Walpole was accused of extortion over the unpopular Excise Bill of 1733 so—

Call'd to order, their *Seconds* appear in their place,
One fam'd for his Morals, and one for his Face;
In half they succeeded, in half they were crossed;
The EXCISE was obtained, but poor DEBORAH lost.

It is similarly tempting to us to make scapegoats of Handel's opponents when thinking of the state of music in England at this time, but in fact the rise of effective parliamentary opposition which came about as a result of these conflicts is of a value far outweighing the temporary inconvenience caused to Italian opera, which was to change its character anyway during the eighteenth century. The opposition to Walpole was associated with a great deal of satire, in which the ballad operas were foremost on the stage, but Walpole knew how to draw their sting;[2] so nothing comes out of the ballad opera fashion to compare with *The Beggar's Opera*. The real value of the new political party becomes evident when we think of the songs associated with their period of supremacy, from 1741 onwards. This is the period of the great patriotic songs, of the notion of the invincible Jack Tar, and of the divine right of commercial expansion. For the new party played up the idea of heroism into a militant nationalism, forced Walpole into the war with Spain known as the War of Jenkins' Ear (1739), and, though he was right in his epigram: 'Today they may ring their bells, but soon they will be

---

[1] But founded nevertheless on the character of Jonathan Wild.
[2] The Lord Chamberlain banned *Polly*, Gay's sequel to *The Beggar's Opera*.

wringing their hands', the desertion of his friends in the City into the militarist and nationalist ranks left him powerless. At such a time came forth the song of *Rule, Britannia*.

The composer was Thomas Augustine Arne, and the occasion an entertainment given before Frederick, Prince of Wales, at Cliveden House, Maidenhead, on 1 August 1740. The famous song appeared at the end of a masque entitled *Alfred*, which was an attempt at a musical and dramatic entertainment following the style of Dryden and Purcell's *King Arthur*. The song we know is simplified from the original *Ode in honour of Great Britain, call'd Rule Britannia*, which in its first form was an inspiring piece with splendid orchestral interludes—trumpets, drums, oboes, and bassoons used in a striking manner. The words are believed to be by James Thomson—poet of *The Seasons*:

> When *Britain* first, at Heaven's command,
>   Arose from out the azure Main,
> This was the Charter of the Land,
>   And Guardian Angels sang this strain;
>   Rule, *Britannia, Britannia*, rule the Waves;
>   For Britons never will be Slaves.

We can admire the melodic curve where Britannia is made to rise like Venus from the sea—the upward swirling on the word 'arose'; Dryden and Purcell would have liked this, but the following verses do not fit the same tune at all well; in particular the second verse requires this rising swirl to accompany the word 'in'. Try singing a short 'i' to a long note without distortion:

> The Nations, not so bless'd as thee,
>   Must in their Turn to Tyrants fall;
> Whilst thou shalt flourish great and free,
>   The Dread and Envy of them all.
>   Rule, *Britannia, Britannia*, rule the Waves,
>   For Britons never will be Slaves.

Remember that the War of Jenkins' Ear proved to be as Walpole had predicted; after a preliminary success at Porto Bello, Admiral Vernon found the odds too great; France saw her interests in the New World in danger, and sent two squadrons to the West Indies. The Tories, however, were coming back into power in parliament, and national pride demanded an ear for an ear at the very least.

Walpole's collapse was imminent, Pitt the Elder's star rising. In such a year—1740—was *Rule, Britannia* [1] brought forth:

> Still more majestic shalt thou rise,
>   More dreadful from each foreign Stroke;
> As the loud Blast that tears the Skies,
>   Serves but to root thy native Oak.
>
> Thee haughty Tyrants ne'er shall tame;
>   All their attempts to bend thee down
> Will but arouse thy gen'rous Flame,
>   And work their Woe, and thy Renown.
>
> To thee belongs the Rural Reign
>   Thy Cities shall with Commerce shine;
> All thine shall be the subject Main,
>   And ev'ry Shore it circles, thine.
>
> The Muses, still with Freedom found,
>   Shall to thy happy Coast repair;
> Bless'd Isle, with matchless Beauties crown'd
>   And manly Hearts to guard the Fair.
>   Rule, *Britannia, Britannia*, rule the Waves;
>   For Britons never will be Slaves.

As stated, this song was made for a masque given before Frederick, Prince of Wales, a thorn in the flesh of Sir Robert Walpole and indeed of his own father. Under Frederick's wing the belligerent elements in British political life found protection. Their views are clearly expressed in *Rule, Britannia*; expansion, territorial and commercial, with the assurance that God would be with us. Here in one song are the sentiments which enabled us to consolidate a great empire, and which lost us thirteen American Colonies.

But what of the spark which set off this patriotic conflagration? Captain Jenkins may have been a liar—he may not have lost his ear at the hands of a Spanish captain who boarded his ship; he may have lost it on the pillory, but this fact was not pursued; the common people were enraged because one of their countrymen had apparently been maltreated and his nation insulted.[2] In an emotional crisis they acted hastily, as men do, and others were ready to take

---

[1] Gramophone record, H.M.V. DLP 1050.
[2] 'I commended my soul to God', said Jenkins, 'and my cause to my country.'

advantage of the situation. Spaniards or Frenchmen might conceivably have done the same had they the same voice in the criticism of their rulers. The theatres responded to the popular outcry.

A turning-point in artistic, as in national, history was 1740, with Italian opera flogged to exhaustion and the ballad opera poisoned with its own physic; then true English songs again came into their own—fanned by a trade wind and warmed by a desire for an ideal national character, brave, honest, and generous to a fault. From an exaltation of the artificially heroic qualities of *opera seria* the public turned to idealized seamen and lasses with delicate airs; [1] English simplicity in song was made elegant with Italianate embellishments, but these were kept closely related. 'What a beautiful mixture it would be', wrote an Italian singing-master of Cuzzoni and Faustina, 'if the excellence of these two angelic beings could be united in a single individual.' The one was expressive and the other highly flexible in song. Simplified, and fitted to English words, this dual ambition dominated the musical style in the theatres from 1740 onwards, especially in the compositions of Thomas Augustine Arne and in the singing of his wife—Cecilia Young—and his sister—Mrs Cibber. Three lines of development were open to English song: (*a*) the popular airs of London pleasure gardens, (*b*) Handelian oratorio, (*c*) English comic opera from Carey's *True Blue* (1739) to the later works of Arne, Shield, and Dibdin. These three lines of development we shall follow in our next chapter.

[1] The well-known song *The Lass with the Delicate Air* is late eighteenth century, by Michael Arne, son of Thomas Augustine.

VIII. IN LOVE AND WAR

'MY WIFE COMES TO ME, to tell me, that if I would see the
handsomest woman in England, I shall come home presently; and
who should it be but the pretty lady of our parish, that did heretofore sit on the other side of our church, over against our gallery,
that is since married—she with Mrs Anne Jones, one of this parish,
that dances finely. And so I home; and indeed she is a pretty black
woman—her name Mrs Horsely. But, Lord! to see how my nature
could not refrain from temptation; but I must invite them to go to
Foxhall, to Spring Gardens, though I had freshly received minutes
of a great deal of extraordinary business. However, I sent them
before with Creed, and did some of my business; and so after them,
and find them there, in an arbour, and had met with Mrs Pierce,
and some company with her. So here I spent 20s. upon them, and
were pretty merry. Among other things, had a fellow that imitated
all manner of birds, and dogs, and hogs, with his voice,[1] which was
mighty pleasant. Staid here till night.'

Samuel Pepys wrote this on 29 May 1666. It is as pleasant a
record of the Vauxhall Gardens and their entertainment as we shall
find anywhere. In Pepys's time they were but newly opened, and
were called Spring Gardens, yet the type of attraction they offered
was so dear to the hearts of Londoners that the gardens continued
in popularity right through the eighteenth century. Dickens saw
Vauxhall in decline, when the entertainment had become cheap
and shoddy, but it was of the same type—popular airs, a band, and
shady arbours for the encouragement of Cupid. Here, too, meals
could be obtained, and originally there was no objection to plucking
the flowers, as on 29 May 1662, when Pepys went 'to the Old Spring
Garden, and there walked along, and the wenches gathered pinks....
Hence to the New one, where I never was before, which much
exceeds the other; and here we also walked, and the boy crept
through the hedge, and gathered abundance of roses.'

Thomas Augustine Arne was appointed composer to Vauxhall
Gardens in 1745; in the same year he became leader of the band

[1] This type of entertainment persisted in the taverns and passed into the music-
halls.

131

at Drury Lane Theatre, and his services were in demand also at Ranelagh and Marylebone Gardens. He was therefore kept fully employed in various rival establishments, from which we may estimate the value set on his genius for dainty pastorals, rousing patriotic songs, and bright music for band or organ. The time was ripe for this harvest; Italian *opera seria* was in decline, Handel had turned to oratorios, and the London theatres were reviving after their dull period at the beginning of the century. Before 1745 instrumental music only had been for some years the rule at Vauxhall, but from the time of Arne's appointment songs too became the vogue. Here were sung the songs he had written for revivals of Shakespeare's plays at Drury Lane—for Shakespeare had raised his head again, after having been so long in disgrace—the pleasant settings we were taught at school of *Where the Bee Sucks, Blow, Blow, thou Winter Wind,* and *Under the Greenwood Tree.* These we may think slight today, but they were intended for comedies which too long had been off the stage. It is only fair, also, to mention that the versions we know are simplified for the use of schools. Such singers as Arne's sister, Mrs Cibber, and his wife, Cecilia Young, had qualities not to be found in school children; these ladies had taste in the execution of smooth English airs and a flexibility learned from the Italians but applied to English song. They sang of country swains in the manner summarized by young Moses in *The Vicar of Wakefield*: [1]

Colin meets Dolly, and they hold a dialogue together; he gives her a fairing to put in her hair, and she presents him with a nosegay; and then they go together to church, where they give good advice to nymphs and swains to get married as fast as they can.

Besides the pastoral songs were the imitation Scottish, of which *Within a Mile of Edinburgh Town* is a fair sample.[2] Then there were what Horace Walpole called 'the singers of roast beef at both Theatres' (Drury Lane and Covent Garden). The theatres, the various gardens,[3] and the concert rooms at the inns all provided meeting-places for people whose innocent delight was in song. There were other, less innocent, delights, such as gambling and

[1] Chapter XVII.

[2] Words based on verses by Tom Durfey (seventeenth century), music by James Hook (1780).

[3] Sixty-four were recorded by Warwick Wroth in *The London Pleasure Gardens of the Eighteenth Century* (1896).

scandal-mongering, but these are to be found in the plays, not in the songs.   As for the roast beef:

> When mighty roast beef was the Englishman's food,
> It ennobled our hearts, and enriched our blood,
> Our soldiers were brave and our courtiers were good,
>   O! the roast beef of old England!
>   And O! for old England's roast beef!

> Our fathers of old were robust and strong,
> And kept open house with good cheer all day long,
> Which made their plump tenants rejoice in this song,
>   O! the roast beef of old England!
>   And O! for old England's roast beef!

> When good Queen Elizabeth sat on the throne,
> Ere coffee, or tea, or such sup-slops were known,
> The world was in terror if e'er she did frown.
>   O! the roast beef of old England!
>   And O! for old England's roast beef!

Richard Leveridge, who wrote that song, was a bass singer who died in 1758 at the age of eighty-eight, and who offered at the age of sixty to sing a song with any man in England for a wager of a hundred guineas. It is a jolly song, but, like all songs about the good old times, assumes that things are not as they were. Moreover this composer got little by his songs, for in his later years he had to be supported by his friends with an annual subscription. It must be said of composers in general in England, that unless one was a foreigner the rewards were meagre.

Thomas Augustine Arne was the son of an upholsterer who would not have had his son a musician; the lad therefore learnt music in secret, and perhaps not too well, for music is not an art to be picked up on the quiet. The father fell on bad times, however, and was glad to drop his scruples about the musical profession when he saw the chance of money in it. His son began to earn a livelihood by music, and his daughter, Susannah Maria, also had a good voice. She went on the stage in 1732 at the age of eighteen, and two years later married Theophilus Cibber the actor, a man ugly in visage and uglier in his habits. In her revulsion against this man, Susannah paid heed to the importunity of a country gentleman named Sloper, apparently to the satisfaction of her husband, who saw a chance of gain at the

*E

expense of his wife's dishonour. Theophilus Cibber threw the pair together as much as he could, and then went away to France to avoid his creditors for a time. He returned in 1738 to sue Sloper for damages; claimed £5,000 and was awarded £10. The court recognized his culpability in the affair.

Yet he made of Susannah Maria a great actress—a worthy partner on the stage for David Garrick in the years to come—and her reputation as a singer was as high as that of any English contralto. For her Handel wrote the contralto arias in *Messiah* and the part of Micah in *Samson*. She it was whom Dr Delaney heard sing for the first time on any stage the aria *He was despised and rejected of men*, and exclaimed: 'Woman, for this thy sins be forgiven thee.'

That was in 1741. The original success of *Messiah* at a charity concert in Dublin must not be misinterpreted, however. Handel's oratorios had to fight their way to popularity in England among a people who believed, as Charles Burney did, that music was 'an innocent luxury, unnecessary, indeed, to our existence, but a great improvement and gratification of the sense of hearing'. While it is true that the period which Handel devoted to oratorio coincided with the establishment of Methodism, the two were not related in the crucial stages, but came together after both had become established among the middle and lower classes. The cathedrals, which accepted Handel's oratorios from the concert-halls and theatres, never broke with Handel as they did with the Wesleys, for music—even on a sacred theme—was an innocent luxury, like hunting the fox.

Handel could have turned to comic opera in 1741 had he chosen. He was master of his craft, and comic opera was on the rise. But Handel chose the serious path, probably because of his temperament. He was drawn in to celebrate national victories (*Judas Maccabaeus* was written for the return of the Duke of Cumberland from routing the Scots after the March of the 'Forty-five', and in the *Occasional Overture* for the same celebrations he made an opening reference to Arne's *Rule, Britannia*), but it was left to the theatres and the pleasure gardens to cash in on the demand for military and naval victories.

Arne's *Masque of Alfred* was refurbished for performance at Drury Lane on 30 March 1745, from which date the popularity of *Rule, Britannia* was established (for the Cliveden performance of 1740 had been private). Again the country was in fear of invasion; it was known that in 1744 the French had collected a force of fifteen thousand men at Dunkirk, with transports for their conveyance across the Channel, but that adverse winds—'those ancient and unsubsidized allies of England', as Pitt called them—had delayed the passage, and a fierce storm had finally shattered the boats. Horace Walpole thought at first that a French invasion would have been accompanied by a general rising, but the country rallied until it was said that the very innkeepers declined to take money for billeting the troops who were brought south to meet the French. The defeat of the British and Hanoverians by the French at the battle of Fontenoy in 1745 made the position more serious, how-ever, and the Young Pretender arrived in Scotland to claim his inheritance, with little to offer, it is true, except his charm of manner, but he raised his standard at Glenfinnan on 19 August; on 18 September he entered Edinburgh, and on 20 September outfought Sir John Cope and his army at Prestonpans.

> Hey, Johnnie Cope, are ye wauking yet?
> Or are ye sleeping, I would wit?
> Oh, haste ye, get up, for the drums do beat!
> O fye, Cope, rise in the morning.
>
> It was upon an afternoon,
> Sir Johnnie marched to Preston town,
> He says, 'My lads, come lean you down,
> And we'll fight the boys in the morning.'
>
> Hey, Johnnie Cope, etc.
>
> But when he saw the Highland lads
> Wi' tartan trews and white cockades,
> Wi' swords and guns, and rungs [1] and gauds,
> Oh, Johnnie he took wing in the morning.
>
> Hey, Johnnie Cope, etc.

Protected as he thought by the marshes, Sir John Cope allowed his men to sleep, but the Highlanders were guided through the marshes in the early morning, fell upon the sleeping men, and all was over in ten minutes. Sir John escaped and brought the news of his own defeat to Berwick, as the song relates:

> Said the Berwickers unto Sir John,
> 'Oh, what's become of all your men?'
> 'In faith,' says he, 'I dinna ken;
> I left them a' this morning.'

[1] Rung = a cudgel.

At first the Government in London had taken no more than adequate precautions to check the Young Pretender, but after his initial victories London grew alarmed. It was then that the theatres roused themselves. First at Drury Lane, and then at Covent Garden, the actors lined up at the end of the performance, and one, stepping forward from the rest, with uplifted hands and eyes, began the first verse of an old anthem called *God Save the King*. The Drury Lane version contained a trio for Mrs Cibber, Beard, and Rheinhold, and Mrs Cibber wrote to David Garrick (then in the country recovering from an illness): 'The Rebellion is so far from being a disadvantage to the playhouses, that I assure you, it brings them very good houses.' [1] Arne arranged the version used at Drury Lane, and his apprentice Charles Burney that used at Covent Garden theatre.

Thus came into general use our National Anthem. It is certainly not a folk-song, yet it is a song which cannot be laid to the credit of any known composer. The phrase 'God save the King' is traditional in the coronation ceremony, having its origin in the Old Testament.[2] We have seen the phrase also in the last verse of the *Agincourt Carol* of the early fifteenth century: 'Now gracious God he saue oure kynge'; it has always in fact been an expression of loyalty and faith until recent times, when perfunctory performance in theatres, parks, and concert-halls has made it commonplace. We cannot blame the actors at Drury Lane and Covent Garden in 1745 for our own errors, however; they did what they could to express the feelings of the London public they knew, hoping, no doubt, that the same public would respond with favour to actors who had volunteered to serve their country.

The tune also is of no one authorship, so far as we can tell. The melodic curve is simple, and phrases of a similar character appear in old dance tunes, a Christmas carol, a catch, and a sonata by Henry Purcell. The seventeenth century may indeed be the crucial stage in the development of this song, for Charles Burney, when he tried to find the source of the song, was told by Mrs Arne (the composer's mother) that 'She had heard it sung, not only in the playhouse, but in the street', in 1688. If this is true, *God Save the King* was at that time a Stuart counterblast to *Lillibulero*—and *Lillibulero* won! The Jacobites, however, made many contributions to Scottish

---

[1] It had been announced that the actors had made themselves responsible for raising two hundred men for the volunteer militia. This would increase their popularity at the time.

[2] In the Old Testament we see this phrase arising spontaneously when Saul was shown to the people (1 Sam. x. 24). It occurs again in 2 Sam. xvi. 16, in 1 Kings i. 39, and again in 2 Kings xi. 12.

song: *Charlie is my Darling, Will ye no' come back again?* and *A Hundred Pipers an' a'* are among the best popular songs of any country, and true indications of the loyalty of the Highlanders to a leader whose cause was lost before he arrived in their territory. Feudalism had held the clans together long after parliamentary democracy had become strong in the Lowlands and England; individual clansmen held allegiance to their chief, and he to their king, Charles Edward Stuart. God saved great George our king with the defeat of the clans at Culloden, and we stole a Stuart song to commemorate the survival of the Hanoverians!

Subsequent uses of this tune in many countries for national occasions are interesting [1]—especially in the U.S.A. (*God Save America, God Save George Washington, God Save the Thirteen States, God Save the President, My Country, 'tis of Thee*), but the general trend has been the same as in England, with the tune taken by any party to serve its ends; in 1688 it was Jacobite, in 1745 Hanoverian, and in 1791 a parody *God Save the Rights of Man* (after Tom Paine's famous republican treatise) was actually revolutionary. We are not concerned with the rights and wrongs of the causes it has been made to serve, but only with the evidence of popularity such practices imply. Charles Burney's view that music was 'unnecessary to our existence, but a great improvement and gratification of the sense of hearing', is true so far as it goes; Jeremy Collier went further, however, when he admitted that popular music was 'not vicious in the composition, yet the design of it is to refresh the *Idea's* of the *Action*, to keep Time with the *Poem*, and be true to the *Subject*'. Thus employed, a tune is indeed 'like a lodestone arm'd', and it would be a distortion of history to attempt to interpret the appeal of popular songs in Burney's terms, whatever modern theorists may proclaim.

No country worthy of the name is ever so resolute as when its way of life is in danger. Patriotic songs are designed to stir the blood in times of crisis. The year 1745 was a time of crisis. A similar situation came in 1759, when an even greater army—eighteen thousand men this time—was ready to embark in a fleet of flat-bottomed boats at Le Havre. For three years we had been engaged with our allies on the Continent in pursuing the Seven Years War, and as usual we had entered into war unprepared. The fleet sent to relieve Minorca had retired under orders from Admiral Byng, who had later been court-martialled for the offence, found guilty,

[1] The authority on *God Save the King* is Percy A. Scholes, whose book *God Save the Queen* (1954) gives Jacobite and other versions of the song in detail.

and shot. On land the Duke of Cumberland (he who had so gal-
lantly massacred the Scots) had been outwitted by the French after
a clumsily fought battle at Hastenbeck on the Weser. We were very
much ashamed of ourselves. The tide began to turn in 1757, with
Clive's victory at Plassey, but the threat of invasion from Le Havre
arose to counterbalance this satisfaction.

The French plan was to employ all their ships together in the
attack, so De la Clue's fleet at Toulon was ordered to sail through
the Straits of Gibraltar, join with Conflans's fleet at Brest, and all
were to sail up the Channel together. La Clue, however, was over-
taken by Admiral Boscawen and his British Mediterranean fleet
off the island of Lagos, near Cape St Vincent; we captured four
French ships and dispersed the remainder. Then Admiral Sir
Edward Hawke, supported by Commodore Howe, found the French
fleet from Brest drawn up among the rocks and shallows of Quiberon
Bay. It was a dirty November night when the French actually found
the British among them, after a feat of seamanship almost as incredible to Hawke's pilot as it was to the French. The majority of
the French ships were captured, burnt, or driven ashore, while the
British lost only forty men in the engagement. Surprise was our
ally, but the invasion boats still remained at Le Havre:

> They swear they'll invade us, these terrible foes,
> They frighten our women, our children, and beaus,
> But should their flat bottoms in darkness get o'er,
> Still Britons they'll find to receive them on shore.

The situation was exactly as it was to be again in the second
world war of the twentieth century, when the whole Continent lay
in the hands of the Nazis, and our shores were lined with the rem-
nants of a defeated army and an as yet untrained Home Guard. In
the air we beat them; but there was no R.A.F. in 1759. Yet, could
we produce in 1940 a better patriotic stimulant than Garrick's song of
1759?

> So cheer up my lads, 'tis to glory we steer,
> To add something new to this wonderful year;
> To honour we call you, not press you like slaves,
> For who are so free as the sons of the waves?
>> Heart of oak are our ships,
>> Jolly tars are our men;
>> We always are ready,
>> Steady, boys, steady.
> We'll fight and we'll conquer again and again.

The music was by Dr William Boyce. And, serious though the situation remained, there was plenty to sing about in 1759. It was indeed a glorious year. On 1 August the battle of Minden had been won, in September the naval battle off Lagos, in October the battle of Quebec, in November the victory in Quiberon Bay. In that year the course of the Seven Years War turned in our favour. As Horace Walpole said: 'We are forced to ask every morning what victory there is, for fear of missing one.'

> We ne'er see our foes but we wish them to stay;
> They never see us but they wish us away;
> If they run, why, we follow, and run them ashore,
> And if they won't fight us, we cannot do more.

The facts were true for both Lagos and Quiberon. There was a final verse sung in the eighteenth century also,[1] which shows still further the topical attraction of these songs:

> We'll still make them run, and we'll still make them sweat,
> In spite of the Devil, and *Brussels Gazette*;
> Then cheer up, my lads, with one voice let us sing,
> Our soldiers, our sailors, our statesmen, and King.

Perhaps a word also should have been added for the taxpayers whose money subsidized the German allies, but taxpayers are not traditionally heroic!

The result of Wolfe's victory at Quebec was to free the British colonies from the restriction put on them by the French, who had previously held a strip of the hinterland extending from Louisiana to the Great Lakes, and had prevented the British colonists from trading with the Indians. After the annexation of Canada we guaranteed to the French Canadians the right to continue in their own cultural traditions—to retain their religion and language—and the benefit of this wise treatment of an honourable former enemy was to be seen fifteen years later, when Benjamin Franklin and two commissioners (named Chase and Carroll) went to urge the Canadians to throw in their lot with the older British colonies against the rule—or misrule—of George the Third's authoritarian advisers; Franklin's propaganda failed; French respect for the nobility withstood the blandishments of republicans, aided by the distrust which

---

[1] Quoted from *The Bull Finch . . . English Songs sett to music and Sung at the Public Theatres and Gardens*. Printed for R. Baldwin, in Pater Noster Row, and John Wilkes, in St Paul's Churchyard, London (N.D.).

the Roman Catholics had for the New England Puritans. We must, however, avoid the fallacy that the war against the American colonists was carried on without the general approval of the English people; popular opinion was as ardent and uninformed as ever, and anyone whom the British had to fight was a 'tyrant' or a 'traitor'. If we would seek the truth about the press-gang or the treatment of soldiers, we should go to folk-songs—and not even to all those. As for the theatres, they played up the role of the altruistic soldier or sailor, loyal to his king (which he was), generous to his friends, and faithful to his love (which he was but rarely). Perhaps it is unfair to quote General Burgoyne, whose surrender at Saratoga in 1777 decided the course of the American War of Independence, for, with his five thousand men surrounded by an army of fifteen thousand determined colonists, he had little choice. General Burgoyne, however, was a writer of popular song lyrics for the theatres, and, though there must have been plenty of stuff to sing about in his experiences, he gave us this instead:

> If I had a beau
> For a soldier who'd go,
> Do you think I'd say no?
>   No, not I!
> When his red coat I saw,
> Not a tear would it draw,
> But I'd give him éclat for his bravery!
>   If an army of Amazons e'er came in play,
>   As a dashing white sergeant I'd march away.
>
> When my soldier is gone
> Do you think I'd take on?
> Or sit moping forlorn?
>   No, not I!
> His fame my concern,
> How my bosom would burn,
> When I saw him return crown'd with victory!
>   If an army of Amazons e'er came in play,
>   As a dashing white sergeant I'd march away.[1]

The theme was not new, for many folk-songs tell of a lass who joined the army without her sex being discovered until necessary for the story. Among these the best known is *Polly Oliver*, telling of a girl who took her brother's place in the regiment, nursed the

[1] Gramophone record, H.M.V. DLP 1019.

Captain through a dangerous illness, and so cherished the brave man that he fell in love and married her. This song is used today in the army, and what could be more fitting for a regimental march? There is, too, a parody quoted in Chappell's *Popular Music of the Olden Time*: [1]

> O pretty Polly Oliver one hot summer's day,
> To Milverton market was making her way,
> With a basket of butter and eggs by the score,
> And cream from the dairy, a gallon or more.
>
> Her basket was heavy so Polly sat down,
> To rest by the wayside a mile from the town;
> She fell fast asleep, and awoke with a scream,
> For her basket was stolen and spilt was her cream.
>
> 'Ah me,' cried Polly Oliver, 'what now shall I do?
> My father he'll beat me till I'm black and blue.
> Kind powers, befriend me, and come to my aid,
> Take pity upon me, unfortunate maid.'
>
> From Bath came that morning the Earl riding by,
> And he sprang from his stirrup when he heard her cry.
> Her story she told, when he said, 'On my life!
> O pretty Polly Oliver, I'll make you my wife.'
>
> The day they were wedded she made him a cake,
> Of eggs, cream and butter, for memory's sake,
> And ev'ry year after she brought him the same,
> And that's how Bath Olivers have come by their name.

After so delightful an explanation who would care to assert the truth that Dr Oliver of Bath left the recipe of his famous biscuit to his coachman by way of a legacy?

The tastes of the officers in the army during the eighteenth century can be judged from their choice of regimental marches such as this. The army bands were kept up by funds subscribed in the officers' mess, and from that point of view the bands were the property of the officers. Without funds subscribed in this way the bands would have made little progress, though drums and fifes were traditional to the common soldiery, and trumpets—the instruments of the king's heralds—were with the cavalry because in earlier years it had been led by the king. The tunes these officers chose are still used for regimental marches: *Begone Dull Care*,

[1] Gramophone record Decca LXT 2797.

The British Grenadiers, and the March from Handel's *Scipio*. There was another march known to all regiments as *The Rogue's March* and used when drumming out a soldier in disgrace.

Before he was drummed out the soldier was flogged, and the flogging he got was a good deal worse than any given to slaves in the colonies—for slaves were valuable. The flogging was carried out by the drummers, each drummer laying on twenty-five strokes before being relieved by the next. By him stood the drum-major with a cane, which he brought down on the drummer if he thought the latter was not striking as hard as he could. The number of the stroke was shouted out loudly for all to hear, so all was strictly just. The man being flogged could ask for the drummer to strike higher or lower, but the effect was the same in the end—his back would be a raw mass of cut flesh. This spectacle had a great attraction for the lucky civilians who lived in garrison towns. After flogging, the soldier was tied to the back of a cart and led through the town, to be discharged at the gate with a parting kick from the smallest drummer-boy in the regiment.

In the navy, punishment was probably worse than in the army, for at sea the ship was a floating prison. Charles Dibdin, who at the end of the eighteenth century was one of the most popular writers of sea-songs, made a tour of England in 1788 and wrote about his experiences. He found London theatrical life dishonest, with the musicians being exploited by the theatrical managers; thus he pin-pointed the tragedy of T. A. Arne—then dead—how he was obliged to overwork to make a living, while foreigners got large sums from the Court; he found cathedral cities generally dull on his tour, agriculture prospering, roads bad, innkeepers indifferent unless there was strong competition from other inns. Highbrow musical societies angered him (he was in fact a little afraid of them, for their members looked down on his comic monologues, and their opinions carried weight), lawyers he detested, doctors he feared to be often incompetent, and, as he was an upholder of colonial policy, he supported slavery against the arguments of humanitarians who would do away with it. Dibdin's reasoning was shaky, but this he honestly did not know; he argued that slavery was not bad because we in England treated our own people worse than the West Indian planters treated their slaves:

Hence all the evils arising from imprisonment for debt, through which the unmerciful creditor has been known to decide upon the liberty, property, and even life of the oppressed debtor. Through which attorneys swarm in this country like locusts. . . . Hence all the distresses to harmless and industrious families by kidnapping and pressing for the army and navy; through which deserted wives and children are committed to the care of merciless overseers, and unthinking boys, in time of peace, flogged to death for desertion.

An instance of this kind lately occurred which plainly evinces that if the laws of this country are mild, the execution of them is cruelly rigorous. In the course of last month, at Dover, a lad of eighteen was sentenced to receive a thousand lashes for desertion. They had given him five hundred when, in terms of the most moving supplication, he implored a respite of the remainder of his sentence, crying out in accents scarcely utterable, that his heart was breaking, and he would die under it if they flogged him any longer. Regardless, however, of his entreaties, they continued their unmerciful work, till at the end of six hundred and fifty lashes, perceiving him actually dying, they removed him to the guardhouse, where he expired next morning.

Query; whether this is not at least a match for any cruelty which has been practised in the West Indies? There is certainly great opportunity for abuses and cruelty to creep into martial laws, and it originates from this. Those who are most likely to commit crimes cannot be tried by their peers. Thus, private soldiers and foremast men are generally punished with rigour, and the crimes of officers are too often palliated and softened into errors.[1]

Dibdin knew the abuses of law and custom as well as anybody. He knew too that a course of strict discipline might have a good effect on some men. 'Depredators who have gone to church to pick pockets have been converted into good citizens in the forecastle of a man-of-war', he said, and quoted a friend as saying:

Their [the sailors'] honesty and good sense are fully accounted for by considering that they have little commerce with mankind. Owing to this they despise money and therefore have no inducement to become knaves; for, as their wants are few, and these soon supplied, they have no occasion to rack invention to keep up a constant deception in their words and actions. Thus their ideas go immediately to the point they want to express, and their tongues transmit those ideas faithfully and without embellishment.[1]

Thomson in *Rule, Britannia*, and Garrick in *Heart of Oak*, had been content to sing the bravery of the sailors and the invincibility of their country, but Dibdin goes into the hearts of men, according to the theory of his time. Men were not naturally depraved, but became so as a result of their environment. One can glimpse the shade of Rousseau behind Dibdin's friend who gave him

[1] Charles Dibdin, *The Musical Tour of Mr Dibdin . . . written by himself* (1788).

the stock explanation for a sailor's reputed innocence: says Rousseau in his *Confessions* (writing of the time when he was apprenticed to a Genevan watchmaker):

Thus I learned to covet, dissemble, lie, and, at length, to steal, a propensity I had never before felt the least inclination to, though since that time I have never been able entirely to divest myself of it. Unsatisfied desire led naturally to this vice, and this is the reason why pilfering is so common among footmen and apprentices, although the latter, when they grow up, and find themselves in a position where everything is at their command, lose this shameful propensity.

The French Revolution was about to break, but, though Dibdin had listened to the new ideas (on a visit to France to escape his creditors), he was too shallow a thinker to understand their full import; he sang of the honest Jack Tar because Carey, Arne, and Boyce had made the honest Jack Tar popular; he wrote about the horrors of flogging because it served his purpose to mitigate the horrors of slavery, for Dibdin got on well with the Liverpudlians, who made money in the slave trade, but he failed to interest the more highbrow Mancunians, who were for abolition of slavery. He was a popular entertainer, with his ear very close to the ground, so *Tom Bowling* was unimpeachable:

> His form was of the manliest beauty,
>   His heart was kind and soft;
> Faithful below, he did his duty,
>   And now he's gone aloft.

Tom Bowling is the song which, of all those by Dibdin, endeared itself to the sentimental Victorians, but it is not his best example of the idealized sailor of the eighteenth century. Such a character must agree not only with Arne's hero of *Thomas and Sally* but with the rich seafaring vocabulary one finds in the works of Smollett. Who nowadays remembers Dibdin's *Poor Jack*?

> Go patter to lubbers and swabs, d'ye see,
> About danger and fear and the like;
> A tight water boat and good sea-room give me,
> And it's not for a little I'll strike.
> Tho' the tempest top-gallant mast smack-smooth should smite,
> And shiver each splinter of wood;
> Clear the wreck, stow the yards, and house everything tight,
> And under reef'd for'sail we'll scud.

Avast, nor don't think me a milksop so soft,
To be taken for trifles aback;
For they say there's a Providence sits up aloft
To keep watch for the life of poor Jack.

Why, I heard the good Chaplain palaver one day
About souls, heaven's mercy, and such;
And, my timbers! what language he'd coil and belay!
Why, 'twas just all as one as High Dutch.
But he said how a sparrow can't founder, d'ye see,
Without orders that come down below,
And many fine things that proved clearly to me
The Providence takes us in tow.
'For,' says he, 'd'ye mind me, let storms e'er so oft
Take the toplights of sailors aback,
There's a sweet little cherub sits perched up aloft
To keep watch for the life of poor Jack.'

I said to our Poll (for you see, she would cry),
When last we weighed anchor for sea:
'What argufies sniv'ling and piping your eye?
Why! what a damn fool you must be!
Can't you see the world's wide, and there's room for us all,
Both for seamen and lubbers ashore,
And if to old Davy I go, my dear Poll,
Why, you never will hear of me more.
What then? All's a hazard, come, don't be so soft—
Perhaps I may laughing come back;
For, d'ye see, there's a cherub sits smiling aloft
To keep watch for the life of poor Jack.'

D'ye mind me? A sailor should be, every inch,
All as one as a piece of the ship;
And with her brave the world without off'ring to flinch,
From the moment the anchor's atrip.
As for me, in all weathers, all times, sides, and ends,
Nought's a trouble from duty that springs;
My heart is my Poll's, and my rhino's my friend's,
And as for my life—'tis the king's.
E'en when my time comes, ne'er believe me so soft
As with grief to be taken aback;
The same little cherub that sits up aloft
Will look out a good berth for poor Jack.

How they loved it! It was just this sort of thing which led Pitt the Younger to employ Dibdin to write songs to inspire men to join the navy during the Napoleonic Wars. Moreover—the trick worked. Men brutally treated were prepared to believe in the ideals shown in Dibdin's songs. During the mutiny at the Nore in 1797, when the Lords of the Admiralty were dealing with the disaffected sailors, Henry Lang, a seaman in the *Champion*, wrote to them: 'Dam my eyes if I understand your lingo or long proclamations, but, in short, give us our due at once and no more of it; till we go in search of the rascals the enemies of our country.' The mutiny was broken by a clever ruse; the marking buoys and lights were removed from the estuary of the Thames, and the sailors dared not trust themselves to the shallows and sandbanks. Their leaders were hanged, and oppressive Acts were put through Parliament; the liberty of the press also was further restricted, but Dibdin's songs brought men into the navy.

If Dibdin avoided political grievances in his songs, however, it was for the same reason that comedians avoid them now. He wanted his songs to offend nobody and inspire all. It is an impossible ideal, but the fiction of the naturally honest Englishmen worked very well. He could be morally uncorrupted without being a milksop.

IX. THE ELEGANT AND
THE GENTEEL

'IT IS PROPOSED to speak of those musical performances with which the public in general were entertained at places of public resort, distinguishing between such as were calculated for the recreation of the vulgar, and those which for their elegance come under the denomination of concerts.' So wrote Sir John Hawkins in his famous *History of Music* in 1776. The distinction was clear: on the one hand the assembly-rooms, on the other the music-houses, which were taverns where musicians were engaged by the master of the house and one paid for one's drinks only. Such taverns still exist, where a pianist is engaged to encourage raucous singing on Saturday nights, and the publican is rewarded with bigger sales of beer than would otherwise be the case. For the present we must leave them, to return to them later, where we think of music-halls; our concern now is with the more elegant places where one paid an entrance fee for the privilege of listening to music, or went by invitation. Roger North (1653–1734) described the character of concert societies in his *Memoires of Musick*:

The Nation (as I may term it) of Musick was well prepared for a revolution. A great means of bringing that forward was the humour of following publick consorts, and it will not be out of the way to deduce them from the beginning. The first of those was in a lane behind Paul's, where there was a chamber organ that one, Phillips, played upon,[1] and some shopkeepers and foremen came weekly to sing in consort, and to hear, and enjoy ale and tobacco; and after some time the audience grew strong.

North describes also the public consort (the name has changed to the French 'concert') started at Whitefriars by John Banister, one of Charles the Second's violinists lately dismissed for impertinence and pilfering from payments he should have made to his subordinates. Banister's room 'was rounded with seats and small tables, alehous [*sic*] fashion. One shilling was the price, and call for what you pleased'. The stand holding the musicians was in the

---

[1] Removed from a church? Probably not, as it is described as a chamber organ.

middle of the room. Then North tells also of a gentleman's meeting

whom I shall not name, for some of them as I hear are still living, that used to meet often for consort after Baptist's [1] manner, and falling into a weekly course, and performing exceeding well with Bass violins [2] (a cours instrument as it was then, which they used to hire) their friends and acquaintance were admitted, and by degrees, as the fame of their meeting spread, so many auditors came that their room was crowded; and to prevent that inconvenience, they took a room in a Taverne in Fleet Street, and the taverner pretended to make formall seats, and to take money and then the society disbanded.

With those three examples we may know the social implications of music-making. Men liked to play or sing together—whether middle class like the shopkeepers and foremen or better class like the gentlemen—and people liked to listen. The listeners were prepared to pay for the entertainment, but this the gentry would not allow; it degraded them. Professional musicians were in another class, for it was their business to make music, so John Banister took money for the entertainment and provided drinks as part of the attraction. The eighteenth century was to see the development of these meetings as concerts of music by professionals, or as concert societies in all the principal towns, where amateur musicians played orchestral music for themselves and their friends, their ranks stiffened by any professional musicians who might be available, and the innumerable glee clubs, where men (and men only) sang together in good company, with their drinks beside them, or after a good dinner. Such a club is the Madrigal Society of London, which still exists, and which dates from 1741.[3]

Madrigals were exceptional, however; the glee was a popular type of composition in the eighteenth century and completely English. Catches were still sung in the glee clubs, and the smut was still in them, but glees were more serious compositions, their verses and music stylized and typical of their period; sometimes they were of trivial musical or literary merit, but at other times of real beauty. Their popularity was enormous; they offered a market to English composers at a time when foreigners were taking all the plums in the opera-house and concert-rooms, and some glees lived on in

[1] Draghi, the composer whom Pepys met at Lord Brauncher's.
[2] The violoncello.
[3] The soprano parts are now sung by ladies, but up to the second world war choirboys had been consistently employed.

public esteem until well into the twentieth century. Spofforth's *Hail, Smiling Morn*, Webbe's *Glorious Apollo*, Stevens's *From Oberon in Fairyland* and *Queen of the Valley*, Danby's *Awake, Aeolian Lyre*, and Tom Cooke's *Strike the Lyre* are fair examples. Tom Cooke belongs to the nineteenth century, however (1782–1848). By the nineteenth century some glee clubs had added orchestras, and the type of entertainment was more mixed, so as to include even so typical a ballad as *John Peel*, written about a hard-drinking, hard-riding yeoman farmer of Cumberland by his friend John Woodcock Graves, and sung to an old Scottish tune known as *The Border Rant*. John Peel was a real character, riding in his grey coat after a mongrel pack to the neglect, apparently, of his farming; he was not therefore representative of the pink-coated, well-mounted huntsmen who have distinguished the hunting-field since the eighteenth century, but he was a man with the primitive urge to hunt strongly within him.

> Yes, I ken John Peel and Ruby too,
> Ranter and Ringwood, Bellman so true.

Where can you find dogs [1] more worthily commemorated?

If we are to think of the Englishman's love of animals, think also of Charles Dibdin's *The High-mettled Racer*, which tells of the fate of horses in those days, passed from the race-track and hunting-field to hacking on the road, and finally to turning a mill. It may be that the English were a long time before they remedied this abuse, but the abuse of men was worse; it is typical of us that the songs pleaded for dumb creatures long before they pleaded for men, and the facts are not all to our credit; but at least we can say that today we have more respect for the suffering of animals and men than they have in many other supposedly civilized countries.

These, then, were some of the songs the English liked at the turn of the eighteenth and nineteenth centuries, along with catches, glees, and innumerable drinking songs. The men's clubs were wide in their appeal, and there were clubs for all social classes.[2] Among the most comprehensive was the Anacreontic Society, which existed in the latter half of the eighteenth century; this was a wealthy and influential club, with a long waiting-list of prospective members.

---

[1] Yes—dogs! None of your social niceties about hounds.
[2] Besides the clubs we should mention the lower class of entertainment from which our music-halls derive, the Comus Courts, meeting in the public rooms or basements of inns. A chairman presided and entertainment was provided by local singers or comedians in return for free drinks.

Their meetings started with a good instrumental concert at which they heard concertos and overtures; then after dinner they were entertained with songs and glees sung by the most accomplished singers. Comic songs were included, sung by performers from the theatres and pleasure gardens, but the society was most distinguished for its theme-song *Anacreon in Heaven*, which all sang to a rousing tune:

> To Anacreon in heaven, where he sat in full glee,
>   A few sons of harmony sent a petition,
> That he their inspirer and patron would be;
>   When this answer arrived from the jolly old Grecian;
> 'Voice, fiddle and flute, no longer be mute,
>   I'll lend you my name and inspire you to boot;
> And besides, I'll instruct you like me to entwine
>   The myrtle of Venus with Bacchus's vine.
> And besides, I'll instruct you like me to entwine
>   The myrtle of Venus with Bacchus's vine.

The full story of this song can be found in the Report on *The Star-spangled Banner, Hail Columbia, America,* and *Yankee Doodle,* compiled in 1929 for the Library of Congress, Washington, and published by them. The tune is that which has served since 1931 as the official National Anthem of the U.S.A. to the words:

> The star-spangled banner, O long may it wave
> O'er the land of the free and home of the brave!

The tune remains, but the Anacreontic Society has gone. Its social standing was its undoing. So famous was the club that the Duchess of Devonshire [1] asked if she might be allowed to remain to one of their after-dinner meetings. The duchess and her party were acccommodated in a space beneath the platform which held the performers, and screened from the view of the audience. The arrangement suited the duchess, but not the comedians, who found at the last minute that they were to sing in the presence of a lady of great social influence. The songs they had prepared had to be hurriedly Bowdlerized, their jokes fell flat, the audience was disappointed, and it is said that one by one they resigned in protest. At any rate the London Anacreontic Society passed out of existence about 1794, and the American song we know is a reminder that societies on this

[1] Georgiana Cavendish (1757–1806), daughter of the first Earl Spencer and wife of the fifth Duke of Devonshire.

model existed in the United States. The verses were written to commemorate the attack by a British battleship on Baltimore, 14 September 1814, and the heroic resistance of the Baltimore patriots. As for Georgiana, fifth Duchess of Devonshire, she was a leader of fashion very different from the kings' mistresses who had for so long bedevilled European politics; she was a woman of high intellectual and spiritual qualities, though an inveterate gambler, but gifted with great natural charm and carefully acquired manners. Her portraits by Reynolds and Gainsborough are well known; she did away with hoops in ladies' skirts and introduced a graceful line of dress. In political life she aided the Whigs to the extent of canvassing for Fox at the election of 1784, exchanging kisses for promises of votes;[1] she 'entered some of the most blackguard houses in Long Acre', and (see how Horace Walpole gives the lie to the idealized sailor of the songs) 'was very coarsely received by some worse than tars'.

Nevertheless she was representative of the age of elegance which was the eighteenth century, and lived to see the change coming into English society as scientific studies applied to agriculture and industry made the fortunes of men with new skills and understanding. This understanding gave men wealth but not necessarily a higher standard of taste. *Rule, Britannia, God Save the King,* and *Heart of Oak* have sincerity, all the more understandable when we know how they came into popularity, but the Napoleonic period seems insincere by comparison; Dibdin the Elder wrote songs to order while Pitt the Younger kept a tight hand on the press. Typical of the period is the following (not by the elder Dibdin):

> Daddy Neptune one day to Freedom did say,
>   'If ever I lived upon dry land,
> The spot I would hit on would be little Britain,'
>   Says Freedom 'Why, that's my own island.'
>   O, what a snug little island,
>   A right little, tight little island;
>   Seek all the globe round,
>   There's none to be found,
>   So happy as this little island.

The tune used was a variant of *The Rogues' March*; the chorus metre that of a limerick.

[1] Go into the Intrepid Fox public-house in Wardour Street, London, and see the plaque in the bar commemorating where she kissed the coalman.

Here we may see emerging a new style of song, not greatly different in form from what might have been used in *The Beggar's Opera*,[1] but lower in intellectual level. The choice of *The Rogues' March* tune for a patriotic song was indeed surprising, but not so surprising as Charles Dibdin the Younger's [2] verses to the same tune, in favour of paper money:

> Ne'er yet was a name so bandied by Fame,
>   Through air, through ocean and through land,
> As one that is upon every banknote,
>   You all must know Abraham Newland.
>   Oh, Abraham Newland!
>   Notified Abraham Newland!
>   I've heard people say,
>   'Sham Abraham' you may,
>   But you must not sham Abraham [3] Newland.[4]

One does not acquire fame by writing such songs, which fawn rather than elevate. If we would seek for heroism it is not here, but in the sufferings of a man who wrote boldly against the deflation of values which Pitt's financial policy brought about. His name was William Cobbett, and he was imprisoned at the time for stating in print his indignation at the treatment of some young men of Ely, in the local militia, who had refused to march without the guinea to which by Act of Parliament they were entitled. They were charged with mutiny, and a body of Hanoverian horse was sent from Bury St Edmunds to compel their sentence to be carried out.

With German mercenaries standing round, the British lads were flogged, and Cobbett, enraged at this indignity to his countrymen, protested in his *Political Register*. He was fined a thousand pounds, imprisoned for two years, and put on strict bail for a further seven years. His printer and bookseller were also imprisoned. So much for Freedom's own little island.

[1] Compare with Macheath's song in Act ii, v, for limerick metre.
> 'At the tree I shall suffer with pleasure,
> At the tree I shall suffer with pleasure;
>   Let me go where I will,
>   In all kinds of ill,
> I shall find no such furies as these are.'

[2] The most interesting of the elder Dibdin's sons. By Harriet Pitt, the dancer.
[3] To 'sham Abraham' was slang for feigning madness—a beggar's trick.
[4] Chappell, *Popular Music of the Olden Time* (1855).

Two famous songs made in rebellion against Pitt's oppressive policy of 1798 are *The Wearing of the Green* and *The Shan Van Voght*—both Irish.

Oh, Paddy dear! an' did ye hear the news that's goin' round?
The Shamrock is forbid by law to grow on Irish ground.
Saint Patrick's Day no more we'll kape, his colour can't be seen,
For there's a cruel law agin the wearin' of the green.
I met with Napper Tandy and he tuk me by the hand,
And he said 'How's poor old Ireland, and how does she stand?'
'She's the most distressful country that ever yet was seen,
For they're hanging men and women there—for wearin' o' the
    green.'

That is truly Irish. If we would seek songs of Irish poets and composers popular in England during the early nineteenth century, there are plenty to be found, but the popular Irish writers for the English market had a genteel style which the new middle class took to their hearts. Tom Moore enjoyed immense popularity in good social circles, for his songs are light, with a sweet nostalgia:

> Those evening bells, those evening bells,
> How many a tale their music tells,
> Of youth and home and that sweet time
> When last I heard their soothing chime!

> Those joyous hours are passed away,
> And many a heart with them was gay,
> Within the tomb now darkly dwells,
> And hears no more those evening bells.

> And so 'twill be when I am gone,
> That tuneful peal will still ring on,
> While other bards shall walk these dells,
> And sing your praise, sweet evening bells.

There was money in it. Moore got a hundred guineas each for the poems published as Irish Melodies, and his publishers made good profits. Who does not know *The Minstrel Boy, The Harp that Once through Tara's Halls*, and *Let Erin Remember?* The formula is always the same, a graceful curve of a tune to which are sung sweet-sad descriptions of scenes distant either in place or time. Others did better, Sir Walter Scott made money out of romantic history, and there were long queues in Albemarle Street for cantos of Byron's *Childe Harold* wet from the press. Did Lord Byron look down on the minor talent of Thomas Moore? Not a bit of it:

My boat is on the shore,
　And my bark is on the sea,
But before I go, Tom Moore,
　Here's a double health to thee;

Here's a sigh to those who love me,
　And a smile to those who hate,
And whatever sky's above me,
　Here's a heart for ev'ry fate.

Tho' the ocean roar around me,
　Yet it still shall bear me on;
Tho' a desert should surround me,
　It hath springs which may be won.

Wer't the last drop in the well,
　As I gasped upon the brink,
Ere my fainting spirit fell,
　'Tis to thee that I would drink.

In that water, as this wine,
　The libation I would pour,
Should be peace to thee and thine,
　And a health to thee, Tom Moore.

Moore was at his best with his native Irish melodies. There was a tune called *Castle Hyde* which in the last decade of the eighteenth century was used for R. A. Millikin's song *The Groves of Blarney* and which we know in a slightly altered form with Moore's verses as *The Last Rose of Summer*. Not only did Beethoven set this air, but Mendelssohn used it for a composition for the pianoforte and Flotow introduced the song into his opera *Martha*. *Martha* was a remarkably successful opera, with a libretto built on the escapade of two English girls of good family who entered into contracts at a hiring-fair by way of a lark and found the contracts binding. All this was socially superior music, fitted for the wealthy families who formed the respectable core of English society in the nineteenth century. In business they were growing ever more powerful; in political life they were largely utilitarian; religion was for them a considerable social bulwark for the upkeep of which they were prepared to pay. Families were large, and entertaining done on a corresponding scale, but sex was unmentionable. To be delicate was to be pretty, to faint was genteel; young ladies sang, played the harp or the piano, but not the violin; young gentlemen sang or played the flute. They cultivated the works of the Viennese classical composers; Beethoven wrote the tune for Moore's *Those Evening Bells*. In the houses of such people Tom Moore sang his own songs—the darling Minstrel Boy of the new age. The compliment we have quoted from Lord Byron was set to music by Sir Henry Bishop, composer of the tunes of *My Pretty Jane*,[1] *Home, Sweet Home*, and arranger of Mozart's operas for English audiences—a great man indeed in his time, Heather Professor of Music at Oxford and the first professional musician to be knighted by a British monarch.[2]

The song *Home, Sweet Home* may be said to symbolize the age in which it was composed. It comes in an opera entitled *Clari, the Maid of Milan*, to a libretto by the American actor John Howard Payne, who took the plot from a French source.[3] *Home, Sweet Home* recurs in this opera like a theme-song, though it is not the first time this device had been used in opera. Bishop's melody had previously been published as a Sicilian Air in an album of national melodies, but was in fact of Bishop's own composition.

What Dr Arne was to the eighteenth century Sir Henry Bishop was to the early nineteenth; both were employed by rival establishments because the public liked their tunes. If Bishop's integrity is less marked than Arne's, Bishop's excuse was that the taste of the public made this necessary:

It is not 'unskilfulness of English musicians' which induced me to retrench any part of that opera [Boieldieu's *Jean de Paris*] but the state of the public taste for music at the time it was produced, which, though it has, I hope, progressively improved, was not then sufficiently cultivated to render otherwise than extremely hazardous the production of an opera without retrenchment of such parts of it as were not likely to be properly appreciated, from their not being understood.

Bishop's methods, which meant the interpolation of his own pieces into the operas of Mozart, and the cutting of Mozart's work

---

[1] Written for Vauxhall Gardens.
[2] Conferred by Queen Victoria in 1842.
[3] J. R. Planché.

to make room for these, and for long ballets which were customary in the second part of the evening's entertainment at the opera house, have brought him into contempt among musical historians. The theatres were dependent on a public not really in sympathy with good theatre. The unit of society which controlled the public taste of the times was the family—that society in which Tom Moore found his *métier*. The best of them avoided the theatres as dens of vice, and Thomas Carlyle in his essay on *The Opera* (1850) saw the Haymarket Theatre as a centre of highly specialized art produced at great expense for a decadent aristocracy. He saw 'improper females' in the boxes visited by 'high-dizened, most expensive persons, Aristocracy so-called, or *Best* of the World'. He moralized. 'Beware, beware, what proofs you are giving here of betterness and bestness.'

Oh worthy Thomas! But the fashionable writers of genteel best sellers moralized too. Who, nowadays, reads *The Belle of the Season*, by Marguerite Gardiner, Countess of Blessington? In it is described the peer of young ladies in the year of grace 1840. Of course she had to be initiated to the opera:

> The night is come—and now to eyes
> Behold the scarlet curtain rise
> Which never novel's page had read,
> But history, voyages, instead,
> With lives of great and virtuous men,
> Such as Plutarch loved to pen;
> For poetry the maid had pleaded,
> And had enjoyed it—wisely weeded:
> Little she dreamed, how much less knew,
> What things Italian playwrights do!
> Judge then—to make her entrance easy,
> The piece was *Norma*, played by Grisi!
> A Priestess breaking vestal vows,
> A mother twice—not once a spouse;
> All frenetic with jealous rage,
> Which nought but vengeance can assuage,
> Grasping a keen and murderous dagger,
> To yon low couch behold her stagger,
> Where sleep her babes: but love prevails,
> The mother stays—the murderess fails!
> When this dark picture Mary saw,
> She trembled—scarcely dared to draw

Photo: Blackpool Tower Company

Tower Ballroom, Blackpool. Industrial Revolutionary Baroque with 'streamlined' alterations to stage. Note the electrical organ grille above the proscenium arch, and compare with plate facing page 93.

The Belle of the Season. One of Chalon's engravings for Lady Blessington's po
1840. The dancer is Taglioni. Note her position on the apron stage forward of
proscenium arch, and the two figures admiring Mary's blush.

Her breath—the while Bellini stole
With magic witching through her soul,
And tears relieved her; then there came
O'er her young brow the blush of shame.
Around she timid glanced her eye,
But none looked shocked, and none looked shy:
Faces, as youthful as her own,
Were placid all—nor there were shown
The feelings wakening in her breast,
By Norma's love and shame confessed!
The curtain falls—the horror's o'er,
And Mary calmer breathes once more!

Lady Blessington was a friend of Lord Byron, who, it will be recalled, found the waltz disgusting. What, then, will Lady Blessington's Mary think of the ballet?

Brisk music gayer scenes announces,
And in a half-dressed *danseuse* bounces,
With arms that wreathe, and eyes that swim,
And drapery that scarce shades each limb.
And lip that wears a studied smile,
Applauding coxcombs to beguile,
As *entre-chat* or *pirouette*
Doth 'Brava!' thundered loud, beget.
When Mary saw her vaunt in air,
Her snow-white tunic leaving bare
Her limbs—and heard that deafening shout
Grow louder as she twirled about,
With one leg pointing towards the sky
As if the gallery to defy;
Surprised, and shocked, she turned away,
Wondering how women e'er could stay,
And thinking men must sure be frantic
Who patronized such postures antic;
She felt abashed to meet the eye
Of every fop that loitered by:
And oh! how rudely did it vex
Her fresh, pure heart, to mark her sex
Thus outraged, while the noblest came
To gaze and revel in their shame.

F

> Her troubled look the mother saw,
> And rose, all pitying, to withdraw,
> Convinced such shows must pain dispense
> To one bred up in innocence.

Perhaps some of us have wondered how Charles Lamb could rail at his generation for neglecting the old comedy on moral grounds. 'The business of their dramatic characters will not stand the moral test. We screw everything up to that.' But the ballet was artificial and wildly applauded! Nevertheless, we can see from Lady Blessington and from Thomas Carlyle that moral judgments, proper in the family circle, were applied in theatrical criticism. Was there a reason? It is possible that Lady Blessington in her innocence has given a reason:

> But there was one who joyed to see
> The pure and shrinking modesty
> Of this fair girl—'twas Deloraigne!

Deloraigne was Mary's approved admirer.

> Ah! stands he at her side again?
> Yes, he now knows that there can be
> No maid more innocent than she;
> And doth with pitying looks survey
> The bolder damsels—pleased to stay
> And watch what makes the indignant blush
> Warm to his idol's forehead rush.

One may see him in Chalon's mezzotint of the belle of the season at the opera, with Mary herself, Mama, the apron stage, and the offending ballerina, and wonder how he would react in due course when Mary had gone a little further in her social education; would he respond (in more genteel terms, of course) like Thackeray's new-rich Cox, speaking of his wife, who similarly had been shocked at first by the ballet, but after three weeks, 'law bless you! she could look at the bally as she would at a dancing-dog in the streets, and would bring her double-barrelled opera-glass up to her eyes as coolly as if she had been a born duchess'.

Mrs Cox was the wife of a barber who had recently come into a fortune, and was therefore being introduced to high society rather later in life than Lady Blessington's debutante, but the moral implication was the same, reoriented for readers of *Punch*. We may well ask how respectable people got into such a state, for this was a debased form of puritanism mixed with rank materialism and dominated by sexual aberration euphemistically disguised as modesty. Within the family orbit the young were educated in a code of manners applicable to blood relations—brothers, sisters, cousins, aunts—but into which marriageable partners were only admitted with parental approval. Young people had claimed the right to choose their partners within the opportunities open to them, but parents could still be very severe when a match was made of which they disapproved. The system, designed as a protection of the young, had its dangers; respectable widows left with unmarried daughters had to strain their social resources to make the most of their daughters' chances:

> Lady Hook was a widow, the wisest and best
> That ever six fatherless daughters caressed;
> A model of prudence, unspotted in fame,
> Her word was a law, and a sanction her name;
> In less than six years from her husband's demise,
> She had married six girls, and each match was a prize.[1]

One of the prizes was a 'prodigious sot', but that was the luck of the game. As for the sons, they no doubt became wary of scheming mothers; mistresses were now almost unthinkable among the middle classes,[2] but there were prostitutes. From these the family box at the opera protected the dandies, but they could go behind the curtain between the end of the opera and the start of the ballet, and flirt with the 'figurantes'—as ladies of the *corps de ballet* were then called—whose wages certainly did not permit them to live without other means. We may recall the character of Mr Dolphin, the theatre manager, in Thackeray's *Pendennis*, 'employed, as he frequently was, in swearing and cursing the ladies of the *corps-de-ballet* for not doing their duty', and recollect how 'he was dragging on his season wretchedly with half salaries, small operas, feeble old comedies, and his ballet company; and everyone was looking out for the day when he should appear in the *Gazette*.' Mr Dolphin was founded on a real character. His theatres were verminous, gin-sodden, and swarming with prostitutes, and he was for a time manager of both the important ones—Drury Lane and Covent Garden. His name was Alfred Bunn.

'The Poet Bunn', they called him, for he had produced some

[1] Mrs Frances Trollope, *The Mother's Manual, or Illustrations of Matrimonial Economy* (1833).
[2] The nobility had their old disregard of conventions, but Victoria and Albert would not have been amused.

minor ballads. He was a manager who could cheesepare and pay lavishly at the same time. He paid Malibran the singer £125 a performance and made money out of it. They were all one to him—*prima donnas*, ballerinas, or performing animals. His name lives as the librettist of a remarkable opera called *The Bohemian Girl*, with music by Balfe—an Irishman who as a youth had fiddled in the orchestra at Drury Lane, had been taken abroad by a patron, and there established a reputation as a baritone singer and composer. *The Bohemian Girl* had everything the genteel heart desired, a kidnapped heiress, an exiled nobleman, tyrants, gipsies, recognition of lost ones by a medallion kept since babyhood, spoken dialogue, melodrama,[1] tuneful music, and the ideal lyric which embraced all that these implied:

> I dreamt that I dwelt in marble halls,
>   With vassals and serfs at my side;
> And of all who assembled within those walls,
>   That I was the hope and the pride.
> I had riches too great to count, could boast,
>   Of a high ancestral name;
> But I also dreamt, which pleased me most,
>   That you loved me still the same.

Nothing had fired the imagination of audiences like this since the days of Polly Peachum. Marble halls arose for popular entertainment, *Marble Halls* sounded from every street organ; 'Gypsy' entertainers appeared in the music-saloons and song-writers could hardly keep up with publishers' demands. Two years before *The Bohemian Girl* first appeared at Drury Lane George Borrow had had a book on the 'Zincali' published, but its sale had been slow; now (1843) it sold out, and Borrow's publisher asked for more. As for the opera itself, it was soon running in three Viennese theatres simultaneously under the title of *Die Zigeunerin*; it saved the fortunes of the Theatre Lyrique in Paris and earned for Balfe the decoration of the *Legion d'Honneur*; it took Italy by storm (sung throughout, though the English version had had spoken dialogue) under the title *La Zingara*, and this Italian version was later sung in London at the opera house in the Haymarket—for English on the stage was there taboo. Travelling opera companies played *The Bohemian Girl* in England until well into the nineteen-twenties.

Nevertheless, the theatres were under suspicion among many people during the nineteenth century, and not without reason.

---

[1] Melodrama—dialogue spoken during orchestral accompaniment.

The real heart of the nation was in the family circle. Gatherings of families were great events, and it was customary for guests to bring their music and to be asked to sing or play. In such gatherings one heard the songs of Balfe—*Killarney*, and his setting of Long-fellow's *The Arrow and the Song*. Sacred songs, too, had a vogue, for the breakers of Victorian unbelief were not yet sapping the foundations of religion. Estate agents would advertise the number of churches and chapels within easy reach of a house they had for sale, for social life depended very largely on the popularity of these, which had far more members than the theatres ever saw. The solidarity of the social scene depended naturally on the conventions being closely observed, and genteel songs bore this in mind; criticism of marriage laws or of woman's status in the home would mark one out for disfavour. Few women risked it; this was the province of the blue-stocking:

> Full many a sorrowful and tragic tale
> Enfolded lies beneath the semblance frail
> Of wedded harmony and calm content!
> How oft the heart in aching bosom pent,
> And careworn thoughts, are borne abroad unseen,
> Veiled in the aspect of a cheerful mien,
> By the sad mourner of a home unblest,
> A faith dishonoured, and a life opprest!

The writer was Harriet Grote, wife of the historian of ancient Greece. She wrote it in 1855, before the Divorce Courts were established. Then, a husband could drag his wife back to live with him if she went away, could deprive her of her children, and had control of her money. We have seen the gradual growth throughout the eighteenth century of the right to choose a mate; this battle at any rate had been won by the middle of the nineteenth century. Mothers who forced their daughters into marriage had to do it secretly. Once married, however, even the woman who had chosen her mate freely was no longer free; the bonds of matrimony were firmly welded, and women themselves generally unwilling to defy the laws or seek to have them amended. Their way was by woman's wiles, as Mrs Grote well knew:

> Thus, since the State directs that woman's fate
> Should hang upon the fiat of her mate,
> Slight hope that private feeling will assume
> A juster tone, or mitigate her doom.

> Bereft of rights, she learns to wear her chain;
> And seeks, by art, the *mastery* to gain.
> Unworthy study, which a juster code
> Might turn aside, or prompt to nobler good.
> The want of will in men—not want of power,
> Defers redemption to a distant hour.
> Far distant! for what eye hath seen the strong
> Relieve the weak because he did them wrong?

The value of the Victorian conscience was that at last a few—a very few—were saying these things. The abuses of which they complained had always existed in a man's world. Harriet Grote was a semi-invalid half her life as a result of the disapproval of her marriage by her husband's father. They had to live at first in a mean court in the City, though wealthy and highly intellectual, by a decision of the elder Grote; she lost her child by puerperal fever and suffered thereafter:

> Man marvels ever—pitying as he goes—
> Th' immense diversity of human woes;
> Yet, with short-sighted folly, fails to see
> How large a share of this vast misery
> Is due to man's own impious agency.
>
> So taught the eloquent recluse, Rousseau.
> In days not quite a century ago.

But what hope had the intellectuals against *The Mother's Manual*?

> Rousseau! good heaven! what put him in your head?
> You'd better study 'Mrs Glasse' instead.

Mrs Glasse was compiler of a popular book on cookery.

Such was the situation. The early Victorians were a haunted people; haunted by their own consciences as their grandparents had not been. John Wesley had not met the challenge of expanding materialism when he awakened the individual to the need for personal salvation, nor had he in his own life understood the misery of the unhappily married woman. One must not seek for enlightenment in Methodist hymns, for they were above it, nor would the genteel songs bring up the cause of disaffected womanhood as Mrs Grote did in her pedantic couplets; but there was one song, by

T. H. Bayly, very popular about 1850 which faced the issue; it was sung in the *salons*, in the music-saloons, and in the streets:

> We met—'twas in a crowd
> And I thought he would shun me;
> He came—I could not breathe,
> For his eye was upon me;
> He spoke—his words were cold,
> And his smile was unaltered:
> I knew how much he *felt*
> For his deep-toned voice faltered:
> I wore my bridal robe,
> And I rival'd its whiteness!
> Bright gems were in my hair,
> How I hated their brightness!
> He called me by my name—
> As the bride of another—
> Oh! *thou* hast been the cause of this anguish, my mother!
>
> And once again we met,
> And a fair girl was near him;
> He smiled and whispered low,
> As I once used to hear him;
> She leant upon his arm—
> *Once* 'twas mine, and mine only—
> I wept, for I deserved
> To feel wretched and lonely:
> And she will be his bride!
> At the altar he'll give her,
> The love that was so pure,
> For a heartless deceiver;
> The world may think me gay,
> For my feelings I smother—
> Oh! *thou* hast been the cause of this anguish, my mother!

.   .   .   .   .

This was Thackeray's world, where the elegant had become the genteel, and the opera, the oratorio, the glee, and the comic song were all part of the normal experience of a gentleman. The music-houses of the earlier centuries had persisted in their humbler way, and had become the Victorian song and supper rooms, with a chairman elevated at the head of the principal table, calling out the names of the songs and toasting the guests in brandy and water. Thackeray looked back on it from middle life, and as usual the old days seemed better than the present:

There was once a time when the sun used to shine brighter than it appears to do in this latter half of the nineteenth century; when the zest for life was certainly keener; when tavern wines seemed to be delicious, and tavern dinners the perfection of cookery . . . when the women of the world were a thousand times more beautiful than those of the present time; and the houris of the theatres especially so ravishing and angelic, that to see them was to set the heart in motion, and to see them again was to struggle for half an hour previously at the door of the pit . . . when the acme of pleasure seemed to be to meet Jones of Trinity at the Bedford, and to make an arrangement with him, and with King of Corpus (who was staying at the Colonnade), and Martin of Trinity Hall (who was with his family in Bloomsbury Square), to dine at the Piazza, go to the play and see Braham in *Fra Diavolo*, and end the frolic by partaking of supper and a song at the Cave of Harmony. . . .

Going to the play then, and to the pit, as was the fashion in those merry days, with some young fellows of my own age, having listened delighted to the most cheerful and brilliant of operas, and laughed enthusiastically at the farce, we became naturally hungry at twelve o'clock at night, and a desire for welsh-rabbits and good old glee-singing led us to the Cave of Harmony, then kept by the celebrated Hoskins, among whose friends we were proud to count.

We enjoyed such intimacy with Mr Hoskins that he never failed to greet us with a kind nod; and John the waiter made room for us near the President of the convivial meeting. We knew the three admirable glee-singers, and many a time they partook of brandy-and-water at our expense. One of us gave his call dinner at Hoskins's, and a merry time we had of it. Where are you, O Hoskins, bird of the night? Do you warble your songs by Acheron, or troll your choruses by the banks of black Avernus?

The goes of stout, the Chough and Crow,[1] the welsh-rabbit, the Red-Cross Knight,[2] the hot brandy-and-water (the brown the strong!), the Bloom is on the Rye [3] (the bloom isn't on the Rye any more!)—the song and the cup, in a word, passed round merrily, and I dare say the songs and bumpers were encored. It happened that there was a very small attendance at the Cave that night, and we were all more sociable and friendly because the company was select. The songs were chiefly of the sentimental class; such ditties were much in vogue at the time of which I speak.

There came into the Cave a gentleman with a lean brown face and long black mustachios, dressed in very loose clothes, and evidently a stranger to the place. At least he had not visited it for a long time. He was pointing out changes to a lad who was in his company; and calling

---

[1] Glee, by Bishop.   [2] Glee, by Callcott.   [3] *My Pretty Jane.*

for sherry-and-water, he listened to the music, and twirled his mustachios with great enthusiasm. . . .

'*Maxima debetur pueris*', says Jones (a fellow of very kind feeling, who has gone into the Church since), and writing on his card to Hoskins, hinted to him that a boy was in the room, and a gentleman who was quite a greenhorn: hence that the songs had better be carefully selected.

And so they were. A lady's school might have come in, and but for the smell of the cigars and brandy-and-water, have taken no harm by what happened. Why should it not always be so? If there are any Caves of Harmony now, I warrant Messieurs the landlords their interests would be better consulted by keeping their singers within bounds. The very greatest scamps like pretty songs, and are melted by them; so are honest people. It was worth a guinea to see the simple Colonel, and his delight at the music. He forgot about the distinguished wits he had expected to see in his ravishment over the glees.

'I say, Clive, this is delightful. This is better than your aunt's concert with all the Squallinis, hey? I shall come here often. Landlord, may I venture to ask those gentlemen if they will take any refreshment? What are their names? (to one of his neighbours). I was scarcely allowed to hear any singing before I went out, except an oratorio, where I fell asleep; but this, by George, is as fine as Incledon.' . . .

And now Mr Hoskins asking if any gentleman would volunteer a song; what was our amazement when the simple Colonel offered to sing himself, at which the room applauded vociferously. . . . The Colonel selected the ditty of 'Wapping Old Stairs' (a ballad so sweet and touching that surely any English poet might be proud to be the father of it), and he sang this quaint and charming old song in an exceedingly pleasant voice, with flourishes and roulades in the old Incledon manner, which has pretty nearly passed away:

> Your Molly has never been false, she declares,
> Since last time we parted at Wapping old stairs,
> When I swore that I still would continue the same,
> And gave you the 'bacca-box mark'd with my name.
> When I pass'd a whole fortnight between decks with you,
> Did I e'er give a kiss, Tom, to one of your crew?
> To be useful and kind, with my Thomas I stayed,
> For his trousers I washed, and his grog, too, I made.
>
> Tho' you promised last Sunday to walk in the Mall,
> With Susan from Deptford, and likewise with Sal,
> In silence I stood, your unkindness to hear,
> And only upbraided my Tom with a tear,
> Why should Sal, or should Susan than me be more priz'd?
> For the heart that is true, Tom, should ne'er be despised.
> Then be constant and kind, nor your Molly forsake,
> Still your trousers I'll wash, and your grog, too, I'll make.

* F

The singer gave his heart and soul to the simple ballad and delivered Molly's gentle appeal so pathetically that even the professional gentlemen hummed and buzzed a sincere applause, and some wags, who were inclined to jeer at the beginning of the performance, clinked their glasses and rapped their sticks with quite a respectful enthusiasm. . . .

Great Hoskins, placed on high, amidst the tuneful choir, was pleased to signify his approbation, and gave his guest's health in his usual dignified manner. 'I am much obliged to you, sir', says Mr Hoskins; 'the room ought to be much obliged to you. I drink your 'ealth and song, sir;' and he bowed to the Colonel politely over his glass of brandy-and-water, of which he absorbed a little in his customer's honour. 'I have not heard that song', he was kind enough to say, 'better performed since Mr Incledon sung it. He was a great singer, sir, and I may say, in the words of our immortal Shakespeare, that, take him for all in all, we shall not look upon his like again.'

X. TRENDS OF SYMPATHY

THACKERAY'S COLONEL was old-fashioned—a relic of the days of elegance when Charles Incledon sang *The Lass of Richmond Hill* in Vauxhall Gardens (which he did first in 1787). If we would know the extent of the decline of Vauxhall we must read what Dickens wrote in 1836:

A small party of men in cocked hats were 'executing' the overture to *Tancredi*, and a numerous assemblage of ladies and gentlemen, with their families, had rushed from their half-emptied stout-mugs in the supper boxes, and crowded to the spot. Intense was the low murmur of admiration when a particularly small gentleman, in a dress coat, led on a particularly tall lady in a blue sarcenet pelisse and bonnet of the same, ornamented with large white feathers, and forthwith commenced a plaintive duet.[1]

The decline no doubt was due to economic changes—a shifting of the patronage towards a larger percentage of the working classes —but even so the programmes aped the better-class entertainments of the time. A change was appearing in the treatment of popular sentiments.

Incledon had served before the mast in his youth and there was a sincerity about his singing of sea songs which carried conviction. He was well served by his contemporary William Shield the composer, who set lyrics like this:

> Come all ye jolly sailors bold,
> Whose hearts are cast in honour's mould,
> While English glory I unfold,
>   Hurrah, for the *Arethusa*!
> She is a frigate tight and brave,
> As ever stemm'd the dashing wave,
> Her men are staunch to their fav'rite launch,
> And when the foe shall meet our fire,
> Sooner than strike we'll all expire,
>   On board the *Arethusa*.

[1] *Sketches by Boz.*

The men aboard Shield's *Arethusa* are represented tough as usual; they meet the French off their own coast, are seriously outnumbered, but nevertheless drive the foe ashore. Our second example from Shield is *The Storm*, describing the sailors' ever-present enemy, the sea itself; it is the song in which Incledon surpassed all other singers, and one can easily guess the reason:

> Cease, rude Boreas! blust'ring railer,
>   List ye landsmen all to me,
> Messmates, hear a brother sailor,
>   Sing the dangers of the sea;
> From bounding billows first in motion,
>   When the distant whirlwinds rise,
> To the tempest-troubled ocean,
>   Where the seas contend with skies.
>
> Now the dreadful thunder roaring,
>   Peal on peal contending clash,
> On our heads fierce rain falls pouring,
>   In our eyes blue lightnings flash;
> One wide water all around us,
>   All above us one black sky;
> Diff'rent deaths at once surround us,
>   Hark! what means that dreadful cry?
>
> O'er the ship wild waves are beating,
>   We for wives or children mourn;
> Alas! from hence there's no retreating,
>   Alas! to them there's no return;
> Still the leak is gaining on us,
>   Both chain-pumps are chok'd below;
> Heav'n have mercy here upon us,
>   For only that can save us now.

Incledon died in 1826, having retired from the London stage in 1822. He lived to see the new era of British mastery of the seas, but not to sing it. With the overthrow of Napoleon the world found a genuine respect for British seamanship, and the navy began an effective protection of the trade routes. Ships no longer needed to carry guns and crews to man them, and a utilitarian age kept a sharp eye on costs and competition from other shipowners. Ships were liable to go to sea undermanned. (Samuel Plimsoll's book, *Our Seamen*, gives the facts.) [1] The sea was an enemy against whom there was no protection but the Almighty. Incledon had sung this in Shield's *The Storm* without bathos; it was a tricky theme, however, for one has to be careful how one plays with the Absolute to please a fickle public. Nevertheless the theatres tackled the problem, and were able in many cases to satisfy their public and yet retain a true conception of humility before God. Andrew Cherry, an Irish actor, wrote the verses of the song *The Bay of Biscay* for an opera called *Spanish Dollars* produced at Covent Garden in 1805, the last verse of which should be recalled when we think of the approaching tendency to sentimentalize about Providence. Cherry treated the situation properly, in the true tradition of the sea:

> Her yielding timbers sever,
>> Her pitchy seams are rent,
> When Heav'n all bounteous ever,
>> Its boundless mercy sent.
> A sail in sight appears,
> We hail her with three cheers,
> Now we sail, with the gale,
>> From the Bay of Biscay, O!

John Davy, a composer hailing from Exeter (and, like Incledon, a pupil of William Jackson), wrote the music to *The Bay of Biscay*. He claimed that the tune was not his own but that he got it from some Negro sailors he heard singing in the London streets.

Similarly we may turn again to Dibdin's *Poor Jack*, whose language does not suggest him to be much of a church-goer, and whose ideas about Providence had to fit the eighteenth-century convention of the ideal sailor:

> But he said how a sparrow can't founder, d'ye see,
>> Without orders that come down below . . .

Mark the use of the biblical reference to the fall of the sparrow,[2] preached to the sailor by the chaplain and retailed by the sailor to

---

[1] The book was published in 1873 and in the same year a temporary Act of Parliament imposed special regulations pending a full inquiry. The results were embodied in the Merchant Shipping Act of 1876, including the Plimsoll 'load line'.

[2] Matt. x. 29.

his Poll as he prepares to sail away. Now see the same biblical reference treated by a later lyricist:

> Rock'd in the cradle of the deep,
> I lay me down in peace to sleep ;
> Secure I rest upon the wave,
> For thou, O Lord, hast pow'r to save;
> I know thou wilt not slight my call,
> For thou dost note the sparrow's fall,
>   And calm and peaceful is my sleep,
>   Rocked in the cradle of the deep.

> And such the trust that still were mine,
> Though stormy winds swept o'er the brine;
> Or though the tempest's fiery breath
> Roused me from sleep to wreck and death!
> In ocean cave still safe with Thee,
> The germ of immortality;
>   And calm and peaceful is my sleep,
>   Rock'd in the cradle of the deep.

Mrs Willard, who wrote the lyric, lacked the imagination of Dibdin, Shield, or Davy, but her song was quite as popular as theirs. Public taste was moving towards a sentimental conception of religion. God was somehow getting popular, and resignation a virtue. The tune of the song just quoted had also a sentimental strain of chromaticism essential to its character, and typical of its period.

As a further example we may take the sentiments concerning the poor, as they were expressed in songs. When C. E. Horn (1786–1849) set Herrick's lines to music he kept the grace of the original:

> Cherry ripe, cherry ripe—ripe, I cry;
> Full and fair ones, come and buy.

G. W. Persley, however, looked at the street-seller entirely through nineteenth-century spectacles when he set these words to music:

> Underneath the gaslight's glitter,
>   Stands a little fragile girl,
> Heedless of the night winds bitter,
>   As they round about her whirl;

While the hundreds pass unheeding,
  In the evening's waning hours,
Still she cries with tearful pleading,
  'Won't you buy my pretty flowers?'

Chorus:

There are many, sad and weary,
  In this pleasant world of ours,
Crying in the night so dreary,
  'Won't you buy my pretty flowers?'

With this song we are reminded of scenes in the novels of Dickens, and of the practical work of the social reformers, political or clerical, kindly or stern, and of the research into the thoughts of the poor themselves noted down in reports of Government Commissioners and in Henry Mayhew's *London Labour and the London Poor*.[1]

Not a loving word to cheer her,
  From the passers-by is heard;
Not a friend to linger near her,
  With her heart with pity stirred;
Homeward goes the tide of fashion
  Seeking pleasure's pleasant bowers,
None to hear with sad compassion,
  'Won't you buy my pretty flowers?'

The concern for the welfare of the poor was so well marked in the middle nineteenth century as to provide a sure sale for songs or literature in which the virtue of charity was eulogized; sympathy with the poor was all the more popular because the laws promulgated by the Benthamites were efficient but inhuman. The way towards improvement was by individual striving for betterment, and this meant the renunciation of vices, cutting of expenses within one's means—however poor—and individual salvation of the soul through prayer and good deeds. Methodism is at once called to mind, and undoubtedly had much to do with the direction of individual consciences of people in all walks of life, but the doctrines preached by the founders of Methodism in the eighteenth century underwent modification and new ideas were introduced. By 1807 the original field preaching such as the Wesleys had used (and which may still be observed in the annual meetings at Gwennap in Cornwall) was being undermined by American methods. The

[1] Cf. Chapter XI, *Buskers*.

revival meetings were called 'camp-meetings', and took place first in the woods and plains in the U.S.A., where hot gospel preachers whipped up religious enthusiasm by hell-fire oratory and infectious hymn singing.

The hymns they used were easy to learn and pleasant to sing. They used rocking, swinging rhythms, and answering phrases—either the leader giving out a phrase to be answered by the mass, or the men and women singing alternate phrases in question-and-answer dialogue. The principles were common in folk-song and in congregational singing in various denominations, but the camp-meetings intensified the means; as a result of this they were able to induce mass hysteria such as Christian teachers had tended to avoid, but which was common enough in primitive or pagan rituals. It has been claimed that the camp-meetings got the technique of this mass hysteria from the negroes, and that it was African in origin. What is more likely is that the slaves heard the white settlers at their worship and recognized the effects as similar to those they knew in their debased and forbidden voodoo rite.[1] Orthodox Christian ritual had made little progress among American Negro slaves during the eighteenth century.

The Constitution of the United States of America makes no provision for an established religion, but this is no oversight; many had fled to the New World in order to worship God in their own way, and the principle of freedom of faith was essential from the first to the American way of life. For that reason unorthodox sects were constantly springing up in America, and as men went further west the inhabitants appeared more rough and ready. Some were hardworking, God-fearing homesteaders while others were bad men, in the west because the eastern states had no use for them except in jail. They came to mock and remained to pray, for the preachers left them in no doubt as to the fate of sinners. Sinners they were, and knew it, and converts they became in their thousands. It is said that in their ecstasy many rolled on the ground or rushed to hide themselves in the woods. It is said also that the sinners there turned to sexual excesses in their ecstasy, as did devotees of more primitive religions in climaxes of religious emotion. The latter statement must, however, be taken with caution (like the Royalist jibe at the Puritan quoted on page 85), for Christianity has always been opposed to sex unless regularized by the marriage ceremony.

[1] Voodoo is a corrupt development in the New World of a phase of African ophiolatry.

Anyway, a preacher named Lorenzo Dow published a book in 1806 entitled *Hymns and Spiritual Songs* with tunes from popular songs (an old practice, as we have noted in Chapter III, condemned by many religious authorities) and introduced to Methodists the American practice of camp-meetings. The first of these was held at Mow Cop, on the Staffordshire-Cheshire border, in 1807; in consequence a schism occurred in Methodist circles, the new sect calling themselves Primitive Methodists.

If we read the pages of John Wesley's *Journal* we shall find some almost incredible descriptions of religious ectsasy, and it may well seem that the Primitive Methodists were right in assuming that title, but on the other hand the original Methodists had learned by 1810 where the real value of conversion lay. The Wesleys had used current events like the March of the 'Forty-five and the earthquakes of 1750 to point the moral of the wrath of God, but the hymns written on these occasions had little merit and no permanence. It is true to say that the leaders in the working-class movements for reform in the nineteenth century were often men trained in Methodist teaching and preaching, but the best of them were the older Wesleyans—not the Primitives. The latter appealed to the less intelligent; their converts were such as would not normally have gone near a place of worship. The tunes they used were rousing and their preaching a rant. 'Ranters' they were rightly called. The Chartists also held camp-meetings at which political hymns were sung. God marched with schemes for reform or showed his loving kindness to the prosperous—it depended on one's point of view or station in life.

Mass singing, then, was known to be influential in directing men's thoughts towards new ideas. The tune gave the pleasure and the words taught the idea. At a time when the working classes were so oppressed that anything might happen to the State, many saw in the workers' love of music a means of reforming their character:

Wherever the working classes are taught to prefer the pleasures of the intellect, and even of taste, to the gratification of sense, a great and favourable change takes place in their character and manners. They are no longer driven, by mere vacuity of mind, to the beer-shop; and a pastime, which opens their minds to the impressions produced by the strains of Handel and Haydn, combined with the inspired poetry of the Scriptures, becomes something infinitely better than the amusements of an idle hour. Sentiments are awakened in them which make them love their families and their homes; their wages are not squandered in intemperance, and they become happier as well as better.

The writer of that paragraph was George Hogarth,[1] music critic and father-in-law of Charles Dickens. Now we may see how the culture of the time was bound up with political and religious thought. The matter has been dealt with more fully elsewhere,[2] and need not be repeated here except for Hogarth's opinion of the force of music: he knew it could influence men in different ways, and just as Plato had done in Ancient Greece, he pleaded for discrimination in the choice of music to be taught. Hogarth says:

Bacchanalian songs and glees may heighten the riot of a dissolute party; but that man must be profligate beyond conception, whose mind can entertain gross propensities while the words of inspiration, clothed with the sounds of Handel, are in his ears.[3]

So the fight was on. Hogarth was right. Out of the conflict came the great choral societies and the British musical renaissance of the late nineteenth and early twentieth centuries, but there also came about the reaction of the modern music-hall and the community sing-song. In the process human nature as usual had to tack with the wind; smutty catches went out of use when women were introduced to singing-classes and choirs, and the reformers took advantage of the situation to compose rounds in praise of temperance, but the period which saw the blackballing of the old catches from the clubs saw also the secret growth of the smutty limerick. *Naturam expellas furca, tamen usque recurret.* In the drawing-rooms could be heard the ballad *Sweet Genevieve*, and from the public houses, too, for its chromatic wail suits the tipsy mind, and in due course the answer came back from the Salvation Army at the street corner— the same tune sung to the words 'Eternity, eternity'.

'There', said their leader, 'but for the grace of God, goes William Booth', and 'Why should the devil have all the good tunes?' The sentiments were not new, but they worked. The 'Army's' brass instruments came from the new manufacturers who supplied instruments to working-class brass bands which were financed in many cases partly by employers, in imitation of the practice of Robert Owen, the pioneer socialist whose only influence on present-day affairs is in the Co-operative trading movement. The tambourines of the Salvation Army came from the nigger minstrels.

Again we see American influence at work on English taste.

---

[1] *Musical History, Biography and Criticism* (1835).
[2] R. Nettel, *The Englishman Makes Music* (1952).
[3] Hogarth, ibid.

When John Davy claimed that he took his tune for *The Bay of Biscay* from something he heard Negro sailors singing in the London streets, he may have been vaguely right, but in fact the tune is as personal to Davy as any of his other tunes. If there was any Negro element in the song Davy said he heard, he cut it out of his tune for *The Bay of Biscay*. Why, then, did he claim Negro origin for his tune? It is likely that he thought it would stimulate human interest in his song. The date was 1805, when interest in the suppression of the slave trade was at its height in Britain. Wilberforce waged his anti-slavery campaign with as much eloquence as he could command, but Pitt kept reforms out of Parliament in order more effectively to overcome the French. In 1806 Pitt died, and was succeeded by a new Government, mainly Whig, called 'The Ministry of all the Talents', which brought in a law to abolish the slave trade;[1] then Fox died and the Government fell. It did nothing for the British labourers, but now the tide of public opinion moved more in favour of Negroes, for we had superior virtue on our side against the slave-owning Americans, who talked of liberty in a French way while owning slaves, just as Wilberforce talked of liberty for the Negroes while supporting any measure to prevent our own people from acquiring collective bargaining power. The nineteenth century was like that. The main propaganda for Negro liberty had to be issued in the U.S.A. and is to be found in Whittier's poems and Harriet Beecher Stowe's *Uncle Tom's Cabin*.

Meanwhile one Thomas Rice of Pittsburg made popular in entertainment his song *Jim Crow*. He blacked his face, and as he sang 'Every time I turn around I jump Jim Crow' he jumped a half-turn. From 1830 onwards this song and 'dance' caught on remarkably, in Britain as well as in America. This stage conception of a nigger was a cheerful, harmless, eccentric figure, quite as artificial as the shepherds and nymphs of the pastoral tradition had been, but Jim Crow packed the halls, and the shops were filled with 'Jim Crow' novelties. The song and 'dance' still remain with us as a children's game. Then in 1843 America produced the Virginian Minstrels, a white company who blacked their faces, and whose best-known entertainer was Daniel Decatur Emmett, the composer of *Dixie*.

There are conflicting explanations of the origin of *Dixie*, which Emmett first sang in 1859. We know it as an affectionate term for the Southern States of the U.S.A., and perhaps as derived from

---

[1] 47 Geo. III, Sect 1, c. 36 (1806–7). This abolished the slave trade but not slavery. The date of Royal Assent of the Bill was Lady Day, 1807.

the Mason and Dixon line, which separated the territory where, before the American Civil War, the Negroes were enslaved, from that where they were free. 'Dixieland' embraces a sentimental notion of an ideal land where Negroes all are happy and beloved of their white massas. A contrary view [1] is that the song commemorates a certain Dixie who was a considerable slave-owner on Manhattan Island, but who, fearing that the abolition of slavery in the U.S.A. would rob him of his property, drafted all his slaves to the Southern States before Abraham Lincoln's campaign had reached a crisis. The Negroes in Emmett's song were therefore longing for a Dixieland which was in fact Manhattan, where they had been better treated than they were in the South.[2] The song *Dixie* was, however, popular among the Confederate troops at the outbreak of hostilities, and became symbolical of the territory and way of life for which they were fighting. Thus an artificial stage sentiment became a patriotic call, not for the first time in history.

> Den I wish I was in Dixie
> Hooray! Hooray!
> In Dixie Land I'll take my stand
> To live and die in Dixie.

The soldiers (or their supporters) changed 'die in Dixie' to 'die for Dixie'.

If Emmett was surprised he need only have considered the fate of *Yankee Doodle*, which was stolen from the Americans by the British troops in the War of Independence, or vice versa—for we cannot be sure who stole it from whom—or the idealized British Jack Tar of the theatres in the eighteenth century, who disguised a type of man treated worse than a Negro slave yet who served Nelson in a way to which the British Navy has ever since looked back with pride. Dixieland may originally have been a sham, but if it has done anything to preserve an ideal of Southern courtesy and resistance to Yankee go-getting then Dixie is as much an historical force as the idealized Jack Tar.

---

[1] See Percy A. Scholes, *The Oxford Companion to Music*, article 'Dixie'.

[2] To a mere Englishman this theory looks suspiciously like propaganda. There is, however, another theory even more diverting. Emmett was himself in New York in 1859 wishing he was in a better climate down South, and the name 'Dix' appeared on bills issued by a New Orleans bank. Thus 'the land of Dix' was the land where this Southern currency passed, and thus became 'Dixieland'. Not all these theories can be right, but rectitude is perhaps of less importance in American song than freedom of opinion!

Greatest of all the singers of the Negro way of life was Stephen Collins Foster, who lived in Pittsburg, just north of the Mason-Dixon line, but who was descended from a Southern family. His fame, like Emmett's, owed much to a black-faced minstrel troupe which sang his songs and which has given its name to this type of entertainment. They were called the Christy Minstrels after their proprietor, under whose name the first edition of *The Old Folks at Home* actually appeared. The theme is purely fictional; there never was a Swannee Ribber except in the hearts of sentimental Americans, but the nostalgic tradition is true enough of the Negroes; it is in their spirituals:

> Deep river, my home is over Jordan,
> Deep river, I'm gonna cross over into camp ground.

Always the Negroes' peace is to be found afar off, and Foster played on the nostalgic yearning of his white audiences. He did reasonably well out of it; his publishers did very well.

> All the world is sad and weary,
>   Everywhere I roam,
> Oh, darkies, how my heart grows weary,
>   Far from de old folks at home.

We might conveniently compare this with an English song just as popular, the history of which we already know:

> Mid pleasures and palaces though we may roam,
> Be it ever so humble, there's no place like home.

We have observed that the popular English songs of that period sought consolation in distant lands or in the past. So it was with those of Stephen Foster:

'Gone are the days when my heart was young and gay', sang Old Black Joe, and *Massa's in de cold, cold ground*; we may never see his like again. Thus it happened to Uncle Tom in Harriet Beecher Stowe's novel; but for all its sentimentality it helped to free the Negroes. Living in Pittsburg, Stephen Foster sighed for *My Old Kentucky Home far away*, and Pittsburg has erected to his memory a fine memorial building, with wonderful facilities for research into Fosteriana, and woe betide the man who dares to hint that Stephen Foster composed best when he was half-seas-over. This is not to be in the Foster tradition.

Foster left about 175 songs, all very simple, with skeleton accompaniments but lovely flowing melodies. Not all are about the Negroes: *I Dream of Jeanie with the Light Brown Hair* is among his best. They were sung by the Christy Minstrels in America and their counterparts in St James's Hall, London, the Moore and Burgess Minstrels. There was at that time a musical clergyman whose books on *Music and Morals* and *My Musical Life* were much read in Victorian England, and who produced in 1861 what is perhaps the best compliment to the Christy Minstrels. To the Rev. H. R. Haweis they were symbolical of the true Negroes:

The Negro mind, at work upon civilized music, produces the same kind of thing as the Negro mind at work upon Christian theology. The product is not to be despised. . . . If we would divest ourselves of prejudice, the songs that float down the Ohio river are one in feeling and character with the songs of the Hebrew captives by the waters of Babylon. We find the same tale of bereavement and sorrow, the same simple faith and child-like adoration, and same wild tenderness and passionate sweetness, like music in the night.

Psalm cxxxvii, *By the rivers of Babylon*, hardly fits Haweis's description, nor is it like the songs of the nigger minstrels. These certainly displayed a simple faith and childlike adoration very different from the Hebrews' fierce cry: 'Happy shall he be that taketh and dasheth thy little ones against the stones'. The error was in taking the merely pleasant as true:

The entertainment is popular, and yet bears some impress of its peculiar and romantic origin. The scent of roses may be said to hang about it still. We cherish no malignant feeling towards those amiable gentlemen at St James's Hall, whose ingenious fancy has painted them so much blacker than they really are.'

Yet the explanation was simple enough. Bondage could be a figurative word—the bondage of sin—and God's banished ones could be called home in due course. There is a hymn by Charles Wesley entitled *On Going to Wakefield to answer a Charge of Treason*, the treason being that Charles had, it was alleged, prayed for the Pretender. This was in 1744, when Britain was afraid of an invasion by Charles Edward Stuart supported by French troops. The presiding magistrate at Wesley's trial was a clergyman. A witness said he heard Wesley 'pray the Lord would call home His banished.[1]

[1] Wesley had in mind 2 Sam. xiv. 14: 'Neither doth God respect any person, yet doth He devise means, that His banished be not expelled from Him.' Cf. Dr Henry Bett, *The Hymns of Methodism* (1945), p. 68.

Wesley's defence was that this was spoken on 12 February 1744, before the earliest news of the proposed invasion.

I had no thoughts of praying for the Pretender, but for those that confess themselves strangers and pilgrims upon earth, who seek a country, knowing this is not their place. The Scriptures, you, sir, know, speak of us as captive exiles, who are absent from the Lord while in the body. We are not at home till we are in heaven.

This explanation the magistrates accepted, and cleared Wesley of the charge brought against him.

Nevertheless the Hebrews had known captivity, and to them the danger of bondage was very real. To the American Negroes in their days of slavery the word 'bondage' had a definite meaning, and they believed not only that death would relieve them from this bondage, but that the Scriptures condemned bondage. (This belief was not altogether true, for St Paul in the Epistle to Philemon accepted the material fact of slave-owning; but one can understand easily enough that the American Negro wished to be free.) Heaven offered the Negro a home, and the hymns he heard white men sing told him that freedom was every man's right, so there were Negroes who believed that the white man was a sinner for owning slaves when his religion denounced this practice. Black and white race-hatred in America depends largely on this hypothesis. True Negro folk-songs have the germs of this disease, but the songs of the Christy Minstrels are in another class. Nothing could be more innocuous.

St James's Hall, where the Moore and Burgess Minstrels played for so many years, was opened in 1858, but according to the evidence of Henry Mayhew's informants [1] this type of entertainment had previously been given at St James's Theatre:

The first came out at St James's Theatre, and they made a deal of money. There was five of them—Pell was bones, Harrington was concertina, I think, White was violin, Stanwood the banjo, and Germaine the tambourine. I think that's how it was, but I can easy ascertain. After them sprang up the 'Lantum Serenaders' and the 'Ohio Serenaders', the 'South Carolina Serenaders', the 'Kentucky Minstrels', and many other schools of them; but Pell's gang was at the top of the tree.

Mayhew got his information from nigger minstrels performing in the streets. Their costumes and style were copied from Pell's 'Ethiopian Serenaders' and are illustrated in Mayhew's book. The

[1] Henry Mayhew, *London Labour and the London Poor* (1851–62), Vol. III, p. 191.

songs they sang were also taken from Pell's performance; imitated, no doubt, for few of the street musicians could read music:

When we started, the songs we knew was *Old Mr Coon, Buffalo Gals, Going ober de Mountain, Dandy Jim of Carolina, Rowly Boly O,* and *Old Johnny Booker.* We stuck to them a twelvemonth. The *Buffalo Gals* [1] was best liked. The 'bones'—we've real bones, rib-of-beef bones, but some have ebony bones, which sound better than rib-bones—they tell best in *Going ober de Mountain,* for there's a symphony between every line. It's rather difficult to play the bones well, it requires hard practice, and it brings the skin off. . . . The banjo is the hardest to learn of the lot. We have kept changing our songs all along; but some of the old ones are still sung. The other favourites are, or were, *Lucy Neale*; *O, Susannah*; *Uncle Ned*; *Stop dat Knocking*; *Ginger Blue*; and *Black-eyed Susannah.*

These men, and the street glee-singers, were the best of the entertainers on the London streets, yet their standards of conduct left much to be desired. They were not above exploiting their nuisance value. It was necessary when people were ill to deaden the noise in the streets, so straw would be laid on the cobblestones outside the house, and the door-knocker would be covered with soft woollen material; these indications of anxiety were sure invitations to street musicians to make as much noise as they could until they were bribed to go away. The 'Ethiopian Serenaders' were no exception. Yet, as men went, they might have been worse:

There are all sorts of characters in the different schools, but I don't know of any runaway gentleman, or any gentleman of any kind among us, not one; we're more of a poorer sort, if not to say a ragged sort, for some are without shoes or stockings. The 'niggers' that I know have been errand-boys, street-singers, turf-cutters, coalheavers, chandlers, paviours, mud-larks, tailors, shoemakers, tinmen, bricklayers' labourers, and people who have had no line in particular but their wits. I know of no connection with pickpockets, and I don't believe there is any, though pickpockets go round the mobs; but the police fling it in our teeth that we're connected with pickpockets. It's a great injury to us is such a notion. A good many of the niggers—both of us here likes a little drop—drink as hard as they can, and a good many of them live with women of the town. A few are married. Some niggers are Irish. There's Scotch niggers too. I don't know a Welsh one, but one of the street nigger-singers *is* a real black— an African. [2]

Mayhew gives examples of the humorous dialogue used by the minstrels, but it is poor stuff. Better opportunities occurred when

---

[1] By Dan Emmett.   [2] Mayhew, ibid.

they were able to play indoors, for there they could present
tableaux. The penny-gaff theatres sometimes served their turn, and
there were music-rooms in public-houses where performers could
go without payment from the management, but where they could
pass round the hat afterwards; in such places the audience did not
pay for admission and were of the roughest kind; in other halls
the entertainers were engaged, and, since Mayhew's informants
were of superior class, as street-singers went, they got such engagements:

Sometimes, when we are engaged for it, we go to concert-rooms and
do the nigger-statues, which is the same as the tableaux vivants. We
illustrate the adventures of Pompey, or the life of a Negro slave. The first
position is when he is in the sugar-brake, cutting the sugar-cane. Then he
is supposed to take it to be weighed, and not being weight, he is ordered
to be flogged. My mate is then doing the orator and explaining the story.
It's as nice a bit of business as ever was done, and goes out-and-out. You
see, it's a new thing from the white ones. The next position is when he is
being flogged, and then when he swears revenge upon the overseer, and
afterwards when he murders the overseer. Then there's the flight of Pompey, and so on, and I conclude with a variety of sculptures from the statues
such as Achilles in Hyde-Park, and so on. This is really good, and the
finest bit of business out, and nobody does it but me; indeed it says in
the bill—if you saw it—'for which he stands unrivalled'.

XI. BUSKERS[1]

~~~~~~

(a) Of Ancient and Modern Street Ballad Minstrelsy

UNDER THE HEAD of the 'Norman Minstrels' Mr Strutt says: 'It is very certain that the poet, the songster, and the musician were frequently united in the same person.' [2]

From this historical sketch it appears evident that the ballad-singer and seller of today is the sole descendant, or remains, of the minstrel of old, as regards the business of the streets; he is, indeed, the minstrel having lost caste, and being driven to play cheap.

The themes of the minstrels were wars, and victories, and revolutions; so of the modern man of street ballads. If the minstrel celebrated with harp and voice the unhorsings, the broken bones, the deaths, the dust, the blood, and all the glory and circumstance of a tournament,—so does the ballad-seller, with voice and fiddle, glorify the feelings, the broken bones, the blood, the deaths, and all the glory and circumstance of a prize-fight. The minstrel did not scoff at the madness which prevailed in the lists, nor does the ballad-singer at the brutality which prevails in the ring. The minstrels had their dirges for departed greatness; the ballad-singer, like Old Alan Bane, also 'pours his wailing o'er the dead'—for are there not the street 'helegies' on all departed greatness? In the bestowal of flattery or even of praise the modern minstrel is far less liberal than his prototype; but the laudation was, in the good old times, very often 'paid for' by the person whom it was sung to honour. Were the same measure applied to the ballad-singer and writer of today, there can be no reason to doubt that it would be attended with the same result. In his satire the modern has somewhat of an advantage over his predecessor. The minstrel not rarely received a 'largesse' to satirize some one obnoxious to a rival, or to a disappointed man. The ballad-singer (or chaunter, for these remarks apply with equal force to both of these street professionals) is seldom hired to abuse.

---

[1] This chapter is quoted direct from Henry Mayhew's *London Labour and the London Poor* (1851), including the two sub-titles, but Mayhew does not use the word 'busker'.

[2] Strutt, *Sports and Pastimes of the People of England*. (R.N.)

I was told, indeed, by a clever chaunter, that he had been sent lately by a strange gentleman to sing a song—which he and his mate (a patterer) happened at the time to be working—in front of a neighbouring house. The song was on the rogueries of the turf; and the 'move' had a doubly advantageous effect. 'One gentleman, you see, sir, gave us a shilling to go and sing; and affore we'd well finished the chorus, somebody sent us from the other house another shilling to go away agin.' I believe this to be the only way in which the satire of the ballad-singer is rewarded, otherwise than by the sale to his usual class of customers in the streets or the public-houses. The ancient professors of street minstrelsy unquestionably played and sang satirical lays, depending for their remuneration on the liberality of their out-of-door audience; so it is precisely with the modern. The minstrel played both singly and with his fellows; the ballad-singer 'works' both alone (but not frequently) and with his 'mates', or his 'school'.

In the persons of some of these modern street professionals, as I have shown and shall further show, are united the functions of 'the poet, the songster, and the musician'. So in the days of yore. There are now female ballad-singers; there were female minstrels, or glee-women. The lays which were poured forth in our streets and taverns some centuries back, for the regalement of a miscellaneous assemblage, or of a select few, were sometimes of an immoral tendency. Such, it cannot be denied, is the case in our more enlightened days at our Cider Cellars, Coal Holes, Penny Gaffs, and suchlike places. Rarely, however, are such things sung in the streets of London; but sometimes at country fairs and races.

In one respect the analogy between the two ages of these promoters of street enjoyment does not hold. The minstrel's garb was distinctive. It was not always the short laced tunic, tight trousers, and russet boots, with a well-plumed cap—which seems to be the modern notion of this tuneful itinerant. The king's and queen's minstrels wore the royal livery, but so altered as to have removed from its appearance what might seem menial. The minstrels of the great barons also assumed their patron's liveries, with the like qualification. A minstrel of the highest class might wear 'a fayre gowne of cloth of gold,' or a military dress, or a 'tawnie coat,' or a foreign costume, or even an ecclesiastical garb,—and some of them went so far as to shave their crowns, the better to resemble monks. Of course they were imitated by their inferiors. The minstrel, then, wore a particular dress; the ballad-singer of the present day wears no particular dress. During the terrors of the reign of Henry VIII, and after the Reformation, a large body of the minstrels fell into meanness of attire; and in that respect the modern ballad-singer *is* analogous.

It must be borne in mind that I have all along spoken—except when the description is necessarily general—of the *street*, or itinerant, minstrel of old. The highest professors of the art were poets and composers, men often of genius, learning, and gravity, and were no more to be ranked with those I have been describing than is Alfred Tennyson with any Smithfield scribbler and bawler of some Newgate 'Copy of Verses'.

How long 'Sir Topas' and the other 'old stories' continued to be sung in the streets there are no means of ascertaining. But there are old songs, as I ascertained from an intelligent and experienced street-singer, still occasionally to be heard in the open air, but more in the country than in the metropolis. Among those still heard, however rarely, are the Earl of Dorset's song, written on the night before a naval engagement with the Dutch,[1] in 1665:

> To all you ladies now on land,
> We men at sea indite.

I give the titles of the others, not chronologically, but as they occurred to my informant's recollection—'A Cobbler there was, and he lived in a stall'—Parnell's song of 'My days have been so wond'rous free', now sung in the streets to the tune of 'Gramachree'. A song (of which I could not procure a copy, but my informant had lately heard it in the street) about the Cock-lane Ghost—

> Now ponder well, you parents dear,
>   The words which I shall write;
> A doleful story you shall hear
>   In time brought forth to light.

the 'Children in the Wood', and 'Chevy Chase'.[2] Concerning this

---

[1] So he said, but actually it was not. (R.N.)

[2] The tune is known by both these names, and appears in *The Beggar's Opera.* Sir Philip Sidney said of *Chevy Chase*: 'I never heard the old song of Percy and Douglas that I found not my heart moved more than with a trumpet; and yet it is sung but by some poor blind crowder [i.e. fiddler] with no rougher voice than crude style; which, being so evil-apparelled in the dust and cobwebs of that uncivil age, what would it look trimmed in the gorgeous eloquence of Pindare.' The song is well-known today in Northumberland. (R.N.)

old ditty one man said to me: 'Yes, sir, I've sung it at odd times, and not long ago in the north of England, and I've been asked whereabouts Chevy Chase lay, but I never learned.'

> In Scarlet town, where I was born,
> There was a faire maid dwellin'
> Made every youth crye, Well-awaye!
> Her name was Barbara Allen.

'*Barbara Allen*'s selling yet,' I was told. 'Gilderoy was a Bonnie Boy', is another song yet sung occasionally in the streets.

'The ballad,' says a writer on the subject, 'may be considered as the native species of poetry of this country. It very exactly answers the idea formerly given of original poetry, being the rude uncultivated verse in which the popular tale of the time was recorded. As our ancestors partook of the fierce warlike character of the northern nations, the subjects of their poetry would chiefly consist of the martial exploits of their heroes, and the military events of national history, deeply tinctured with that passion for the marvellous, and that superstitious credulity, which always attend a state of ignorance and barbarism. Many of the ancient ballads have been transmitted to the present times, and in them the character of the nation displays itself in striking colours.'

The 'Ballads on a Subject' of which I shall proceed to treat, are certainly 'the rude uncultivated verse in which the popular tale of the times is recorded,' and what may be the character of the nation as displayed in them I leave to the reader's judgment.

(b) Of Street 'Ballads on a Subject'

There is a class of ballads which may with perfect propriety be called *street* ballads, as they are written by street authors for street singing (or chaunting) and street sale. These effusions, however, are known in the trade by a title appropriate enough—'Ballads on a Subject'. The most successful workers in this branch of the profession are the men I have already described among the patterers and chaunters.

The 'Ballads on a Subject' are always on a political, criminal, or exciting public event, or one that has interested the public, and the celerity with which one of them is written, and then sung in the streets, is in the spirit of 'these railroad times'. After any great event, 'a ballad on a subject' is often enough written, printed, and sung on the street, in little more than an hour. Such was the case with a song 'in honour', it was announced, 'of Lord John Russell's resignation'. Of course there is no time for either the correction of the rhymes or of the press; but this is regarded as of little consequence—while an early 'start' with a new topic is of great consequence, I am assured; 'yes, indeed, both for the sake of meals and rents'. If, however, the songs were ever so carefully revised, their sale would not be greater.

It will have struck the reader that all the street lays quoted as popular have a sort of burthen or jingle at the end of each verse. I was corrected, however, by a street chaunter for speaking of this burthen as a jingle. 'It's a chorus, sir,' he said. 'In a proper ballad on a subject, there's often twelve verses, none of them under eight lines—and there's a four-line chorus to every verse; and, if it's the right sort, it'll sell the ballad.' I was told, on all hands, that it was not the words that ever 'made a ballad, but the subject; and more than either,—the *tune*!' Indeed, many of the street-singers of ballads on a subject have as supreme a contempt for words as can be felt by any modern composer. To select a tune for a ballad, however, is a matter for deep deliberation. To adapt the ballad to a tune too popular or common is injudicious; for then, I was told, any one can sing it—boys and all. To select a more elaborate and less-known air, however appropriate, may not be pleasing to some of the members of 'the school' of ballad-singers, who may feel it to be beyond their vocal powers; neither may it be relished by the critical in street song, whose approving criticism induces them to purchase as well as to admire.

The licence enjoyed by the court jesters, and, in some respects, by the minstrels of old, is certainly enjoyed, undiminished, by the street-writers and singers of ballads on a subject. They are unsparing satirists, who, with a rare impartiality, lash all classes and all creeds, as well as any individual. One man, upon whose information I can rely, told me that, eleven years ago, he himself had 'worked' in town and country, twenty-three different songs at the same period and on the same subject—the marriage of the Queen. They all 'sold',—but the most profitable was one 'as sung by Prince Albert in Character'. It was to the air of the 'Dusty Miller'; and 'it was good', said the ballad-man, 'because we could easily dress up to the character given to Albert'.

> Here I am in rags,
> From the land of All-dirt,
> To marry England's Queen,
> And my name is Prince Albert.[1]

'And what's more, sir,' continued my informant, 'not very long after the honeymoon, the Duchess of L—— drove up in her carriage to the printer's, and bought all the songs in honour of Victoria's wedding, and gave a sovereign for them and wouldn't take the change. It was a duchess. Why I'm sure about it—though I can't say whether it were the Duchess of L—— or S——; for didn't the printer, like an honest man, when he'd stopped the price of the papers, hand over to us chaps the balance to drink, and *didn't* we drink it! There can't be a mistake about *that*.'

Of street ballads upon political subjects, or upon themes which have interested the whole general public, I need not cite additional instances. There are, however, other subjects, which, though not regarded as of great interest by the whole body of the people, are still eventful among certain classes, and for them the street-author and street-singer cater.

I first give a specimen of a ballad on a Theatrical Subject. The best I find, in a large collection of these street effusions, is entitled 'Jenny Lind and the Poet B'. After describing how Mr Bunn 'flew to Sweden' [2] and engaged Miss Lind, the poet proceeds,—the tune being *Lucy Long*:

> After Jenny signed the paper,[3]
> She repented what she'd done,
> And said she must have been a cake,
> To be tempted by A. Bunn.
> The English language she must decline,[4]
> It was such awkward stuff,
> And we find 'mongst our darling dames,
> The one tongue's quite enough.

[1] At the time of Victoria's ascending the throne republicanism was rife (her predecessors had been unpopular) and before her marriage Albert was said to be a princely pauper marrying for money. The ballads only restated the opinions of upper classes. By 1851, however (the date of the Great Exhibition), we realized that whatever was wrong with Saxe-Coburg-Gotha, it was in industrial England that we should look for the land of All-dirt. (R.N.)

[2] and [3] Not Sweden but Berlin, Jenny Lind signed the contract hurriedly in the private box of the British Ambassador between the acts of an opera. Bunn did not sign her copy. (R.N.)

[4] She spoke no English. Opera in Drury Lane was generally performed in English. (R.N.)

So take your time Miss Jenny,
Oh, take your time Miss Lind,
You've only to raise your voice,
John Bull will raise the wind.

Says Alfred, 'In the public eye
My name you shan't degrade,
So birds that can and won't sing,
Why of course they must be made.'
This put Miss Jenny's pipe out,[1]
Says Bunn, 'Your tricks I see,
Altho' you are a nightingale
You shan't play larks with me.'

The Poet said he'd seek the law,
No chance away he'd throw;
Says Jenny if you think I'll come,
You'll find it is no go!
When a bird-catcher named 'Lummy',[2]
With independence big,
Pounced down upon the Nightingale,
And with her 'hopp'd the twig'.

I am inclined to think—though I know it to be an unusual case
—that in this theatrical ballad the street poet was what is tenderly
called a 'plagiarist'. I was assured by a chaunter that it was written
by a street author, but probably the chaunter was himself in error
or forgetfulness.

Next, there is the ballad on a Civic Subject. In the old times the
Lord Mayor had his laureate. This writer, known as 'poet to the
City of London', eulogized all lord mayors, and glorified all civic
pageants. That of the 9th November, especially 'lived in Settle's
numbers one day more,'[3]—but Elkanah Settle was the last of such
scribes.[4] After his death, the City eschewed a poet. The office has
now descended to the street bard, who annually celebrates the great

---

[1] Bunn was a hard bargainer; his threats frightened her. (R.N.)

[2] Benjamin Lumley, director of the Italian opera at the Haymarket. He engaged
her and paid the fine of £2,000 awarded to Bunn for her breach of contract. (R.N.)

[3] Alexander Pope, *The Dunciad*, I. 183.

[4] Not only the Lord Mayor of London, but other mayors kept their civic poets.
(R.N.)

Photo: Republic Pictures International Inc.

ABOVE. The Charleston. BELOW. Improvised Jazz. Benny Goodman is on the left.

Photo: Howarth, Blackp(

Photo: Butlins L

ABOVE. The Luton Girls' Choir. BELOW. Holiday Campers' Choir, Filey, Yorks.

ceremony. I cite two stanzas and the chorus from the latest of these civic odes:

> Now Farncombe's out and Musgrove's in,
>   And grand is his position,
> Because he will be made a king
>   At the Hyde Park Exhibition;
> A feast he'll order at Guildhall,
>   For hypocrites and sinners,
> And he has sent Jack Forrester to Rome,
>   To invite the Pope to dinner!

> A day like this we never saw,
>   The truth I am confessing,
> Batty's astonishing menagerie
>   Is in the great procession;
> There's lions, tigers, bears and wolves,
>   To please each smiling feature,
> And elephants in harness drawing
>   Drury Lane Theatre.

>> It is not as it used to be,
>>   Cut on so gay and thrifty,
>> The funny Lord Mayor's Show to see,
>>   In eighteen hundred and fifty.

There is, besides the descriptions of ballads above cited, the Ballad Local. One of these is headed the 'Queer Doings in Leather-Lane', and is on a subject concerning which street-sellers generally express themselves strongly—Sunday trading. The endeavour to stop street trading (generally) in Leather Lane, with its injurious results to the shopkeepers, has been already mentioned. The ballad on this local subject presents a personality now, happily, almost confined to the street writers:

> A rummy saintly lot is there,
>   A domineering crew,
> A Butcher, and a Baker,
>   And an Undertaker too,
> Besides a cove who deals in wood,
>   And makes his bundles small,
> And looks as black on Sunday
>   As an Undertaker's pall.

G

You must not buy, you must not sell,
    Oh! is it not a shame?
It is a shocking place to dwell,
    About sweet Leather Lane.

The Butcher does not like to hear
    His neighbours holloa, 'Buy!'
Although he on the Sunday
    Sells a little on the sly;
And the Coffin Maker struts along
    Just like the great Lord Mayor,
To bury folks on Sundays,
    Instead of going to prayers.

There are yet three themes of these street songs of which, though they have been alluded to, no specimens have been given. I now apply them. The first is the election ballad. I quote two stanzas from 'Middlesex and Victory! or Grosvenor and Osborne[1] for ever!'

Now Osborne is the man
    To struggle for your rights,
He will vote against the Bishops,
    You know, both day and night.
He will strive to crush the Poor Law Bill,
    And that with all his might,
And he will never give his vote
    To part a man from his wife.

        Then cheer Osborne and Lord Grosvenor
            Cheer them with three times three,
        For they beat the soldier, Tommy Wood,
            And gained the victory.

I have not forgot Lord Grosvenor,
    Who nobly stood the test,
For the electors of great Middlesex
    I know he'll do his best;

[1] Ralph Bernal Osborne, elected member for Middlesex, 1847. (R.N.)

He will pull old Nosey o'er the coals,
    And lay him on his back,
And he swears that little Bob's head
    He will shove into a rat trap.[1]

Then come the 'elegies'. Of three of these I cite the opening stanza. That on the 'Death of Queen Adelaide' has for an illustration a figure of Britannia leaning on her shield, with the 'Muse of History' (as I presume from her attributes) at Britannia's feet. In the distance is the setting sun:

Old England may weep, her bright hopes are fled,
    The friend of the poor is no more;
For Adelaide now is numbered with the dead,
    And her loss we shall sadly deplore.
For though noble her birth, and high was her station,
    The poor of the nation will miss her,
For their wants she relieved without ostentation,
    But now she is gone, God bless her!
      God bless her! God bless her!
    But now she is gone, God bless her!

The elegy on the 'Death of the Right Honourable Sir Robert Peel, Bart., M.P.', is set off with a very fair portrait of that statesman

Britannia! Britannia! what makes thee complain?
    O why so in sorrow relenting?
Old England is lost, we are borne down in pain,
    And the nation in grief is lamenting.
That excellent man—the pride of the land,
    Whom every virtue possessed him,
Has gone to that Home, from whence no one returns,
    Our dear friend, Sir Robert, God rest him.[2]

[1] Middlesex was in the lead in bringing to light the abuses of the new Poor Law system. In West Middlesex a Radical coroner, Dr Wakley, held inquests on paupers and had the body of a pauper named Thomas Austin exhumed. This man had fallen into a copper full of boiling water in Hendon workhouse and had been quietly buried. The authorities were censured, at which the workhouse master sneered in the Bumble manner: 'The jury have found a verdict, but they have not identified the body.' To which Dr Wakley replied: 'If this is not the body of the man who was killed in your vat, pray, sir, how many paupers have you boiled?' 'Old Nosey' was the Duke of Wellington. (R.N.)

[2] N.B. the word 'God' in the last line of this and the preceding ballad, introduced without any suspicion of petty blasphemy. Sir Robert Peel the younger died in 1850. (R.N.)

The verses which bewail the 'Death of H.R.H. the Duke of Cambridge', and which are adorned with the same illustrations as those upon Queen Adelaide, begin:

> Oh! death, thou art severe, and never seems contented,
> Prince Adolphus Frederick is summoned away,
> The death of Royal Cambridge in sorrow lamented,
> Like the good Sir Robert Peel, he no longer could stay;
> His virtues were good, and noble was his actions,
> His presence at all places caused much attraction,
>   Royal Cambridge, we'll behold thee no more!

The third class of street ballads refers to 'fires'. The one I quote, 'On the Awful Fire at B. Caunt's, in St. Martin's Lane', is preceded by an engraving of a lady and a cavalier, the lady pointing to a column surmounted by an urn. I again give the first stanza:

> I will unfold a tale of sorrow,
>   List, you tender parents dear,
> It will thrill each breast with horror,
>   When the dreadful tale you hear.
> Early on last Wednesday morning,
>   A raging fire as we may see,
> Did occur, most sad and awful,
>   Between the hours of two and three.

In a subsequent stanza are four lines, not without some rough pathos, and adapted to move the feelings of a street audience. The writer is alluding to the grief of the parents who have lost two children by a terrible death:

> No more their smiles they'll be beholding,
>   No more their pretty faces see,
> No more to their bosoms will they fold them,
>   Oh! what must their feelings be.

I find no difference in style between the ballads on a subject of today, and the oldest which I could obtain a sight of, which were sung in the present generation—except that these poems now begin far less frequently with what at one time was as common as an invitation to the Muse—the invitation to good Christians to attend to the singer. One on the Sloanes, however, opens in the old fashion:

> Come all good Christians and give attention,
>   Unto these lines I will unfold,
> With heartfelt feelings to you I'll mention,
>   I'm sure 'twill make your heart run cold.

I will now conclude this account of street-ballads on a subject with two verses from one on the subject of 'The Glorious Fight for the Championship of England'. The celebration of these once-popular encounters is, as I have already stated, one of the points in which the modern ballad-man emulates his ancient brother minstrel:

> On the ninth day of September,
>   Eighteen hundred and forty-five,
> From London down to Nottingham [1]
>   The roads were all alive;
> Oh! such a sight was never seen,
>   Believe me it is so,
> Tens of thousands went to see the fight,
>   With Caunt and Bendigo.
>
> And near to Newport Pagnell,
>   These men did strip so fine,
> Ben Caunt stood six feet two and a half, [2]
>   And Bendigo five foot nine;
> Ben Caunt, a giant did appear,
>   And made the claret flow,
> And he seemed fully determined
>   To conquer Bendigo.
>
> With their hit away and slash away,
>   So manfully you see,
> Ben Caunt has lost, and Bendigo
>   Has gained the victory. [3]

.   .   .   .

[1] Nottingham was Bendigo's birthplace, and a Nottingham printer continued to reprint ballads of his fights until the present century. (R.N.)

[2] Correct; and weighed fourteen stone, seven pounds. (R.N.)

[3] The referee awarded the fight to Bendigo (whose real name was William Thompson) after two hours fighting. There were ten thousand spectators. The purse was £200. According to *D.N.B.* the place was near Sutfield Green, Oxfordshire. (R.N.)

The ballads were crudely printed, as Mayhew states, with wood-cut illustrations. Some of these were stock blocks with a cut-out section into which a different figure could be inserted to make the block serve for another character. Especially so in illustrations of executions. Gradually, however, such business passed to the news-papers. Charles Mackay, when editor of the *Illustrated London News*, introduced the attraction of a new song printed in every number; the Sunday papers later adopted this practice and kept it up until the coming of radio. In the early part of the twentieth century came the craze for picture postcards, some of which bore illustrations and the verses of songs like *Barbara Allen*, *The Volunteer Organist*, or *The Lost Chord*. Even so, sheets containing a large selection of popular hits—pantomime or seaside minstrels' songs—were sold for a penny well into the twentieth century. Nowadays we have the juke-box. (R.N.)

XII. MAINLY GILBERTIAN

FOREIGNERS COMING INTO BRITAIN have for long been inclined to regard us with suspicion on account of our topsyturvy character. To many of them we are no less than hypocrites, and we can do little to disillusion them so long as Mrs Grundy haunts our dreams, for she is the kind of fiction which can persist only in a guilt-ridden nation. Nevertheless, she is outmoded; her period was truly Victorian.

Mrs Grundy appeared first as a character in a play by Thomas Morton called *Speed the Plough*, and the author died a year after Victoria came to the throne. He would have been surprised to learn how seriously this absurd character's notions were to be taken by the Victorians. We have seen them already at work, poisoning the minds of mothers and daughters until the sight of a ballet-dancer's legs shocked them, yet characters like Mrs Grundy cannot stand alone; they exist as covers for something unmentionable, just as 'nether garments' existed as a euphemism for 'trousers'.

One can understand how this veneer of deception gained credence. It was the counter-attack against an amoral elegance which persisted throughout the reigns of the Georges and was anything but dead when Victoria and Albert married in 1840. The rakes at court were frowned on by Albert, but their passing was slow. The utilitarian philosophers, moreover, had to achieve their economic supremacy before they could work their moral revolution; the sins the middle classes abhorred were, to be found out in a sexual irregularity, or to become a bankrupt. In the second half of the nineteenth century, therefore, Mrs Grundy thrived, and we can see her sham philosophy dictating to popular artists and writers. When she was at the height of her power, however, a remarkable advance took place in the theatre, and took place with a full acceptance of the true character of Mrs Grundy. Gilbert and Sullivan wrote their successful series of comic operas. If you want a practical illustration of the fruit of Jeremy Bentham's aim at 'the greatest happiness of the greatest number', look for it not in his political reforms but in the by-blow of the Savoy operas.[1]

But first we must turn to two other people who knew how to satisfy Mrs Grundy and the public. The trick was to keep out of the theatres, with all their immoral associations, and to present plays and musical entertainments in places of undoubted respectability such as church halls, temperance halls, etc. Mr and Mrs German Reed were old troupers, but they turned their attention to these new markets, and earned for themselves a good middle-class reputation. Among other places, they performed in St Martin's Hall, Long Acre, which had been built for Dr John Pyke Hullah's singing classes. Mr and Mrs German Reed sought for clean comedy and found it in a little comic interlude called *Cox and Box*, libretto by F. C. Burnand—later editor of *Punch*—and music by Arthur Sullivan. This entertainment had been first performed privately at the home of Arthur Lewis, a wealthy amateur of music living at Campden Hill. It set a pattern in topsyturvy plots, pleased respectable families, and abounded in likable tunes. The composer was to hand; all that was required was an author able to work in the topsyturvy medium and a theatrical manager willing to finance a venture in English comic opera along these lines. W. S. Gilbert was such an author and Rupert D'Oyly Carte was such a manager. He was producing light French *opéra bouffe* at the Royalty Theatre in Soho and got Gilbert and Sullivan to collaborate in a curtain-raiser called *Trial by Jury*.[2] The work struck fire. It became the model for a series of larger comic operas.

W. S. Gilbert had been trained as a lawyer and knew the humorous side of the law's conventions; he had also served in the army, knew parliamentary procedure very well, and the course of constitutional history. The constitution had suffered numerous changes within the memory of members of his audiences. The Benthamites were due for a shaking anyway, and Gilbert was a natural conservative. So Gilbert found plenty of opportunities for introducing legal and social paradoxes. His audiences were ready for these: the army, navy, Houses of Lords and of Commons, the arts—all were centres of old conventions and targets for reformers. To Gilbert the reforms themselves were funnier than the old conventions. So he devised innumerable dilemmas in the British way of life, mixed up his peers with fairies, a pirate with a nonconformist conscience,

---

[1] Not the least interesting side of Victorian history is how Gilbert dreamed Bentham's dream and achieved it by poking fun at it.

[2] First produced 1875.

Darwin's theory of evolution with snobbish heredity in Pooh-Bah,[1] and denounced modern art in *Patience*:

> Oh, to be wafted away
>> From this black Aceldama of sorrow,
> Where the dust of an earthy today
>> Is the earth of a dusty tomorrow.

Look at a Rossetti or Burne-Jones picture and note the sick look on the faces of the characters—'greenery-yallery, Grosvenor Gallery, foot-in-the-grave young men,' [2] with a vengeance.

Gilbert respected the Church of England, and it follows from what we have already observed that the English family was sacrosanct. He pilloried the traditional wicked squire and the new Victorian puritanism in the same opera—*Ruddigore*. In *H.M.S. Pinafore* he hit at the reformed Civil Service, for which since 1870 entrants had been chosen as a result of a competitive examination instead of through family influence; so the advice of a First Lord of the Admiralty in that opera is:

> Stick close to your desks and never go to sea,
> And you all may be the rulers of the Queen's Navee.

The Army was reformed in 1871 on the German model which had successfully trounced the French in the Franco-Prussian War. (We did not, however, introduce conscription.) We were not a militaristic nation, but we were becoming an Imperialist one. When Victoria came to the throne we sang of our tight little island, but Disraeli in 1876 made the Queen Empress of India by the Royal Titles Act, and Jingoism was on the way. Jingoism implied a boastful attitude towards other nations, so, to paint its absurdity, Gilbert and Sullivan made the Mikado's army ridiculous:

> Our warriors in serried ranks assembled,
>> Never quail, or they conceal it if they do,
> And I shouldn't be surprised if nations trembled
>> Before the mighty troops of Tittipoo.

---

[1] Pooh-Bah: 'I can trace my ancestry back to a protoplasmal primordial atomic globule. Consequently my family pride is something inconceivable. I can't help it. I was born sneering.' *The Mikado*, Act I.

[2] *Patience*, Act II.

* G

But in *Utopia Limited* they got more sardonic:

> Our pride and boast—the Army and Navy—
> Have both been reconstructed and remodelled
> Upon so irresistible a basis
> That all the neighbouring nations have disarmed—
> And War's impossible!

If we are to understand the full import of late Victorian thought we should try to imagine what the reception of that verse would be today, if introduced into a musical comedy. Gilbert and Sullivan were above suspicion, yet their age was more unsettled in some ways than ours. Republicanism, never quite dead, revived in 1871 under the leadership of Charles Bradlaugh, Joseph Chamberlain, and Sir Charles Dilke. Queen Victoria was attacked for staying so long in retirement after the death of her husband, and the cost of the Monarchy was fiercely criticized. Now turn again to *The Gondoliers* and enjoy those parts where republican equality is reduced to absurdity:

> When everyone is somebody
> Then no one's anybody.

This sort of thing did not make Gilbert and Sullivan reformers —they were never that except in entertainment—but it shows how closely they had their ears to the ground. *The Gondoliers* was first produced two years after Victoria's Golden Jubilee, when the Queen's popularity was established beyond doubt, and the brunt of the republican attack had been met in the 'seventies, but as late as 1885 a fashionable men's paper called *Town Talk* (not, be it noted, a working-men's journal) published a 'programme' for the Jubilee stating that 'The Queen will come to London and stop a whole week, Her Majesty will spend five shillings with two London tradesmen'. The 'programme' ended with a procession of '10,000 children who have had no meat for a year' and '100 workmen who have been sent to prison for being poor'. Then came 'Prince Lagerbeer of Stunkenstein, in his carriage and four, accompanied by his English princess, fed and clothed and housed by the English ratepayers'. This was cheap propaganda lingering on after its time, but it is well to realize that not until the Jubilee of 1887 was the Crown given the respect which it enjoys to this day.[1]

---

[1] One may find music-hall songs in 1888 like:

> 'We sing "God save the Queen"
> Though she's very seldom seen,'

but such stuff was unimaginative at that date.

As for 'ballads on a subject', they persisted—*Goodbye, little yellow Bird*, and *Mrs Dyer the Baby Farmer*—relics of the fate of the 'fallen woman' in a Grundiesque society:

> Poor girls who fall from the straight path of virtue,
>   What could they do with a child in their arms?
> The fault they committed they could not undo,
>   So the baby was sent to the cruel baby farms.

Chorus:

> The old baby farmer, the wretched Mrs Dyer,
>   At the Old Bailey her wages is paid;
> In times long ago we'd ha' made a big fire,
>   And roasted so nicely that wicked old Jade.

As in all true ballads of the sort we have observed since Thomas Deloney, the moral issue was never in doubt:

> To all these sad crimes there must be an ending,
>   Secrets like these for ever can't last;
> Say as you like, there is no defending
>   The 'orrible tales we have heard in the past.

This is Victorian balladry of the type issued from the cheap presses situated at Seven Dials. It was intended for the streets and is of the streets. Gilbert and Sullivan used ballad form extensively, but for respectable audiences; they could make their best appeal by turning upside-down the moral platitudes of the balladiers, reducing law and order to absurdity in the sure belief that these were not in any danger at the Savoy Theatre:

> When the enterprising burglar's not a-burgling,
>   When the cut-throat isn't occupied in crime,
> He loves to hear the little brook a-gurgling,
>   And listen to the merry village chime.
> When the coster's finished jumping on his mother,
>   He loves to lie a-basking in the sun;
> Ah, take one consideration with another,
>   The policeman's lot is not a happy one.

Can you imagine Albert Chevalier, the coster character comedian in a music-hall, singing about jumping on his mother? The music-halls idealized the working-class in the nineteenth century as the theatrical composers had idealized the sailor in the eighteenth.

It would be ridiculous to expect Gilbert and Sullivan to treat the facts of life as seriously as George Bernard Shaw (for whom the London theatres were unready) or even Oscar Wilde. Gilbert and Sullivan were creating an artificial musical comedy, proper to the English theatres at that time. Not only is this evident in their treatment of topical notions, but in the style of composition adopted by Sullivan. Nowhere is it advanced; everywhere it summarizes all that was most enjoyable to Victorian audiences.

The Victorians were familiar with drawing-room ballads, glees, part-songs, Italian and French opera, and they had had the benefit of good musical educationists who had classified the forms and harmonies of their age and made them known intimately to a wide variety of people. (The public schools alone were backward in musical education in the late nineteenth century.) Consider, then, the styles employed by Gilbert and Sullivan in comparison with those familiar to their audiences. First, the very respectable part-songs of the Victorians, the voices moving together in block harmonies—in their serious moments never very far from hymn-tune style. Secondly the older form of popular part-singing—the glee. This style was properly for a single voice to each part, unaccompanied, but during the nineteenth century orchestral accompaniment became not unusual, especially in the theatres. There were many glee and madrigal societies in being, which seems to have led W. S. Gilbert into a belief that these musical styles were much the same: at any rate the 'madrigal' in *The Mikado* is more like a glee than anything else.

From the opera house Gilbert and Sullivan took the duets, trios, quartets, and quintets for principal singers, the grand finales with all the company on stage for a climax, and of course the solo songs. Coloratura sopranos were expensive and D'Oyly Carte did not want them, but the patter-song—after the manner of Rossini's *Largo al factotem* but with English words—Gilbert and Sullivan could manage extremely well; there was also the trick known to Bellini, Donizetti, and Rossini, of using the orchestra in a simple guitar-like manner; one finds it in the song *Take a Pair of Sparkling Eyes*, in *The Gondoliers*.

This kind of song went down well in the Victorian drawing-rooms when guests brought their own music and liked to be asked to sing it.

Gilbert and Sullivan had discovered a formula for popular entertainment of a socially acceptable order which gave their audiences what they wanted—'the greatest happiness of the greatest number'.

Admittedly this theory had been conceived in philosophy a century earlier—Erasmus Darwin expressed it—and had been the cry of the Benthamites in the early nineteenth century, but so was everything that Gilbert and Sullivan touched; their genius was to sum up what was familiar to their audiences, and to use those things which their audiences liked. Their audiences were not composed of advanced people, but of romanticists of the older school; on their ideas were impinging the new romanticism of Wagner, and of leaders of the Aesthetic Movement, which the more serious among them were inclined to accept, but neither Gilbert, Sullivan, nor D'Oyly Carte were ready to serve the modernists; Aestheticism was mocked in *Patience*, Darwinism and women's emancipation in *Princess Ida*, socialism in *Utopia Ltd*, and the chance to parody Wagner in *The Grand Duke* was thown away by Sullivan.

The results are well known. *The Sorcerer* ran for 175 nights, *H.M.S. Pinafore* for 700, *The Pirates of Penzance* 400, *Patience* 408. Long runs meant profits undreamed of before, and more—for with long runs in view greater capital could be employed for staging each production. A new standard of production in the commercial theatres became possible, and, once D'Oyly Carte had established this principle, others had to copy it or fall into the second rank. D'Oyly Carte built the Savoy Theatre for further operas by Gilbert and Sullivan, and *The Mikado* ran for 672 nights. From this time on musical comedy has been gay, and expensively produced, attractive but inoffensive, never 'advanced' except in new spectacle. The coming of the talking film made even greater outlay of capital reasonable, for the possible market was many times larger than for a 'live' company. Decisions were taken on the margin of profit likely to accrue, and success had to be measured solely in financial terms.

D'Oyly Carte was the hero of the Savoy; Gilbert and Sullivan quarrelled on a trivial point, but behind all was the fear in Sullivan's mind that he had prostituted his art by associating himself with Gilbert and the commercial theatre. If he seemed to be in danger of forgetting this, his professional rivals reminded him. Looking back on their opinions we can only suggest that W. S. Gilbert was right:

> Our attitude's queer and quaint;
> You're wrong if you think it ain't.

They lived, however, in the age when Mrs Grundy was at her worst, so everything was presented in a seemly manner: there must be no men dressed in women's clothes, nor women in men's; suggestive sallies must be avoided; sex conventionalized, and so on. More than these—the theatre itself must be cleaned out; drunks and whores were to be put in their places, and the fight outside the doors of the pit to gain admission was stopped by a new system called the queue. A visit to the Savoy Theatre was quite in keeping with the best behaviour of a respectable family—one was not even exposed to the lure of classical ballet—all one got was a chorus of fairies or pretty girls who *never* kicked their little toes above their ankles.

XIII. THE MUSIC-HALLS

THERE HAS SURVIVED into the twentieth century an army song not to be found in print for an obvious reason; in its crudest form it is unprintable—but the version following will just, perhaps, pass:

My name is Captain Hall, Captain Hall, Captain Hall;
My name is Captain Hall, Captain Hall;
My name is Captain Hall, and I've only had one brawl,
But it's better than none at all,
Damn your eyes, blast your soul,
But it's better than none at all, damn your eyes.

They say I killed a man, killed a man, killed a man;
They say I killed a man, killed a man;
I hit him on the head with a bloody lump of lead,
And now the fellow's dead,
Damn his eyes, blast his soul,
And now the fellow's dead, damn his eyes.

And now I'm in a cell, in a cell, in a cell;
And now I'm in a cell, in a cell;
And now I'm in a cell, and on my way to hell,
Perhaps it's just as well,
Damn your eyes, blast your soul,
Perhaps it's just as well, damn your eyes.

The Chaplain he will come, he will come, he will come;
The Chaplain he will come, he will come;
The Chaplain he will come, and he'll look so bloomin' glum,
As he talks of Kingdom come,
Damn his eyes, blast his soul,
As he talks of Kingdom come, damn his eyes.

Now this is my last knell, my last knell, my last knell;
Now this is my last knell, my last knell;
Now this is my last knell, and you've had a [jolly] sell,
For I'll meet you all in hell,
Damn your eyes, blast your soul,
For I'll meet you all in hell, damn your eyes.

Now I feel the rope, feel the rope, feel the rope;
Now I feel the rope, feel the rope;
Now I feel the rope, and I've lost all earthly hope,
Nothing but the Chaplain's soap,
Damn his eyes, blast his soul,
Nothing but the Chaplain's soap, damn his eyes.

Now I am in hell, am in hell, am in hell;
Now I am in hell, am in hell;
Now I am in hell, and it's such a [blooming] sell,
'Cos the Chaplain's here as well,
Damn his eyes, blast his soul,
'Cos the Chaplain's here as well, damn his eyes.

This song is a variant of a 'hit' song of the early Victorian period,[1] made famous by W. G. Ross—known to his audiences as 'The Great Ross'. He would sing it in the Cider Cellars and the Coal Hole (two famous singing-taverns which preceded the modern music-halls) sitting astride a chair, dressed in dirty rags, a blackened clay pipe in his mouth, which he removed only when he wanted to spit or swear. He was insignificant as an actor; his 'greatness' depended entirely on his foul-mouthed venom, of so blasphemous a nature that his singing of this song was regarded as the height of audacity. Men flocked to hear Ross sing *Sam Hall* (the 'Captain' of the army version is a variant) as they would to see the monkeys mating in the zoo, and for the same reason—it would have been stopped if the Mrs Grundies had had their way.

But the Mrs Grundies were not there. The haunts where this song had its beginning were for men only, and, like the obscene catches of the eighteenth century, they went out of fashion when women were admitted to the mystery. This is not a reflection on the baseness of men and the refinement of women,[2] but an acknowledgment of the facts of social life. Women there were who would enjoy such 'art'—Gay has shown us a glimpse of them in *The Beggar's Opera* —but the presence of such women in such circumstances was injurious to the reputation of taverns. It would be absolutely wrong to pretend that the taverns where music was provided were concerned in moral uplift—they were concerned solely with making

[1] In its turn a variant of *Jack Hall*, an eighteenth-century ballad about the hanging of a chimney sweep for murder.

[2] See quotation from Thackeray at end of our Chapter IX. The 'Cave of Harmony' was like Evans's Song and Supper Rooms, for men only, but careful to avoid giving offence.

money—but as the industrial revolution took effect, the women from the factories sought relaxation and entertainment with the men who shared their working life; the sales of food and drink were greater in those places where women were admitted, but less of drink was sold than of food. Cook Taylor was emphatic enough:

The operatives of Manchester have shown their taste and capability for higher enjoyments than smoking and drinking. I have gone into the concert-rooms attached to favoured public-houses which they frequent, and have never been in a more orderly and well-behaved company. The music is well selected, the songs perfectly unobjectionable; the conversation, in the intervals between the pieces, not only decorous, but to some degree refined, and the quantity of liquor consumed by each individual very trifling. But I have also been in houses where music was prohibited, and the scenes that I have witnessed will not bear description.[1]

It all depends on what you mean by refinement. We have described the Italian opera, however, and heard the comments of Lady Blessington on its 'indecencies'; now let us glance inside another 'Temple of the Muses', this time attached to a public-house in the industrial north.

The proprietor, called Chaffing Jack, was dressed like the head waiter of a London tavern—in black silk stockings, silver knee-buckles, white waistcoat, and diamond pin. A Polish lady ('The Signora sings in English like a new-born babe') sang *Cherry Ripe*, and bowed to the applause like a *prima donna*. Long after she had been shut off, Chaffing Jack remained, bowing to his guests. 'It's almost too much,' he exclaimed; 'the enthusiasm of these people. I believe they look on me as a father.' [2]

Disraeli is more useful to us probably than Thackeray, whose description of *The Cave of Harmony* we have already given, or Dickens, who knew the Grecian Hall behind the Eagle in the City Road (it appears in *Sketches by Boz*). Disraeli goes into greater detail, and shows the interplay of motives behind the entertainment business; the dreamlife of the factory girl:

'Well, what do you think of it?' asked Caroline of Harriet, in a whisper as they entered the splendid apartment.

'It's just what I thought the Queen lived in,' said Harriet, 'but indeed I'm all of a flutter.'

'Well, don't look as though you were.'

[1] Cook Taylor, *Tour in Manufacturing Districts of Lancashire* (1842), p. 131.
[2] Disraeli, *Sybil*, Chapter 10.

With Caroline and Harriet is Dandy Mick, spending his wages in style, and getting, no doubt, his money's worth of admiration:

'It's pretty, Miss Harriet,' said Dandy Mick, looking up at the ceiling with a careless *nil admirari* glance.

'Oh! it is beautiful,' said Harriet.

'You never were here before; it's the only place. That's the Lady of the Lake,' he added, pointing to a picture; 'I've seen her at the circus, with real water.'

Contrasted with the easy-going Mick is his friend Devilsdust, a foundling brought up, not in a home, but in a factory:

Devilsdust had entered life so early that at seventeen he combined the experience of manhood with the divine energy of youth. He was a first-rate workman and received high wages; he had availed himself of the advantages of the factory school; he soon learnt to read and write with facility, and at the moment of our history was the leading spirit of the Shoddy-Court Literary and Scientific Institute. His great friend, his only intimate, was Dandy Mick. The apparent contrariety of their qualities and structure perhaps led to this. It is indeed the most assured basis of friendship. Devilsdust was dark and melancholy; ambitious and discontented; full of thought, and with powers of patience and perseverance that alone amounted to genius. Mick was as brilliant as his complexion; gay, irritable, evanescent, and unstable. Mick enjoyed life; his friend only endured it; yet Mick was always complaining of the lowness of his wages and the greatness of his toil; while Devilsdust never murmured, but read and pondered on the rights of labour, and sighed to vindicate his order.

It is interesting to compare Devilsdust with Cassius in Shakespeare's *Julius Caesar*. 'He thinks too much; such men are dangerous,' though the process is often strange:

'I have some thoughts of joining the Total Abstinence,' said Devilsdust; 'ever since I read Stephen Morley's address it has been on my mind. We shall never get our rights until we leave off consuming excisable articles; and the best thing to begin with is liquors.'

'Well, I could do without liquors myself,' said Caroline. 'If I was a lady, I would never drink anything except fresh milk from the cow.'

'Tea for my money,' said Harriet; 'I must say there's nothing I grudge for good tea. Now I keep house, I mean always to drink of the best.'

'Well, you have not yet taken the pledge, Dusty,' said Dandy Mick; 'and so suppose we order a go of gin and talk this matter of temperance over. . . .'

We have said before that popular entertainment is a two-way traffic; the proprietor must please his patrons and his patrons look for their money's worth from the proprietor. We can tell from Disraeli's character-studies what the patrons want; they want distraction from everyday life offered within the scope of that life; so the decorations belong to a romantic world, yet a world into which one can be admitted in spirit; the 'Polish' lady sings *Cherry Ripe*, the 'principal harpist of the King of Saxony' is seen and heard because she in her turn wants to visit 'the world-famous scenes of British industry'. All this is sham, no doubt, but shams exercise the imagination. The hot sausages are not sham, nor the gin, but these are nevertheless special luxuries to be enjoyed while the money lasts, and dreamed of for the rest of the week. Devilsdust stands apart from the rest of the community. He thinks. But even his thinking is applied to a theory which he has somehow knit into a dream of the future.

But what about Chaffing Jack, the proprietor? He will not make profits out of disgruntled theorists; he makes them out of gregarious masses seeking confidence in themselves. By themselves they are lonely and unsure, but when three hundred of them applaud the same song, or shout the same chorus, how can they all be in doubt? Besides, are not three hundred satisfied patrons desirable to Chaffing Jack, with no trouble from the police? Had he been content with a mere gin-shop he would have had constant trouble, for he would have had no reputation. 'Must have a name, Mr Morley,' said Jack, 'name's everything; made the fortune of the Temple; if I had called it the Saloon it would never have filled, and perhaps the magistrates would never have granted a licence.'

Such was the business policy and its social counterpart. There was one Charles Morton, who kept the Canterbury Music-hall, and actually gave the first performance in England of Gounod's *Faust*. Think of the pictures round the walls of Disraeli's Temple of the Muses and consider the prestige which would follow the mounting of a romantic opera, more or less grand, on Chaffing Jack's stage! Charles Morton lived to a healthy old age; when he was eighty no less a person than Mrs Beerbohm Tree recited a complimentary poem containing this verse:

Sixty or seventy years ago, in the days of the 'drinking den',
The jokes they made and the songs they sang were sorrow to
    Englishmen.
If you doubt my word, take Thackeray down, and Colonel New-
    come call
To tell the tale of the days of Ross, and then shudder at vile 'Sam Hall'.

But he dreamed of the Madrigal, Grand Old Man, and the English
    Catch and Glee,
And murmured, 'Pleasure it should be pure, and Art it must be free'.
So he opened a 'Sing Song' bright and gay, Vice took to its heels
    and ran!
Said the women, 'Oh Governor! Let us in!' 'You shall come,'
    said the Grand Old Man.

Complimentary verses to Grand Old Men are no more to be
trusted than the verses on tombstones, however. The English glee
was sung continually in Evans's Song and Supper Rooms until
the 'seventies, and this was the last stronghold of the men.[1] It was
patronized by people like Thackeray, and clean-minded to the point
of smugness. Its shutting-out of women was a hang-over of anti-
feminism as much out of date in the 'seventies as the refusal of admission of women to the membership of the Oxford Union is today
when women are fully enfranchised. Charles Morton, of the Canterbury Music-hall, was not the originator of the sing-song; this
communal pleasure is as old as inebriation and religion, and has
always had its place in public-houses. The glee clubs met upstairs
in the eighteenth-century pubs. and the Comus Court in the base-
ment, and in both they sang. Sometimes a singer who had appeared
upstairs would come downstairs to amuse the lower classes, along
with whoever happened to be there, and, directed by their chairman
—even as the others were in the catch and glee clubs—they would
sing and listen to the 'turns' of visitors.[2] The song and supper
rooms of the early nineteenth century continued this entertainment,
but women were at length admitted (except at Evans's) and the
chairman, seated in state at the main table, called the 'turns' and
added his humour in the gaps between. The 'turns' grew more and
more popular, the stage bigger, and the refreshments were gradually
relegated to the far end of the room. The law in 1872 made it an
offence to serve meals after 12.30 at night, and that was the end of
Evans's, but already the music-hall as we know it was developed.
The stage held the attractions. The promenade behind the auditorium became the haunt of prostitutes, and an object of scorn among
puritans. Reform had to be undertaken, and the excuses of the pro-
prietors sound very mercenary today.[3]

[1] The first part of the night's entertainment usually employed choir boys and men to
sing glees, madrigals, and part-songs.
[2] Many of these were trivial, like simple conjuring tricks or imitation of animal
noises.
[3] The Empire in Leicester Square took the brunt of the attack.

Nevertheless, it was possible to take a woman into most music-halls even in the so-called naughty 'nineties without her being molested. The 'turns' were clever, and the lewdnesses in the patter generally disguised from recognition by clean-minded people; the songs were simple and convivial:

> Champagne Charlie is my name!
> Champagne Charlie is my name!
> Good for any game at night, my boys!
> Good for any game at night, my boys!
> Champagne Charlie is my name!
> Champagne Charlie is my name!
> Good for any game at night, boys!
> Who'll come and join me in a spree?

Anyone who cannot repeat this after a first hearing would spend his money better on a baby's rattle than on a music-hall seat. It was sung by George Leybourne, who had a good voice, and liked to act the 'heavy swell' type of character. This glorification of the gentleman's minor vices always was popular, for in their own way the working classes could copy them. Southend and Blackpool, Wigan Wakes or Hampstead Heath were all hardy annuals in vulgar distraction. The ladies had their moments too:

> A smart and stylish girl you see,
> Belle of good society;
> Not too strict, but rather free,
> Yet as right as right can be!
> Never forward, never bold—
> Not too hot, and not too cold,
> And the very thing, I'm told,
> That in your arms you'd like to hold.
>
> Ta-ra-ra Boom-de-ay.
> (8 times.)

This chorus was even easier to learn than that of *Champagne Charlie*. Lottie Collins first sang it in 1891, and had to keep giving encores until she was exhausted; the public could never have enough.

> I'm a timid flower of innocence—
> Pa says that I have no sense,
> I'm one eternal big expense;
> But men say that I'm just immense.

Ere my verses I conclude,
I'd like it known and understood,
Though free as air I'm never rude,
I'm not so bad and not so good.

Ta-ra-ra Boom-de-ay.[1]
(8 times.)

Lottie's calculated mixture of sauce and innocence were of the music-hall. The inhibitions of romantic opera, and their opposite, the treacheries and the lurid crimes, were of the theatre and the opera house, with earnest reformation preached *ad nauseam* in scientific and literary institutes, singing-classes, temperance societies, and mission-halls. And just as vast capital transformed the early individualist music-halls into 'emporiums' of entertainment, so capital entered into the mission field. The gospel songs of Sankey and Moody were in the music-hall style, with easily learnt choruses. The gospel missions were in fact founded on the communal sing-song as were the music-halls. But the American Negro could not, or did not, follow in the wake of the white man to this extent; his spirituals are successors to a purer stock; wishful thinking, certainly, but sincere. The white niggers, again, are another line of development, with a good deal of sham morality in their sentiment, and though nigger minstrel troupes did appear in the music-halls, these were not their true home. The individual black-faced coon was another type, the most famous of them Eugene Stratton, who sang a song composed for him by Leslie Stuart:

It's de same old tale of de palpitating nigger ev'ry time, ev'ry time;
    It's de same old trouble of a coon,
    Dat wants to be married very soon;
It's de same old heart dat is longing for its lady ev'ry time, yes,
    ev'ry time.
But not de same gal, not de same gal.
    She is ma Lily, ma Lily, ma Lily gal!
She goes ev'ry sundown, yes, ev'ry sundown, calling' in de cattle
    up de mountain;
I go 'kase she wants me, yes, 'kase she wants me help her do de
    callin' an' de countin'.
She plays her music to call de lone lambs dat roam above,
    But I'm de black sheep and I'm waitin'
    For de signal of ma little lady love.

[1] Gramophone record, H.M.V. C 1592.

Chorus:

> She's ma lady love, she is ma dove, ma baby love;
> She's no gal for sittin' down to dream,
> She's the only queen Laguna knows;
> I know she likes me, I know she likes me,
> Bekase she says so;
> She is de Lily of Laguna, she is ma Lily and ma Rose.[1]

This was to the nineteenth-century music-hall what the pastoral songs were to the eighteenth-century pleasure gardens—a convention of entertainment. If we would really see the influence of America on the English music-hall we should look to the dance. There came into popularity in the very early years of the twentieth century the cake-walk—a vulgar dance done by two lines of dancers, men on one side, women on the other; each line advanced towards the opposite line, heads down, until nearly touching, then all bent their heads back and retreated in time to the music. The music itself had a distinctive rhythm, the rhythm of the phrase which comes oftenest in the most popular song for dancing the cake-walk:

> When we are married we'll have sausages for tea
> Sausages for tea
> Sausages for tea;
> When we are married we'll have sausages for tea
> Sausages for you and me.

It was sufficiently lucrative for managers and publishers to take a chance on a further development of the rhythmic force of syncopation, which came a few years later in Ragtime, and later still in Jazz. But we anticipate—these things had not arrived in their commercial varieties at the turn of the century, but a subtle change had come about in the character of popular songs.

The music-halls were always under attack from puritanical people and from the theatres. The Theatres Act of 1843 had allowed the lesser theatres to play legitimate drama (previously by law a monopoly of the patent theatres, Drury Lane and Covent Garden) but had insisted that meals or drinks should not be consumed in the auditorium. This distinguished the theatres from the song and supper rooms. But we have seen how Morton wanted to perform opera on a music-hall stage. The music-halls were rebels all along, trying to evade the law in order to expand their business. In the latter part of the nineteenth century they had become quite different

---

[1] Gramophone record, H.M.V. C 1592.

from the saloon-theatres from which they had sprung, and could put on any sort of stage show.[1] In particular they provided comedians who transformed the character of the English panto-mime in the theatres; at Drury Lane in particular. Pantomime had grown out of the Italian *comedia dell' arte*, with its traditional figures of Harlequin, Clown, Pantaloon, Columbine, etc. Harlequin had originally been the prime actor, but had given place to Clown. The greatest clown of the English stage was undoubtedly Joe Grimaldi, who has given his name 'Joey' to English circus clowns for all time. Grimaldi sang a song called *Hot Codlings*, and lived during the transitional stage of pantomime into its fairy-tale en-vironment. His most famous pantomime was *Mother Goose*. He wore the traditional clown's costume which we still see in the circus. Compare him with the most famous of modern English clowns, Charlie Chaplin, and we may then understand how the character changed. Chaplin is nearer to the 'little man' within us. No one man could do this, but one name stands out in the process —Dan Leno.

When Leno started his career, the 'heavy swell' was all the rage (he is still 'on the boards') and the satire of the music-hall comedians was directed against the puritanical laws which forbade Sunday entertainment, found fault with raw jokes, or libelled the working class. The latter might libel themselves, all in the course of fun, but they resented others doing so.

This is a consistent factor in popular entertainment. The lofty individualist sneers at the masses, and, though he was as welcome as Devilsdust in the old music-hall after he had bought his ticket, he had little chance of popularity there. The positive side of music-hall entertainment was that which glorified working-class virtues. A warm humanity cleansed a sordid society: 'Paddle your own canoe', 'A little of what you fancy does you good', 'All good pals and jolly good company'—the catchwords of the music-halls persist like the quotations from *Hamlet*. Meanness was a vice unpardonable—a mark of austerity mixed somehow with moral reform; denial of present mirth for an unsure future never was a philosophy for Chaffing Jacks or Dandy Dicks:

> Up and down the City Road,
> In and out the Eagle,
> That's the way the money goes;
> Pop goes the Weasel.

[1] Ballet was popular at the Alhambra in Leicester Square, and at the Empire.   For the social background read Sir Compton Mackenzie's novel *Carnival*.

That song comes from the London of Dickens, but here is one of modern Glasgow, sung by the late Will Fyfe:

> I belong to Glasgow,
>   Dear old Glasgow toun;
> There's only one thing wrong wi' Glasgow,
>   It's goin' roun' an' roun';
> I may be a common old working chap,
>   As anyone here can see,
> But when I get a skinful of beer on a Saturday,
>   Glasgow belongs to me.

The god is in him; he is uplifted as once his primitive ancestors were rendered divine by inebriation. This is the spirit of the music-halls—the uplifting of man as he is, not into something which he ought to be. The songs have it, and especially the choruses. More, it is in the very architecture of the 'halls'. Their steel girders are hidden behind plaster, moulded in voluptuous curves and embellished with a wealth of ornament. It might well be called vulgar, for this is the term that once was applied to baroque architecture, and a comparison of Wren's theatre in Dorset Garden [1] with the interior of the Tower Ballroom at Blackpool illustrates the similarity of taste. Both were aggrandizements of their environments. We may even follow the trend of taste into the next period, and see in the Blackpool illustration how the streamlining of our own age has imposed itself on this Industrial Revolutionary Baroque in the adaptation of the stage to modern requirements, but we should also note the grille above the proscenium arch made for the output end of the synthetic organ (the console is on stage) and observe that this is in the same position as Wren's music-room in the illustration from Elkanah Settle's *Empress of Morocco*. The age of the music-halls was the age of a new baroque at a time when artists sneered at that style of art.

But we should recollect that Dryden spoke of 'heroic' verse, and Sir James Thornhill of 'heroic history painting' when they meant what we call baroque. Where is the heroic in the Industrial Revolutionary Baroque?

It is right in the picture. The common man was made the hero—put on a pedestal in his Sunday best just as the industrialists in their frock-coats were put on pedestals in their market-places, to gaze

[1] See plate facing page 93.

benevolently on town halls and bus queues. Jenny Hill used to sing a song about a man in his Sunday best:

> Oh, 'Arry, what 'Arry,
> There you are then, 'Arry.
> I say, 'Arry!
>   By jove! you are a don!
> Oh! 'Arry! 'Arry!
> There you are then, 'Arry!
> Where are you going on Sunday, 'Arry,
>   Now you've got 'em on?

A working man often felt out of countenance in a new suit, but he could be reconciled:

> 'Arry likes a jolly good joke;
>   Quite right 'Arry.
> 'Arry won't mind the fun that I spoke;
>   What say, 'Arry?
> The 'upper ten' may jeer and say
>   What 'cads' the 'Arries are;
> But the 'Arries *work* and *pay their way*
>   While doing the La-di-da.

This virtue of independence through earning power was a great resource to the working man. One finds it well expressed in the play by Stanley Houghton, *Hindle Wakes*, when the erring daughter gets turned out. In the old tragedy she would have wept, but the Lancashire girl says: 'I've got trade i' my fingers, an' as long as theer's mills i' Lancashire I shall get along somehow'.

Why should the 'Arries and the 'Arriets not have thought themselves the salt of the earth? The middle classes did, and the aristocracy. It is part of human nature to think well of oneself; all classes combined in Jingoism:

> We don't want to fight, but, by Jingo, if we do,
> We've got the ships, we've got the men, we've got the money too.

This song—by G. W. Hunt—was made to cash in on the Russo-Turkish situation of 1887; it was thrown into prominence by the Liberals, who accused Disraeli's party of excessive bellicosity. The Imperialists were dubbed 'Jingoists' and a new word came into currency. The Jingoistic period was short but lively, ending with the defeat of the Unionists in 1906. It had its peak in the Boer War, when the largest expeditionary force ever to leave Britain up to that time was sent out, to the strains of *Good-bye, Dolly, I must leave you.*

It served its turn, and has worn better than Kipling and Sullivan's *Absent-Minded Beggar* which was used to raise funds (in the name of charity) to help carry on the war. The best of the martial songs of that time, however, is *Soldiers of the Queen,* in which the pageantry of the old Queen's jubilee is well reflected. These songs catch the spirit of the time, but have no depth of thought. If we would have ideas we should seek them in parodies of music-hall songs, of which there was—and is—a never-ending stream. In fact, the politicians rarely had any originality in tunes; their best practice was that of the balladeers, to take a tune already popular and tack on to it the words which suited their policy. When the music-hall singer took to politics he rarely made the mistake of pleading an unpopular cause; his blurb was for the edification of the mob. Women's rights we have already seen disputed,[1] but it needs little imagination to guess that when the final phase of the fight for these was in progress, the comedians were on the side of law and order:

> Put me upon an island where the girls are few;
> Put me among the most ferocious lions in the zoo;
> You can put me upon a treadmill and I'll never, never fret,
> But for pity's sake, don't put me near a suffragette.

The unthinking public can be very cruel in its humour. It is at its best, however, when in touch with low-life problems which could happen to anyone. The brokers' men in the pantomime are an example; Baron Hardupp and the Ugly Sisters in the Cinderella story are others. There is the episode of the 'midnight flit' (a common enough occurrence in the early years of this century) which Arnold Bennett put into his novel *The Card,* and its comic counterpart which used to be sung by Marie Lloyd.

> My old man said 'Follow the van,
>   And don't dilly-dally on the way.'
> Off went the cart with the home packed in it;
>   I walked behind with my old cock linnet.

---

[1] See Chapter IX for Mrs Grote's opinion.

But I dillied and dallied, dallied and dillied,
  Lost the van and don't know where to roam.
I stopped on the way to have the old half-quartern
  And I can't find my way home.

Marie was perhaps the greatest of them all, though she never
knew where to draw the blue line, and is said to have confounded
a bench of magistrates on one occasion by asking them if they
thought Lord Tennyson a proper poet, and then to have quoted to
them in her inimitable style *Come into the garden, Maud*. Her end was
in character. She collapsed on the stage while singing *One of the
Ruins which Cromwell Knocked about a bit*, and died soon after.

Already, however, a challenge to the cheerful conviviality of the
music-hall song was being made. In 1911 a new tune by Irving Berlin
was heard, *Alexander's Ragtime Band*. This used syncopated features
which had been heard in the cake-walk, but more intensively.
The orchestration for popular consumption was more vigorous
than anything previously heard in this type of entertainment and
the words glorified not the common man, nor played on his everyday humours, but glorified the music of Irving Berlin. The old
chorus songs had been propaganda for a way of life; ragtime was
propaganda for ragtime. Business acumen was in charge as never
before. The titles of the songs are significant: *Everybody's Doing it*
(Ragtime, of course), *Ragtime Cowboy Joe, Hitchy-coo*:

Oh, you should ought to hear 'em sing,
It's the cutest little thing,
With the cutest little swing,
  Hitchy-coo, hitchy-coo, hitchy-coo, hitchy-coo.

They linked up with coon songs and songs about the American
South, so using the not yet sour milk of Stephen Foster and Leslie
Stuart to suckle the new babe. Old Uncle Joe with his banjo kept
bobbing up, and there were soon old homes in Carolina, Texas,
Maryland—anywhere—as well as the original old one in Kentucky.
Trombones *portamentoed* up from dominant to tonic before a new
phrase, and the trap drummer (often a Negro) clowned across the
break. They worked to the Marxist theory (though they did not own
it) that all art is propaganda, and this art was propaganda for itself!

The revolution was upon us. A new style was sold to us. It is
still with us, though pepped up and remodelled to suit the experts.
Undoubtedly these boys know their stuff in music, but something
nevertheless is lacking. The Ragtime musician lost touch with God.

XIV. DEUS EX MACHINA?

WHAT A WEALTH of significance there is in that one song—
Land of Hope and Glory! After fifty years, with an empire crumbling
about us, we still sing on national occasions:

> Wider still and wider
>   Shall thy bounds be set;
> God, who made thee mighty,
>   Make thee mightier yet.

In what environment does this song really belong; the coronation
service or the Empire Music Hall in Leicester Square, opened in
1884 and demolished after the first world war? We know that the
words were written for a coronation and the tune for a march
dedicated to an amateur conductor in Liverpool—A. E. Rodewald;
if the music-halls come into the picture it is because they were in
some way not divorced from national aspirations. Consider, then,
the character of the monarchy to which Edward VII succeeded.
As W. S. Gilbert wrote: [1]

> Great Britain is that monarchy sublime,
> To which some add (but others do not) Ireland.

We were a monarchy but not a nation in the accepted sense.
Nationalism implies a union of the state with a community having
its own traditional culture. There are in Great Britain at least three
national traditions—Irish, Scottish, Welsh, and in England a freer
mixture of influences ranging from the Northern Counties to Celtic
Cornwall, and these split again by the Industrial Revolution, which
brought Victorian 'progress' to the towns and did much to im-
poverish the agricultural areas by importing cheap food from
abroad. All these were represented in parliament, and to all these,
and those in the innumerable dominions overseas, the king dedicated
himself in a Coronation Service which is in fact an elaboration of
the Communion Service of the Church of England. Other nations
gaining power would try to mix their nationalism with imperialism,

---

[1] *Utopia Limited*, Finale.

making Africans into good Germans or good Frenchmen, with results which we know. For a time—say from 1874 to 1906—Britain tried to mix nationalism and imperialism, but the idea had no basis in fact, for there is no British nation.

The reaction against this was in the work of the Folk Song Society, with which we are not concerned in these pages.[1] It was more than a reaction against a sham conception of nationality, however; it was a reaction against industrialism, which was herding people together in ugly towns and subjecting them to mass rule and propaganda. Among such people *Land of Hope and Glory* was accepted without question as a national song.

By the time of the election of 1906, however, the cause of Joseph Chamberlain was in decline, and the verses of Kipling—who after all made his protest in the *Recessional*—are today little revered; but Elgar's song [2] lives on because of its heroic tune, just as *God Save the King* lived on after the Stuarts had given way to the Hanoverians on the throne of Britain. At the opposite pole to *God Save the Queen* today is *The Red Flag*, the words of which were written by Jim Connell and are sung now to a German tune *Der Tannenbaum*. To this same tune James Ryder Randall of Baltimore wrote the patriotic song *Maryland, my Maryland*, to aid the cause of the Southern States in 1861. The fact is that there is nothing about these 'national' tunes of a distinctive national character; all come within the scope of a general culture springing from Western civilization.

It follows, therefore, that songs so broadly based can command a wide acceptance, and, given the necessary capital and means of distribution, a monster market can be opened up in which to sell them. Such has been the fate of popular entertainment throughout the twentieth century.

Sweet are the uses of advertisement, but every advertiser knows that he can only make popular a product which has in it something which the public wants. Popularity is a two-way traffic in which the safety beacons are well-worn clichés like the comic mother-in-law, the idealization of one's better qualities—love of friends and love of country—fear of danger and especially of death, or (most potent of all) association of oneself with God. The latter is a high stake for which to play, but the reward is great if it can be won. 'God, who made thee mighty, make thee mightier yet'; or

---

[1] See R. Nettel, *Sing a Song of England* (1954). Note that the word 'English' did not appear in the title of the original Folk Song Society.
[2] The verses of *Land of Hope and Glory* are by A. C. Benson.

on a lower plane, 'God, who took away my eyes, that my soul might see'.

Here we come to grips with a moral problem in popular songs. The sentiments may be thin, or even ridiculous, as in the ballad of *The Blind Ploughman*:

> Set my hands upon the plough,
> My feet upon the sod;
> Turn my face towards the east
> And thanks be to God.

It is unlikely that a blind man could drive a straight furrow with the best horses in the world, and certainly the east has nothing to do with ploughing, but all the songs are not materially accurate in this way—they appeal to some deep sense of rightness inside us, and an easy-flowing tune makes the whole thing memorable. A song may be about love, sorrow, friendship, danger, or the ruling monarch, and in every case God can be naturally associated with the theme. The clever lyric-writer holds God in check, as a good composer holds back his trombones, until the climax. The best rough test of a bad song, as Frank Howes pointed out in the nineteen-twenties, is God in the last line.[1] One need not be a churchgoer to be captivated by this device; in fact the most interesting thing is that so many people claiming to be irreligious give themselves away by applause or even tears at the end of such a song.

The type of song in which this device was most practised was known as the royalty ballad. The composer and lyric-writer might get royalties on every copy sold, but more often the term referred to the practice of paying a royalty to a famous singer to feature it in his programmes. Ballad concerts were highly respectable in the early part of the twentieth century, but the word 'ballad' now meant the innocuous royalty ballad and not the ballad about topical events which had earlier coaxed the pennies from the pockets of semi-illiterate working men. As time went on there came into being the Performing Rights Society, which was able to collect royalties for performances of songs and distribute these among copyright owners; so the machine was geared to meet a coming situation; when radio became general, sales of songs in published form fell off, but funds came in from performance rights. The trick of paying performers to feature songs which needed to be made known then ran into a

[1] Frank Howes, *The Borderland of Music and Psychology* (1926).

devious channel called 'song plugging', and if you ask why the word 'plug', which means 'to stop up', should be applied to opening up a channel of approach, the reply is that the plug inserted into an electrical circuit opens up that circuit (or channel) into the further one plugged into it.[1] We are moving with the times!

This, then, is the thought of the new age, sufficient at least to satisfy our curiosity without destroying our faith in the slogan (plugged, of course) that 'the customer is always right'. Strange to say, the principle is not so dishonest as it may appear, for it is wellnigh impossible for a composer to carry conviction if he does not believe in his theme, and, just as the world is made up of men who respond to God in the last line, there are men whose minds work naturally in this way, and they are neither fools nor dishonest men. One of the most successful lyric-writers was F. E. Weatherly, an eminent barrister. Eric Coates has described him well in his autobiography,[2] one side of his desk piled with song-lyrics and the other with legal documents. These were the two ways in which Weatherly's mind functioned; Coates guessed as much and Weatherly confirmed it:

I was right in both cases, for during the conversation which followed he told me he wrote poems while working out difficult problems of law.[3]

When reading his verses to you he would adopt a listening attitude and croon his lines in a most extraordinary manner. If the words were particularly moving he would frequently break down with emotion and have to wait until he could compose himself sufficiently to continue.

His knack of painting pictures with his poems ('word pictures' he called them) was uncanny, for with a few delicately chosen words he could conjure up a scene which it would have taken anyone else a whole page to describe.[4]

As for composers, there were Wilfrid Sanderson, Guy d'Hardelot, Haydn Wood, Teresa de Riego, and of course Coates himself. They all had or have a gift for well-turned and easily singable melody; but, more than this, the melody satisfies so completely that it disarms criticism; the tunes live on when their detractors' opinions are forgotten.

[1] 'Circuit' is in the wired track of an electric current, 'channel' a frequency in the ether.
[2] Eric Coates, *Suite in Four Movements* (1953).
[3] Ibid., p. 118.
[4] Ibid., p. 118.

Nevertheless there are rewards for higher standards of art not always appreciated. We should bear in mind when studying the relative popularity of music that there are compositions like Puccini's opera *Madama Butterfly*, which continue in the repertory without having the spectacular distinction of a long run. But the plot of *Madama Butterfly* comes from a musical comedy called *The Geisha*, which had a long run in the 'nineties; its best-known song was *Chin-chin Chinaman, muchee muchee sad*. It appealed to a facile audience, had its wave of popularity, made its considerable profit, and is remembered now as a period piece. The total attendances at *Madama Butterfly* must be greatly in excess of those at *The Geisha*, reckoned over the last half-century, but the profits are nothing like the same. Judged by commercial standards *The Geisha* was the greater success; judged by staying-power, *Madama Butterfly* is an easy winner. The division of opinion on the merits of such music is largely dependent on opposing standards of judgment, and we carry on our backs that Old Man of the utilitarian philosophies of the nineteenth century, 'The greatest happiness of the greatest number.'

It all depends on the meaning of happiness, and how it is to be measured. In terms of profit and loss we have distributed more happiness if we have sold the music to a wider audience, and popular art is mostly distributed for money. The machine, then, must be geared to speed up delivery; the product itself stream-lined.

Such is the principle. But remember that in an age of technical efficiency such as ours the most attractive presentation of the generally acceptable object is the one which will capture the market. The old composers of musical comedy—Rubens, Lionel Monckton, and their kind—were superior in their day. Later composers, like Jerome Kern, Ivor Novello, and Irving Berlin, won success by superior presentation. Just as criticism will find the flaws in a pretentious composition it will find the flaws in a simple one. Everyone knows *It's a Long Way to Tipperary*, because it was given publicity as a song sung by the British troops in the first world war. It came out, however, in 1912, had its run of popularity, but its sales had already declined when the war broke out. It then had a second chance,[1] but went down before the onslaught of such new songs as Ivor Novello's *Keep the Home Fires Burning*.[2] The words of

---

[1] Among the troops *Tipperary* lost favour, but entertainers at home stuck to it because their audiences did not know this.

[2] Gramophone record, H.M.V. C 4080.

H

Tipperary are by a cripple, Harry Williams, son of a Warwickshire innkeeper, and the tune by Jack Judge, of Oldbury, in the Black Country—both of them poor men. Ivor Novello wrote the other song at the request of his mother, Clara Novello Davies, a member of a famous musical family. She felt that *Tipperary* was becoming a bore after several months' reiteration—which it was; but why?

The flaw lies in the tune of *Tipperary*; the repetition of the first line of the melody in line three is good, but its repetition in line five is redundant. That error of judgment killed a tune twice! There is more repetition in Ivor Novello's tune, but it is varied in pitch, becoming not mere repetition but melodic imitation at different levels; the return to the original phrase in line five is acceptable. As for the third hit song of the first world war, *Pack up Your Troubles in your old Kitbag*, this was American, the words by George Asaf and the tune by Felix Powell; it will be noted that the initial musical phrase, though not a plagiarism, is very close to the first phrase of *Tipperary*.

The songs we have quoted—*Tipperary*, *Keep the Home Fires Burning*, and *Pack up your Troubles*—were all music-hall songs which had the effect of cheering up people in a time of strain. They went along with the songs of character-comedians who idealized the sentiments of the poor, turned topsyturvy their worries, or appealed through a familiar turn of tune. Harry Lauder's song *The Wedding of Sandy MacNab* has a chorus almost entirely pentatonic—and what Scotsman does not feel he is at home with his five-note scale? The comedian Fred Karno became, in the first world war, the hero of a soldiers' song which is still to be heard in the army, though the men now serving never saw him. The men in *Fred Karno's Army* represented the limit of inefficiency, but muddled through:

> We are Fred Karno's army,
>   Fred Karno's infantree;
> We cannot fight, we cannot shoot,
>   So what damn good are we?
> But when we get to Berlin
>   The Kaiser he will say: [1]
>   Hoch, hoch, mein Gott,
>   Vot a bloody fine lot,
>   Fred Karno's infantry!'

[1] In the second world war (1939-45) they changed 'The Kaiser' to 'Old Hitler'.

At home the pubs ran out of stock. There was joking at a situation which had not happened before in this country:

> We used to gather at the Old Dun Cow,
>> But the Old Dun Cow,
>> She's done for now;
> Got no beer, got no gin,
> And next week they're going to have the brokers in;
> So now we gather at the Fountain,
>> Each night at half-past nine,
>>> And take a cup,
>>> And drink it up,
> For the sake of auld lang syne.

It is a fact that when they had to do without beer men learnt more about teetotalism than all the moralists of the nineteenth century had taught them. In civilian life it had been a common sight to see drunken men helpless in the gutters on Saturday nights before the war; after the war this offence was practically unknown except in some of the ports.

This effect of a beer shortage was remarkable, especially when we consider what happened in America during the period of the Prohibition Laws. There, an illicit trade in booze caught the whole of great cities in a vicious grip, and through the speak-easies went a strain of art bred in the brothels of the transport centres in the U.S.A., but now revised for big city titillation; it was called jazz.

Jazz arrived in Chicago before the passing of the Prohibition Laws, and it was there, in 1915, that the word 'jazz' was applied to Tom Brown's Band from Dixieland.[1] It was apparently first used in derision by Brown's rivals, for in Chicago—at any rate at that time—jazz was a slang term for the motions of copulation. This is but one of many theories in etymology attached to this form of music; but the very confusion of facts is interesting, for while we may believe easily enough that history in the past has been corrupted at the orders of tyrannical rulers who were in a position to control what was written, the history of jazz has been played out in the public eye within the lifetime of people living, yet it is practically impossible to get at the truth of it. Certainly it was introduced into Chicago from New Orleans and was associated with public dancing.

---

[1] This band came to London in 1919 and appeared at the Hippodrome in de Courville's revue *Joy Bells*. They played also at Martan's Club, Reclar's Club, and Hammersmith Palais de Danse.

Certainly it was associated with public dancing in Britain from the year 1918. I myself remember seeing in an illustrated paper a photograph of an actress whose name I have now forgotten, but who was described as showing 'how the fox trots and the pigeon walks'; the pigeon-walk cannot have caught on with the public, but the foxtrot did. This, like jazz music, hailed from the U.S.A., being, according to the *Dancing Times* of January 1915, 'a nerve wrecking [*sic*] movement arranged by a vaudeville artist named Fox'. The Oxford English Dictionary is more cautious, but states that it is thought to have been the invention of a dancing-master named Fox. The 'Jazz, or 1919 Foxtrot' is also described in that dictionary, which mentions also that there are Straight Jazz, Side Jazz, and Jazz Roll. Under the heading *Jazz*, we may read:

(Origin unknown; generally thought to be Negro). A kind of Ragtime dance (three steps to four musical beats) introduced from the United States to Europe towards the end of 1918. Hence, the kind of music to which this is danced, jazz music; often loosely applied to any syncopated dance music.

This is an example of how even the most erudite of Britishers can turn a fact topsyturvy, for there is little doubt that the music came before the dance was invented, and probably the word 'jazz' was loosely applied to any irregular oscillatory motion, be it copulation, a drunken gait, or syncopation of the particular sort employed in jazz music. This syncopation is anticipatory—i.e. striking a note *before* the beat on which it would normally arrive—and is combined with a complication essentially polyrhythmic, wherein a straight line of eight beats is set against eight beats arranged in two groups of three and a two (thus, there are three variations commonly employed against the straight eight—3+3+2; 3+2+3; 2+3+3, but the first of these is most used). An interesting feature is the figure used so much in the earlier cake-walk, for this persists in jazz and became known in the late 'twenties as the 'Charleston' rhythm! But what's in a name?

As regards the dance in Britain with which this syncopation was mostly associated, I am authoritatively informed [1] that:

At this time and for some years afterwards there was a great variety of steps in the Foxtrot which were taken from other dances, such as the Maxixe and the Tango. . . . At a meeting of teachers and band-leaders in

---

[1] By A. H. Franks, managing editor of the *Dancing Times*, 17 August 1955.

October 1924 it was agreed that at this time there were essentially two different kinds of Foxtrot in existence [1]—one suitable for music at a fast tempo and the other at a tempo of 44 to 46 bars a minute. It was then agreed that the one suitable for the faster tempo should be entitled either Quick Step or Quick Time Foxtrot. For some time the title Quick Time Foxtrot remained in vogue, but after the advent of the Charleston and the influence of that dance on the Quick Time Foxtrot, this dance became known as the Quickstep.

In so far as he was required to provide music for dancing teachers, the jazz musician was a servant of the crowd, but servility is actually the antithesis of all that jazz stands for. Jazz is rebellious, and individually so to the true jazz player:

Extemporization is, and always will be, the basis of true jazz. The soloist has, or should have, something to say, and he uses the theme of a number as his starting-point. Jazz is a doctrine of self-expression. This self-expression must come from the heart and not from the head if it is to be true jazz. 'Think' music is not real music—merely a demonstration of man's ability to be clever.

Complicated orchestrations are all very well when a band has to dress up Tin Pan Alley tripe for the benefit of the Great (and Dumb) British and/or American public. Otherwise a mere framework of chords and figures is all that is necessary to back up the soloists. Where hot team work is scored this is merely a logical development of single line extemporization. . . . Pretentious orchestrations and alleged 'New Music' are just so much hooey, and their perpetrators know it.[2]

Down with logic! Down with 'think'! Down with the public! It is easy to see the dichotomy in this propaganda, for nobody thinks less than a great 'dumb' public; but there is no rational antidote; this anti-social vein is but the counterpart of the wish for self-assertion.

This 'modernism' is as old as history. It is quite correct to say that jazz is based on a very old tradition of performance, known in folk music but never taught in the academies of Western music culture. Musicologists call it heterophony. It consists of playing a known tune with individual variations, in association with other players who also embellish the music according to their own ideas. The effect is invariably original, and can be excellent of its type when

---

[1] The types previously mentioned had evidently fallen into disuse.
[2] Jeff Aldam, in *Swing Music*, April 1935.

done by players who can enter into the communal spirit of the group and who also have a good training in the oral tradition to which the style belongs. This is performers' music, and with practice gets more and more interesting to the players and more and more complex to the uninitiated listener. By the normal processes of development 'hot' jazz has, under competition from specialist players, become a rarefied art, with adherents who look down on the taste of the common man with as much disdain as any other resident in a cultural ivory tower. There is no purist so unrelenting as a jazz style purist.

His, however, is not popular music. It is music for the few. We are concerned with the workaday world, and this means the association of jazz rhythms with the dance. Foxtrot influence we have already noted. By 1927 a dance called the Charleston had come into vogue,[1] the distinctive feature in which was a side-kick from the knees. Ladies' dresses were now worn short; the knees could be seen beneath an outdoor dress for the first time in civilized history. Hail emancipation! It was not unladylike to smoke, work for money, drink in public bars—cocktails came in fashion—or cast one's vote. The reforms for which so many blue-stockings had fought in the Victorian and Edwardian periods were now won. Ladies had neither breasts nor hips, corsets were irrelevant to a stove-pipe figure,[2] God and Mrs Grundy equally irrelevant to a girl who could buy contraceptives at any chemists and cocaine (at a price) from some Mayfair bootlegger. But above all it was a dancing age: the joke of the town was a definition of syncopation as 'an irregular movement from bar to bar'. The spirit of the 'Bright Young Things' is nowhere better displayed than in a song from Noel Coward's *This Year of Grace*.

> Dance, dance, dance, little lady,
> Youth is fleeting to the rhythm beating
>   in your mind;
> Dance, dance, dance, little lady,
> So obsessed with second-best, no rest
>   you'll ever find.

Noel Coward, who wrote the music and verses of the above, is master of every device known to the theatre. Lady Blessington's *Belle of the Season* would have had to change her views to win a

---

[1] First found in U.S.A. in 1923.
[2] But not for long; a stove-pipe type arrived!

husband in 1928, and who can say the result would not have been better? The young lady of 1928 had read something at any rate of a psychology which taught that behind every prudery there stands an obscenity. Alas, that this wisdom could not be rewarded with a more hopeful outlook on life. Coward's *Cavalcade* came in 1932, only to end on this note:

> Blues, Twentieth Century Blues, are getting me down.
> Who's escaped those weary Twentieth Century Blues?
> Why, if there's a God in the sky, why shouldn't he grin?
> High above this dreary Twentieth Century din.

The age to which this relates passed, but *Cavalcade* kept its popularity in a film version. As for *Twentieth Century Blues*, the purists of jazz style hate it worse than the patrons of good drama. Blues originally were improvised and uninhibited; during the repetition of the first line the singer thinks up a third:

> You can take me, baby, put me in your big brass bed;
> You can take me, baby, put me in your big brass bed;
> Go ridin' me, baby, till my face turns cherry-red.

This was in the true jazz tradition, from the underworld of New Orleans where sex was often a disappointment but never an embarrassment. It was not, however, the spirit of the English theatre, where conventional morality still boosted the dividends paid to a civilization in decline.

Jazz was truly an American product and has never been properly assimilated by the British. Only the experts can do justice to it. The common man wants his jazz watered down, and when he takes matters into his own hands his line of development in Britain is quite different from that of the residents of 'Anderson's County'.[1]

In case this statement should raise a scholarly eyebrow we should point out that there is plenty of evidence still to be seen that the Welsh and English can, in times of adversity probably as hard as those by which the originators of jazz were oppressed, strike out on their own. The year 1926 saw the miners of Great Britain locked out of their jobs until they accepted lower wages. This was the year of the General Strike, when the most powerful trade unions struck work in an effort to assist the miners to obtain a fair deal. The

---

[1] Anderson kept the biggest saloon in the dockside district of New Orleans, into which the disreputable section of the population was forced by a municipal effort to clean up the morals of the city. In the slums around the docks, therefore, jazz flourished.

strike failed, and with it the only serious threat of Syndicalism in Britain. We are concerned not with the rights and wrongs of capital and labour, however, but with a cultural offspring of the year 1926.

In the South Wales coal-field during the troubles of 1926 a group of miners, with nothing but time on their hands, formed themselves into a band. The instruments they used were called in the musical trade 'kazoos' and by the miners themselves 'bazoukas'. They were metal tubes with a side-vent, and operated on the comb-and-paper vibratory system. Anyone could hum a tune into a kazoo and get results. To these they added drums and other percussive instruments—either home-made or loaned from boys' brigades—and the band was complete. There was nothing like it elsewhere. Their womenfolk made fancy costumes for the bandsmen—again like nothing to be seen elsewhere—and with a splendour befitting the finale of a Drury Lane pantomime these men paraded the stricken area in which they lived, bringing a splash of glory into an apparently doomed community. The songs they played were the popular songs of the day. A new line of folk-culture was making a beginning.

They called these bands 'jazz bands' for want of a better name. Jazz they were not, but the word 'jazz' had already been made to cover so many sins that it had little claim to distinction in 1926. (The jazz 'purists' came later.) The craze spread, and 'carnival bands'[1] came out all over the Rhondda area—Oriental, Ruritanian, Futurist, Arabian, military, or just vaguely musical comedy. The craze did not die out with the ending of the lock-out, but spread to the industrial midlands and even into Lancashire. Every band was original in its choice of costume and interpretation of the music on the march, or in dance movements in set displays. They found people to offer prizes, and organized themselves in leagues, like football teams, to compete for these prizes. The proceeds collected from spectators were given to local charities. Throughout the nineteen-thirties such bands were conspicuous in the areas we have mentioned, but they never penetrated to London or the southern English counties.[2]

No government or large industrial concern encouraged them, but the various mayors' charities committees soon saw the value of these attractions for their purpose, and undoubtedly the industrial

---

[1] The distinction between 'jazz' and 'carnival' is significant. 'Carnival' bands had a scheme in their costumery while 'jazz' bands were a medley.

[2] Some of the more famous of them now receive engagements with South Coast holiday resorts (1955).

districts during the great depression of those years were the better for them. Down the streets moved the bands, headed by a resplendent figure, followed by his men with the instruments, and then a long train of girls in costume, marching smartly in white rubber shoes with a quick step the Guards could not have kept up. The drums rolled, the cymbals clashed, and the kazoos buzzed:

> There's a good time coming, be it ever so far away,
> That's what I says to myself, says I, jolly good luck, hooray!

Look closely at the face of the leader and as likely as not you would see the yellow complexion of one who had for years seen more dinner-times than dinners. In 1933 twenty-two per cent of the working population were unemployed, and these were not spread evenly over the whole country but were most numerous in the districts of the heavy industries. Most men in the 'jazz bands' were 'on the dole'.

This was one reaction to the difficulties of the times; the other was communism, a creed not in the British socialist tradition, but now for the first time adopted by many who had lost faith in their old leaders. From the U.S.A. also came the same two popular reactions; on the one hand the spectacular film—now allied to sound—with glamorous singers and luscious harmonies all dolled up in the richest tone-colours available in a symphony orchestra, and at the other extreme a song lamenting the distress of the down-and-out in a land where financiers had for long regarded a boom-and-bust economy as divinely ordained:

> Once I built a tower to the sun,
> Bricks and rivets and lime;
> Once I built a tower—now it's done—
> Buddy, can you spare a dime?

It was in the nature of the American popular song to boom or bust. Either it attained to the swiftest means of escape or descended to a blue moan. It is useless to claim that we in Britain were able to resist these influences, but we never gave in completely to them. When we philosophized, cheerfulness would keep breaking in, for, as the working classes put it: 'It's being so cheerful as keeps you going'. The most popular gramophone records sold in the industrial areas during the slump were not of hot jazz but of a Yorkshire comedian named Sandy Powell. Sandy did character sketches

* H

in a well-worn path; *Sandy the Policeman* and *Sandy the Doctor*
were characters as screamingly incompetent as *Fred Karno's Army*,
but the biggest winner of all was *Sandy on the Dole*.[1]

> I'm signing on—signing on—
> Every morning you can see me signing on,
> And when the roll is called up yonder
> And from loving friends I've gone,
> You will find me at the counter signing on.

By some means the degradation of unemployment relief had
became a joke. The topsyturvy British were at it again, somehow
expecting to muddle through.

Muddling through had brought us to a crisis in 1931, when the
pound sterling became a scrap of paper, and according to expert
opinion this ought to have been the end of us. On the night that the
news was broadcast, however, the radio kept us going with a spate
of good cheer from a dance band. It was an American song popular
at the time:

> Give yourself a pat on the back,
> Pat on the back, pat on the back,
> And say to yourself,
> 'Here's jolly good health,
> We've had a good day today.'

This song came on with such persistence that we might have
accused the B.B.C. of 'plugging' it, but for the fact that the B.B.C.
had denounced that shameful practice. It must, then, have been
quite by accident that this song kept bouncing into the general
gloom on that particular night! Whether it complied with the topsyturvy genius of the British or the high seriousness of the propa-
gandists is perhaps irrelevant, for the truth is that nobody believed
it; nor was it the sort of fiction we enjoyed.

Propaganda we suspect. Advertising is another matter. We know
that somebody is persuading us to buy an article because he wants
our money, and we like being courted. Advertising is essential to
full production in a machine age—a part of our way of life. Meanwhile the machine runs faster and faster, for its very existence
depends on increased production.

This works two ways; for if the machine is made to feed the

---

[1] Very well then—the *second* biggest winner on the theme of industrial materialism,
the other being Charles Chaplin's film *Modern Times*.

common man, the common man is made to feed the machine. Increased production means a streamlining of work into simpler and simpler operations, and the process is soul-destroying. Time-and-motion-study cuts out every action not absolutely essential, and men are treated like automatons. But men are not machines. They get bored with mechanical efficiency—irritable; they make mistakes, go slower at the job, and then what happens? 'Music', say the philosophers 'has no useful purpose whatever.' But not so to an industrial psychologist. He switches on pleasant tunes half-way through the working shift, and what he calls 'morale' improves. The boredom ceases, work goes on apace.[1] This is the materialist conception of music. Musicians despise it; some employers hate it, but can they stop it? Not they. The workers insist on having their musical anodyne.

'Music has no useful purpose whatever.' It depends, of course, on what we call music. Bach's *Goldberg Variations*, Beethoven's *Variations on a Theme of Diabelli*, Brahms's *Variations on a Theme of Haydn*, Vaughan Williams's *Fantasia on a Theme of Thomas Tallis*, none of these need any justification but themselves. They serve no material master. Turned on for 'Music While You Work' they would ruin the job. So, too, would hot jazz, which is either pure music or a rhythmic aphrodisiac. Only a succession of clichés preserves from boredom the slaves of the endless belt. If the work becomes interesting the need for music is less; a skilled craftsman ignores it, a manager finds it an annoyance. In a materialist environment bad music is as ever-present as death on the roads.

Yet popular music is not, fortunately, so circumscribed. If this sort of thing goes on during working hours, the entertainment most enjoyed in factories in the lunch-hour is varied, with the tastes of the old music-halls still in evidence. Some of the workers like to make their own entertainment, and what they like to do themselves is better for our purpose than what they draw from the supply-line. We have seen how, in the worst years of the economic depression, men went so far as to invent a recreation of their own in their carnival bands, and heartlessly preferred *Sandy on the Dole* to Greenwood's play *Love on the Dole* (which was a London success but in the Provinces was attended for the sake of the swear-words). So the old familiar music-hall tradition went on in those grey years in the person of Gracie Fields, who sang like the Lancashire lass she was

---

[1] An opposite—i.e. depressing—effect might here be mentioned: Dr Goebbels 'plugged' *I'm dancing with tears in my eyes* to British troops in the early part of the second world war.

about *The Biggest Aspidistra in the World*, or *I took my Harp to a Party* (both of which smack very strongly of the nineteenth century) or the warmest-hearted sentiment of all time:

> Sally, Sally, pride of our alley,
> You're more than the whole world to me.

Meanwhile the propaganda machine did its worst in Germany, and for a second time in the twentieth century the poor foolish British had to demonstrate that they did not know when they were beaten.

When the R.A.F. waited for the Messerschmitts to appear in the Battle of Britain they sang sardonically:

> 'They'll be flying in formation when they come,'

or the commonest song of all:

> Bless 'em all, bless 'em all;
> The long and the short and the tall.
> Bless all the sergeants and W.O. ones,
> Bless all the corporals and their bastard sons,
> For we're saying goodbye to 'em all,
> As back to our billets we crawl;
> You'll get no promotion this side of the ocean,
> So cheer up, my lads, bless 'em all.

John Moore, who served in the Fleet Air Arm, records [1] that his own service sang a parody of *The Mountains of Mourne* with a grim last line:

> When a poor bloody pilot goes down in the sea.

And he mentions also the Navy's favourite: sung as they sailed towards Normandy on D-day:

> I don't want to join the Navy!
> I don't want to go to sea!
>   I'd rather muck around
>   Piccadilly underground
> Living on the earnings of
> A high-born ladee!

[1] *In the Season of the Year* (1954).

All of which suggest that the British are a cowardly crew, if you don't know the British. The truth is, they don't like boasting about their deeds, so they sing about their follies:

> Roll me over in the clover,
> Roll me over, turn me down and do it again.

W. S. Gilbert had the right idea:

> To lay aloft in a howling wind
>   May tickle a landsman's taste,
> But the happiest hour a sailor sees
>   Is when he's down
>   In an inland town
> With his Nancy on his knees,
>   And his arm around her waist.

It should, however, be mentioned that the rural singers in the past had no shame in singing about themselves and their occupations. There are many fine folk-songs about jolly ploughmen, carters, sheep-shearers, or just farmers' boys, and if the girl in the modern factory fails to sing about her job the reason is obvious—her job is nothing to sing about; it bores her; the less intelligent she is, the more adaptable to her task. But there are nevertheless industrial songs to be heard; they do not tell of the rolling belt, but here is one about the rolling truck:

> You may sing of your soldiers and sailors so bold,
> But there's many and many a hero untold,
> Who sits at the wheel in the heat and the cold
>   Day after day without sleeping.
>
> So look out for cops and slow down at the bends,
> Check all your gauges and watch your big ends,
> And zig with your lights when you're passing old friends,
>   You'll be champion at keeping 'em rolling.[1]

Such songs, however, are not in the tradition of modern popular songs, for they are limited in their appeal. They mark out the lorry-driver as a specially fine fellow, whereas the true popular song tries to collect all within its fold. It assumes we are companionable. The rousing chorus is its finest feature; then the timid are made brave (for is not unity strength?) and our dreams are not so silly after all

[1] Ewan MacColl, *The Shuttle and Cage*, Industrial Folk Ballads (1954).

when we find a hundred other people in agreement. And are our dreams always so far from reality? The pin-up girl is a dream, but the girls in bikinis at the holiday resort are real enough. You may not live in a Tudor palace, but the brewery companies do their best, and think of the possibilities? Olde Englyshe teashops, Viennese ballrooms, or, if these are fakes, the Industrial Revolutionary baroque of the Tower Ballroom at Blackpool is genuine period stuff and likely to last a long time yet. The spirit of all is gregarious:

> The more we are together,
> The merrier we shall be;
> For your friends are my friends,
> And my friends are your friends,
> The more we are together,
> The merrier we shall be.

Think of what these things mean. The Cider Cellars, Coal Hole, and saloon-theatres of the early nineteenth century—and, even worse, Kate Hamilton's 'Night House'—were the gregarious delights of a century ago. Between them and us stretches the long line of the music-halls and thirty years of sound radio leading at last to television. The aim of it all has been entertainment, but by choice of entertainment may a people be judged. There are obscene songs as there are obscene books, but the obscene songs circulate in private, like sexual perversions, or radiate from comedians euphemistically called 'daring'. Friendliness *en masse* has no use for smut; it elevates the common man into a good fellow and the common girl into a charmer. You may see them in their thousands on any Sunday afternoon, and read their opinions in any popular paper. Here is a letter from a naval chaplain's wife who went to a British holiday camp with her husband and children:

By birth and upbringing I am a Canadian, and often found the people of Britain rather aloof and reserved . . . as we say in Canada, living and breathing 'the old school tie'! This aloofness simply does not exist on these camps but a blissful state of communalism which we long to see percolating into our Parish Churches.[1]

Communalism! A risky word, surely? But she explains:

I know nothing at all about politics but one hears a lot about communism, that it is a philosophy and so on—all this is beyond my understanding. Writing as a wife and mother I believe that the communalism you

[1] Isobelle Derby, article in *Butlin's Holiday Camp Church Review* (1954), p. 5.

find on a Butlin's Camp may well be the answer to the fear of communism. . . .

So often I have seen, and indeed, have once suffered myself, in having a child refusing to be ORDINARY, yet after a week or two at these Camps the children do become ORDINARY and SELF-RELIANT.[1]

Then how is it done? Let me quote an example. Here is *The Beavers' Song*, sung to the tune of *We're all Friends Here*:

> If you're a Butlin Beaver you're a friend of mine;
> If you've the Butlin Spirit then the world is fine.
> In our lodge you'll find good company,
> To be a Butlin Beaver is good fun you'll all agree.
> We are the Eager Beavers and we promise true,
> To keep the golden rule in everything we do.
> Come and join us—wear a badge—learn the secret sign,
> Be an Eager Beaver—Busy Eager Beaver—
> If you're a Butlin Beaver you're a friend of mine.

Levelling again, says the individualist. What can you expect in this age of the Common Man?

> Our city we have beautified—we've done it willy-nilly—
> And all that isn't Belgrave Square is Strand and Piccadilly
>   We haven't any slummeries in England!
> We've solved the labour question with discrimination polished,
> So poverty is obsolete and hunger is abolished—

This, however, is not from a play of the nineteen-fifties but from Gilbert and Sullivan's *Utopia Limited*, and is criticism of a theory rather than of an accomplishment. We have now a good measure of social security in England, and with it a good deal of change from the conditions Gilbert and Sullivan knew. We see how mass-production of materials is accompanied by mass-production of ideas, and the world is in terror of the consequences. There are many people like the lady who went to a holiday camp and discovered that in fellowship is a possible antidote to evils which are present but which we cannot understand. She thought of Communism—we might think of other things. The fact that it was necessary for Parliament in 1955 to bring out an Act to purge the country of 'horror comics' (surely an obvious case of what Orwell

---

[1] Ibid.

calls 'double-think', for since when has the horrific been comical?)
should make us pause to consider. Is music also clean?

This is a strange situation, for though there is much bad art in
popular songs, and much flabby sentiment, it is in serious music
that we find most evidence of the appeal of the horrific. Such things
as the *Ride to the Abyss* in Berlioz's *Damnation of Faust*, Dvořák's
The Spectre's Bride, Weber's *Der Freischütz*, and the romantic ballet
Giselle are where we must go to feel the effects of necromancy.
These works are not vulgar, as the music-hall songs were, and it
should still be possible for well-wishing people like the Canadian
lady referred to, to find in popular—even vulgar—songs, the antidote she knows society needs. If so, she has not discovered something new in history, but recovered that which was well known to
all men in the days of carols and miracle plays. Admittedly it is
against the interests of the music-halls to improve anybody—their
function is to please, even when it means stripping the ladies of
the cast to nudity, and this they have done. But, just as the profit
motive caused Chaffing Jack to think of his reputation, so there are
forces working today which show that popular art can be made
even more popular when allied to beauty, truth, and common
happiness.

In the Bedfordshire town of Luton a man and some eighty girls
between the ages of fourteen and twenty-three have set out 'to
use' as they proudly state, 'our talents in the interests of those
less fortunate than ourselves'. They have brought joy to innumerable people and have given, so far, over £50,000 to
charities.

The Luton Girls' Choir is modern, but the humanitarian thought
which inspires them goes back to the nineteenth-century singing-
classes, which fought tooth and nail against the evils of their time.
Gone, now, is the old music-hall with its hefty chuckers-out; now
we have the air-conditioned cinema with its smart usherettes. So with
the Girls' Choir. They are smart, happy, and absolutely modern.
Their appeal is natural; they are ordinary girls in their happiest
mood, delightful to see and hear, and happy in making us happy.
They sing nothing likely to be unpopular; their repertory in-
cludes film music, royalty ballads, Victorian part-songs like *The Lost
Chord* and *The Holy City*, music of Mendelssohn and Handel, waltzes
and polkas by the Viennese Strausses, and songs of Schubert.
Singing these they make the be-bop specialists, working in the sweat
of their brows, sound merely clever, and no doubt some will think
it unfair that school, shop, and factory girls, obviously enjoying

themselves, gain more popularity than qualified and long-experienced ecdysiasts,[1] but such is the way of the world.

How do these young amateurs succeed? Professionals compel our admiration in this expert age, but the Luton girls represent an ideal. In our irreligious society they are perhaps the best reminder we have of the biggest best seller of all time—the Virgin Mary in the three centuries before the Reformation. That they are a poor reminder they themselves would be the first to admit, but the public cannot analyse its own dreams, and is embarrassed beyond measure when faced with essential truths. So the public sidetracks God and finds a devious path to happiness through Tin Pan Alley:

> I think that I shall never see
> A poem lovely as a tree,
> A tree whose hungry mouth is pressed
> Against the earth's sweet flowing breast,
> A tree that looks to God all day,
> And lifts its leafy hands to pray.

It may be said of the Luton girls as Mendelssohn said of Jenny Lind: 'She sings bad music divinely.' Jenny did not know that the songs Mendelssohn referred to were bad, however, and it may cause some embarrassment to learn that the song *Trees* is not artistically a good one; but trees do not think of God, nor pray; neither should a poem in praise of nature be related to a tune from an Eastern harem; yet the tune of *Trees* is a variant of the Hindu Song from Rimsky-Korsakov's *Sadko*, simplified almost to the commonplace. This practice causes much concern to modern composers of Rimsky-Korsakov's standing, for if a tune has in it the elements of popularity there is no knowing to what purpose it may be put in the process of commercialization. Modern musicians therefore hive off into strange idioms, difficult to understand and safe from imitation at least during the lifetime of their creators. In the past, great music has owed much to popular art, but now the process is reversed; popular art draws on great music, simplifying —often (but not always) marring—while greatness eschews the vulgar. Jazz styles have been used by serious musicians, but the idiom of jazz will not mix comfortably. It seems that the musicologists are right when they talk of 'musics' in the plural, for jazz

---

[1] Ecdysiast. From the Greek *ecdysis*—riddance. Used by naturalists to describe the way a snake removes its skin, and in the entertainment profession to indicate exponents of 'a formal and rhythmic disrobing of the body in public'. In other words —strip-tease.

will no more sit at ease with symphony than Bach will run with
Chinese percussion. Yet it is the educated public which experiences
these difficulties and sees the world split into uncompromising
sects; the common man believes we can hold our pleasures in
common; but this is an example of faith—not of intelligence.

Not everything that modern mechanism brings is bad. There has
been a new interest in ballet brought about through television and
the coloured films, and we should also give a thought to the lovely
old German Christmas song, *Silent night, holy night*, which came
to us from the U.S.A. by way of the cinema. If I have said hard
things about the Luton Girls' Choir for their choice of *Trees* [1] I can
balance them with a whole-hearted admiration for their singing of
Silent night.[2]   It is not in feeling we err so much as in education.
We lack the natural aesthetic selection which the old folksingers
knew, and the reason is that we are not given time to test for values
before another 'winner' is foisted on us. God moves in a mysterious
way, and it may well be that it is no part of his plan to offer material
resources and good taste at the same time, but just as Sinbad in the
pantomime carries on his back the Old Man of the Sea, so we carry
in the back of our minds the old philosophy of 'the greatest happiness of the greatest number' into an age which mistakes acquisition for happiness. The drama of history has moved to a climax,
when disaster seems imminent and unavoidable. This is a familiar
situation in drama, however, for which the classical writers had a
remedy. They called on the stage carpenter for that marvel of his
art, the *Deus ex Machina*—the god from the machine—and the god
put all things right with a few immortal phrases. We are waiting for
a *Deus ex Machina* to sort out the muddle we have made of our
society, and we assume that because we live in a machine age the god
will come that way; but we forget that in the classical drama the god
only removed a crisis which has been devised by the man who
manipulated the god, and none of our dictators has proved himself
capable of this. The way which history shows is always one which
comes from within ourselves, and grows in strength as it is fed by
human aspirations. We have seen such aspirations reflected in our
songs, and not all are creditable, but taken for what they are they
add to our understanding of ourselves.

[1] Gramophone record, Parlophone R 3212.
[2] Gramophone record, Parlophone R 3146.

Bibliography

BAILY, Leslie, *The Gilbert and Sullivan Book*, 1952

BETT, Henry, *The Hymns of Methodism*, 1945

BRIDGE, J. C., *Town Waits and their Tunes*, 1928
(Proceedings of the Royal Musical Association)

BURNEY, Charles, *A General History of Music*, 1776

CARLYLE, Thomas, *Essay on the Opera*, 1850

CHAPPELL, William, *Popular Music of the Olden Time*, 1855–9

COATES, Eric, *Suite in Four Movements*, 1953

COBBETT, William, *Autobiography* and *Rural Rides*

COLE, G. D. H., *The Common People, 1746–1928*, 1938.

COLLIER, Jeremy, *A Short View of the Immorality and Profaneness of the English Stage, together with a Sense of the Antiquity of the Argument*, 1698

Coventry Play of *The Nativity*

DAVENANT, Sir William, *The First Dayes Entertainment*, 1656
The Siege of Rhodes, 1656

DEARMER, Percy (ed.), *The Oxford Book of Carols*, 1947

DELONEY, Thomas, *Thomas of Reading, Jack of Newbury*, etc., ed. F. O. Mann, 1912

DENT, E. J., *Foundations of English Opera*, 1928

DIBDIN, Charles, *Musical Tour*, 1788

DICKENS, Charles, *Sketches by Boz*

DISRAELI, Benjamin, *Sybil*

DRYDEN, John, *Prefaces to the Plays*

DURFEY, Thomas, *Love for Money, Pills to Purge Melancholy*, 1719

EASTLAKE, Lady Elizabeth, *Mrs Grote—a Sketch*, 1880

'ESQUIRE', *The Jazz Book*, 1947

EVELYN, John, *Diary*

FELLOWES, E. H., *The English Madrigal*, 1921

GARDINER, Margaret, Countess of Blessington, *The Belle of the Season*, 1840

GAY, John, *The Beggar's Opera*, 1728

GILBERT, W. S., *The Savoy Operas* (libretti)

GOLDSMITH, Oliver, *The Vicar of Wakefield*

GREENE, R. L., *Early English Carols*, 1935

GROTE, Harriet, *Collected Papers*, 1842–62

HAWEIS, H. R., *Music and Morals*, 1871
My Musical Life, 1884

HAWKINS, Sir John, *History of Music*, 1776

HIBBS, Leonard (ed.), *Swing Music*, 1936

HOGARTH, George, *Musical History, Biography and Criticism*, 1835

HOGGART, Richard, *The Use of Literacy*, 1956

HOWES, Frank, *The Borderland of Music amd Psychology*, 1926

LAING, Ian, *Background to the Blues*

McKECHNIE, Samuel, *Popular Entertainment Through the Ages*

MANN, F. O., *Deloney's Works*, 1912

MAYHEW, Henry, *London Labour and the London Poor*, 1851

MOORE, John, *The Season of the Year*, 1954

New Oxford History of Music, Vol. II, 1954

NICOLL, Allardyce, *Restoration Drama*, 1940

NORTH, Sir Roger, *Memoires of Musick*, 1728 (published 1845)

PEPYS, Samuel, *Diary*

PLAYFORD, John, *The Dancing Master*, 1651

REESE, Gustav, *Music in the Middle Ages*, 1941

SANDS, Milly, *Invitation to Ranelagh, 1742–1803*, 1946

SCHOLES, Percy A. *The Puritans and Music*, 1934
God Save the King, 1942

SCOTT, Harold, *The Early Doors*, 1946

SETTLE, Elkanah, *The Empress of Morocco*, 1673

SONNECK, Oscar, *Report on the Star-Spangled Banner*, etc

STERNHOLD & HOPKINS, *The Whole Booke of Psalms, etc.*, 1562

STOWE, Harriet B., *Uncle Tom's Cabin*

TATE, W. E., *The Parish Chest*, 1939

TAYLOR, Cook, *Tour of the Manufacturing Districts of Lancashire*, 1842

THACKERAY, W. M., *Pendennis, The Newcomes, Cox's Diary*

TREVELYAN, G. M., *English Social History*, 1946

TROLLOPE, Mrs Francis, *The Mother's Manual, or Illustrations of Matrimonial Economy*, 1833

WADDELL, Helen, *The Wandering Scholars*, 1932

WESTRUP, J., *Purcell*, 1947

WHITE, Eric W., *The Rise of English Opera*, 1951

Index